INDUSTRIAL BONDS
AND THE
RATING PROCESS

New Titles from QUORUM BOOKS

Supply-Side Economics in the 1980s: Conference Proceedings
FEDERAL RESERVE BANK OF ATLANTA AND EMORY
UNIVERSITY LAW AND ECONOMICS CENTER, SPONSORS

Deregulation and Environmental Quality: The Use of Tax Policy to
Control Pollution in North America and Western Europe
CRAIG E. REESE

Danger: Marketing Researcher at Work
TERRY HALLER

OPEC, the Petroleum Industry, and United States Energy Policy
ARABINDA GHOSH

Corporate Internal Affairs: A Corporate and Securities Law Perspective
MARC I. STEINBERG

International Pharmaceutical Marketing
SURESH B. PRADHAN

Social Costs in Modern Society: A Qualitative and Quantitative
Assessment
JOHN E. ULLMANN, EDITOR

Animal Law
DAVID S. FAVRE AND MURRAY LORING

Competing for Capital in the '80s: An Investor Relations Approach
BRUCE W. MARCUS

The International Law of Pollution: Protecting the Global Environment
in a World of Sovereign States
ALLEN L. SPRINGER

Statistical Concepts for Attorneys: A Reference Guide
WAYNE C. CURTIS

Handbook of Record Storage and Space Management
C. PETER WAEGEMANN

INDUSTRIAL BONDS AND THE RATING PROCESS

ahmed
belkaoui

Q

Quorum Books
Westport, Connecticut • London, England

332.632
B43 i

Library of Congress Cataloging in Publication Data

Belkaoui, Ahmed, 1943–
  Industrial bonds and the rating process.

  Bibliography: p.
  Includes indexes.
  1. Bonds—Ratings. I. Title.
HG4651.B44 1983   332.63'23   83-4600
ISBN 0-89930-046-4 (lib. bdg.)

Copyright © 1983 by Ahmed Belkaoui

All rights reserved. No portion of this book may be
reproduced, by any process or technique, without the
express written consent of the publisher.

Library of Congress Catalog Card Number: 83-4600
ISBN: 0-89930-046-4

First published in 1983

Greenwood Press
A division of Congressional Information Service, Inc.
88 Post Road West
Westport, Connecticut 06881

Printed in the United States of America

10 9 8 7 6 5 4 3 2 1

To Hedi J. and Janice M. Belkaoui

UNIVERSITY LIBRARIES
CARNEGIE-MELLON UNIVERSITY
PITTSBURGH, PENNSYLVANIA 15213

CONTENTS

EXHIBITS

PREFACE

The best known measures of prospective bond quality are the bond ratings assigned by the rating agencies: Moody's, Standard and Poor's, and Fitch. Their ratings provide a judgment of the investment quality of a long-term obligation and a measure of default risk. Accordingly, they may affect the interest rate an organization pays on its bonds. Although each rating agency has defined the meaning of its ratings, the agencies have not explicitly specified the process they use to arrive at these ratings. Given the importance of these ratings, various researchers have attempted to explain and/or predict them based on the financial and/or statistical characteristics of the bonds and issuing firms.

Models to explain or predict bond ratings have been reported to have been useful to the rating agencies themselves and to the investors. Above all, however, the models should be useful to the issuers themselves by providing them with vital information on how the rating agencies operate and especially by indicating how the rating of their bonds might turn out. If managers could predict the ratings of their bonds, they may also approximate the risk premiums prior to issuing debt, given the observed high correlation between bond ratings and yields to maturity.

The main purpose of this book is to develop and test a multiple discriminant for predicting industrial bond ratings that may be useful to the rating agencies, the investors, and the issuers. It should be of interest to practicing investment and credit analysts, bond raters, and the financial managers of the issuing firms. It is also intended for second-year master's degree students in business and for final-year students in undergraduate accounting or business programs.

The book consists of five chapters. Chapter 1 asks the reader to examine the nature, folklore, and implications of bonds, bond ratings, and the rating process. Chapter 2 elaborates on the format and content of published financial statements and introduces the reader to univariate ratio analysis as a tool of bond evaluation. Chapter 3 presents a survey of the various attempts made in the literature to develop bond rating models using various financial variables and various statistical approaches. Chapter 4 is used to develop and test a multiple discriminant model for predicting industrial bond ratings. Finally, Chapter 5 is aimed at guiding the bond rater, the bond issuer, or any other interested analyst to a practical implementation of the bond rating prediction model.

Many people helped in the development of this book. Considerable assistance was received from University of Illinois at Chicago students—especially Jeny Lau, Chris Paly, Patricia Aird, Vikram Sharma and Lois Yee. Anne Tyree and the secretarial pool at the College of the Business Administration of the University of Illinois at Chicago provided professional secretarial support. Financial assistance from the College of Business Administration and the Department of Accounting at the University of Illinois at Chicago provided both time and resources to ensure the manuscript was completed in adequate time. Finally, to Hedi J. and Janice M. Belkaoui thanks for making "everything" possible and agreeable in spite of the uncivilized 2 o'clock feedings.

INDUSTRIAL BONDS AND THE RATING PROCESS

1

BONDS, BOND RATINGS, AND THE RATING PROCESS

Polonius' admonition, "Neither a borrower nor a lender be," ranks as some of the least-heeded advice in history. In a modern economy, it is impossible to avoid being both. The choice is one of degree, and for the last few decades the smartest choice for corporations, as well as for governments and individuals, has been to be in debt up to the hilt.

—*Business Week*, July 26, 1982

It is by now an established fact that individuals, firms, and governments resort to financial leverage through debt financing as a way of financing growth more readily and more efficiently. For firms to be able to accomplish this financing task readily and efficiently, their bond issues need to have interesting investment features of profitability, stability, and liquidity, to name only a few. Above all, the investors need to assure themselves that the issuers will be able to fulfill their obligations. Fortunately, the market provides the investor one way of judging the quality of a bond through the unbiased opinions of informed and experienced professionals working for the bond rating agencies. These professionals rate bonds by assigning to them known bond ratings designed essentially to rank the issues in order of the probability of default, that is, the inability to meet interest obligations, sinking-fund payments, or repayment of principal. Given the complexity and importance of bonds, bond ratings, and the rating process, this chapter introduces the reader to an examination of their nature, folklore, and implications.

DEBT FINANCING

NATURE OF DEBT FINANCING

Debt financing consists of issuing bonds, publicly sold or privately placed, with maturities in excess of ten years. The basic bond is a long-term contractual IOU by which the firm (borrower) agrees to pay the bondholders a specified interest each year and then redeem the principal at the maturity date. Various factors may motivate a firm to issue long-term debt in the form of bonds, including the politics of corporate control, maintaining an adequate debt/equity ratio, expectations about the term structure of interest, and, most of all, its capacity to absorb debt. The capacity to absorb debt is determined by the capacity to repay the fixed interest payout periodically and a stated principal sum at maturity. This capacity is important because missing an interest payment may lead the bondholders' trustee to declare the entire principal and debt due and payable. To prevent such a situation from happening, a bond contract or indenture contains sufficient provisions or protective covenants to safeguard the bondholders' claims by restricting the firm's ability to extend itself. The bond indenture or contract is the legal agreement between the issuing firm, the bondholders, and the trustee representing the bondholders. It spells out in detail the specific rights of the bondholders and the powers of the trustee.[1] It is intended to control the bondholder-stockholder conflicts. Examples of bondholder-stockholder conflicts include the areas of dividend payment, claim dilution, asset substitution, and underinvestment. Categories of covenants are generally included in the bond indenture to control for these conflicts. They are production/investment, dividend, financing, and bonding covenants.[2]

The restrictions on the firm's production/investment policy consist of explicitly specifying the projects that the firm is allowed to undertake, restricting the extent to which the firm can become a claimholder in another business, restricting the sale, lease, transfer, or disposition of some of the assets, pledging some of the assets until the bonds are paid in full, restricting some mergers, and requiring a strict maintenance of the firm's properties and working capital.

The restrictions on the payment of dividends consist of placing a limit on distributions to stockholders by specifying an inventory of funds available for dividend payments over the life of the bonds.[3]

The restrictions of subsequent financing policy consist of controlling the creation of claims with a higher priority and also controlling the rentals, lease, and leaseholders of property owned prior to the date of the indenture.

The restrictions modifying the pattern of payoffs to bondholders consist of creating a sinking fund to amortize part or all of the indebtedness prior to its maturity, creating convertibility provisions that give to the holder of the bond the right to exchange them for shares of the firm, and including callability provisions that give to the firm the right to redeem the bonds before maturity at a stated price.

The restrictions specifying bonding activities by the firm include committing the firm to issue periodic financial reports, specifying the accounting techniques to be used, providing an annual officers' certificate of compliance, and requiring the firm to purchase insurance. For example, Leftwich presents evidence of the types of measurement rules contained in lending agreements summarized as follows:

(i) Definitions of accounting numbers in lending agreements consistently refer to generally accepted accounting principles (GAAP). GAAP is used as a benchmark and any modifications to those principles consist of specific inclusions and exclusions.

(ii) The definitions of accounting numbers require that contractual accounting numbers be determined by generally accepted accounting principles in force at the date of calculation, not at the date of issue of the debt; i.e., the definitions rely on "rolling" GAAP, not "frozen" GAAP.

(iii) Variations from generally accepted accounting principles are more frequent (and more elaborate) in private debt agreements than in debt indentures.

(iv) If modifications to generally accepted accounting principles are made in lending agreements, those modifications state that certain *increases* in income and asset values are *not* allowed, and ensure that *decreases* in income and asset values *are* recorded.[4]

As may be expected, there are advantages and disadvantages to long-term debt financing.

The advantages include a lowering of the firm's after-tax cost of capital, the ease to sell to a broad market of institutional investors, the lower than stock flotation costs, the absence of threat to management control, and the favorable financial leverage with increased earnings per share.

The disadvantages include an increase in the financial risk, the larger cash flow requirements to meet the fixed charges payment and the sinking fund, the unfavorable leverage when operating cash flows do not cover the financial charges, and the loss of policy flexibility resulting from the restrictive nature of the bond indenture covenants.

TYPES OF INDUSTRIAL BONDS

There are various types of industrial bonds and they vary as to the mode of interest payment, the nature of the claim, the type of guarantee, and the repayment.

With regard to the mode of interest payments, bonds are either coupon bonds or registered bonds. A coupon bond (or bearer bond) is a basic bond, ownership of which is evidenced by possession rather than record. Each of the coupons attached to the bond represents an interest payment date and is presented for payment at that date. A registered bond is also a basic bond, ownership of which is evidenced by record on the books of the corporation. Interest is paid by check in the name of the bondholder.

With regard to the nature of the claim, bonds are either debenture bonds or mortgage bonds. Mortgage bonds are secured bonds with a specific lien on particular assets of the firm. Upon liquidation holders of mortgage bonds may acquire title to the pledged assets and sell it to satisfy their claims. The mortgage bonds may be first mortgage bonds, where the claimants have first claim on the pledged assets, and second or third mortgage bonds, where the claimants have second and third claim on the pledged assets. Mortgage bonds may also be closed-end mortgage bonds which restrict the borrowing to a fixed sum of bonds which the firm may sell under the mortgage, or open-end mortgage bonds, which allow the firm to sell additional bonds with the same claim on the pledged assets. Finally, mortgage bonds may be general mortgage bonds, where the firm pledges all or most of its assets as security instead of specific assets. Mortgage bonds are not the only secured bonds. Other secured bonds include collateral trust bonds and equipment trust certificates. Collateral trust bonds are secured by a lien on stocks and bonds of other corporations and of the firm's subsidiaries. Equipment trust certificates are issued by the transportation industry to finance the purchase of rolling stock and aircraft. They may take place under either the Philadelphia lease plan or the direct obligation plan. Under the Philadelphia lease plan, a trustee (a bank or trust company) issues the certificate, guarantees the payment of principal and interest, and keeps the title until the transportation company completes paying the interest and the principal. Under the direct obligation plan, the transportation company issues the certificate, and the trustee still keeps the title without guaranteeing the payment of principal and interest.

Debenture bonds are unsecured bonds with no specific liens on any particular assets of the firm. They are also referred to as subordinated debenture bonds, given their lowest claim on earnings and assets of all the firm's bonds. The subordination is indicated in the indenture. Subordination has no impact on the firm's obligation to meet payments of interest and principal on the subordinated debt except in case of difficulty. Subordination takes effect only in the event of liquidation, dissolution, bankruptcy, or reorganization. Robert W. Johnson viewed subordinated debentures as a debt that serves as equity given that it may be regarded as "preferred stock with a due date."[5] Other types of unsecured bonds include the income bonds, the receiver's certificate, and the convertible debenture bond.

The income bond is an unsecured debenture whose interest is paid only when earned. They are usually issued by firms experiencing financial difficulties or which have been reorganized after a bankruptcy and are not sufficiently profitable to guarantee the payment of an interest. They are definitely junior debt instruments, but they are senior to preferred stock and common stock. This point is made by Bierman and Brown as follows:

Income bonds may give their holders a position preferred to that of general business creditors but below other bondholders in the hierarchy of creditor's rights. Preferred stockholders are placed below the general business creditors. The effect of this hierarchy is to make credit a little more difficult to secure when income bonds are outstanding than where preferred stock is outstanding. If the income bonds were made junior to the business creditors, the risk of the income bondholders getting nothing in the event of liquidation would be increased. Nevertheless, the bondholders would still be in a better position than the preferred stockholders.[6]

Another reason for the superiority of income bonds over preferred stock is that unlike preferred stock, whose dividends are not tax deductible, the interest payments of income bonds are tax deductible expenses. As a result, a firm may obtain necessary funds for expansion at a cost substantially lower than the cost of preferred and common stock.[7] Other advantages of income bonds, suggested by Sidney M. Robbins, include an excellent opportunity to strengthen the capital structure, raise new capital, and affect exchanges arising out of mergers.[8] The major disadvantage against income bonds is that they may indicate a "weak market position" when used by a firm.[9]

The receiver's certificate is issued by the bankruptcy court when it takes over the firm's activities in receivership. Because these certificates have priority over all other claims, they allow the receiver to raise funds.

The convertible debenture bond is an unsecured bond which carries an option to exchange the bond for common stock at the holder's option. A firm's motivation in issuing convertible debt is the desire to get a bargain rate of interest or to avoid repayment of principal or both. When firms have deeply discounted debt and no longer wish the conversion feature (that is, they wish to eliminate any potential dilution), they use the discounted convertible bond exchange to replace convertible debt with nonconvertible debt. A discounted convertible bond exchange (DCBE) has been defined as "an offer by a corporation to its bondholders of new bonds for its outstanding (deeply) discounted convertible bonds, where the par value of the new bonds offered is less than the par value of the old bonds."[10] These exchanges have the effect of changing the firm's debt/equity ratio, its reported income, and its potential dilution.[11]

With regard to the types of bonds carrying a guarantee, bonds are either guaranteed bonds, assumed bonds, joint bonds or industrial revenue bonds. These bonds are guaranteed as to payment by a third party other than the borrower. The guaranteed bonds are unsecured bonds of subsidiaries whose interest and principal are guaranteed by the parent firm or a more credit worthy corporation. The assumed bonds result from a merger when one firm takes over the debt of the other firm. The joint bonds are issued by a joint venture and are guaranteed by the firms forming the venture. The industrial revenue bonds are issued by a local government to provide funds and/or buildings for a firm.

With regard to repayment, provisions include sinking funds, serial bonds, call provisions and premiums, deferred call privilege, balloon payment, and commodity-linked bonds.

A sinking fund consists of periodical depositing of a portion of the principal into an escrow account to be used to retire part or all of the issue by maturity. Serial bonds have a common date of issuance under the indenture, but are redeemed at random from a list of the serial numbers printed on each bond. Call provisions allow the borrower to call the bond for redemption at a specified price before maturity. To protect themselves from the call provision, investors demand a call premium, an excess over the face value. The value of the call privilege to the borrower is a function of the expected declines in the future market rates of interest. The greater the expectations of a fall in interest rates, the greater the value a borrower places on the call provision. Similarly, in periods of high interest rates, the borrower may have to offer a higher yield in order to convince the investors to accept the call privilege.[12] Deferred call privileges may be negotiated in the indenture to cancel or avoid the call provision.[13] The balloon payment provision gives the firm the right to redeem the bond at maturity rather than gradually retiring it over its life. More and more companies are issuing commodity-linked or commodity-backed bonds.[14] For example, the Sunshine Mining Co., an operator of the largest silver mine in the United States, made in 1980 two $25 million bond issues backed by silver. Similarly, in 1979, an agency of the Mexican government issued bonds in local currency backed by oil. The reason may be that the issuer is "willing to share the potential price appreciation of the underlying commodity with the purchaser of the bond, in exchange for a lower coupon rate, more favorable bond indentures, or the acceptance of a weaker currency by foreign investors."[15] In fact, commodity-linked bonds have been suggested as a way for less developed countries to transfer a substantial proportion of commodity price risks to the financial markets.[16]

BOND RATINGS

NATURE OF BOND RATINGS

The following statements from *Moody's* and *Standard and Poor's* publications give some insight on what does a bond rating measure:

A municipal bond is a judgment of the investment quality of a long-term obligation issued by a state or one of its subdivisions. It is based on an analysis that must ask, first, what has the debtor pledged to pay and, second, what is the likelihood that he will be able to keep his promises. The rating . . . is a statement about the debtor's condition and the probability that he can and will do what he says regarding the debt. It is an evaluative assessment of the protections afforded the bondholder.[17]

A Standard and Poor's corporate and municipal debt rating is a current assessment of the creditworthiness of an obligator with respect to a specific obligation. This assessment may take into consideration obligors such as guarantors, insurers, or lessees.

. . . The debt rating is not a recommendation to purchase, sell or hold a security, inasmuch as it does not comment as to market price or suitability for a particular investor.[18]

Above all, a rating is intended to indicate how likely it is that the issuer will be able to meet principal and interest payments on time; in other words, it is intended to measure the default risk.

Corporate bond ratings were developed prior to World War I to provide independent and reliable judgment about the quality of corporate bonds. The development was spurred by the interest and the efforts of men like Roger Babson, Freeman Rutney, Jr., and John Moody. In fact, the first ratings were published in 1909 by John Moody in his *Analyses of Railroad Investments*. Rutney was associated with the development of corporate bond ratings by Poor's Publishing Company in 1916.[19]

Today corporate bond ratings are prepared by Fitch, Moody's Investors Service and Standard and Poor's Corporation. These companies provide the financial community with a regular record of their opinions on the quality of most large, publicly held corporate, municipal, and governmental issues. Moody's Investors Service, Inc. (a subsidiary of Dun and Bradstreet Companies, Inc.) and Standard and Poor's Corp. (a subsidiary of McGraw-Hill, Inc.) are the two agencies principally involved in wielding the enormous power of bond ratings. They rate all corporate bond issues as well as private placements, commercial paper, preferred stock, and some large debt offerings of foreign companies and governments. As we will see later, their rating systems are similar, although the labels differ somewhat. Besides, their respective ratings differ only on an estimated 10 percent of all issues.[20] Fitch Investors Service Inc. rates fewer firms than the two main rating agencies and enjoys special clout in the rating of banks. In fact, the rating of banks is reported to be today the principal one in which Fitch's judgments have much influence.[21]

Besides these three main rating agencies, other agencies are gradually entering the rating market and game. For example, Duff and Phelps Inc., an independent rating agency in Chicago, is involved in utility ratings. Unlike Moody's, Fitch, and Standard and Poor, which charge variable fees to the companies they rate, Duff and Phelps is paid by investors.[22]

BOND RATING SYSTEMS

As stated earlier, Moody's and Standard and Poor's are the most important rating agencies in terms of the variety and the number of securities they rate and in terms of their power and importance in the market. In what follows the bond rating systems of each of these two agencies is explicated.

Moody's Bond Rating System

Moody's is the oldest of the rating agencies. It began rating corporate bonds in 1909 and municipals as well as all tax-exempt issues in 1919. Moody's corporate bond ratings are letter coded.

Aaa.   Bonds which are rated Aaa are judged to be of the best quality. They carry the smallest degree of investment risk and are generally referred to as "gilt edge." Interest payments are protected by a large or by an exceptionally stable margin, and the principal is secure. While the various protective elements are likely to change, such changes as can be visualized are most unlikely to impair the fundamentally strong position of such issues.

Aa.   Bonds which are rated Aa are judged to be of high quality by all standards. Together with the Aaa group they comprise what are generally known as high grade bonds. They are rated lower than the best bonds because margins of protection may not be as large as in Aaa securities or because fluctuations of protective elements may be of greater amplitude or there may be other elements present which make the long term risks appear somewhat larger than in Aaa securities.

A.   Bonds which are rated A possess many favorable investment attributes and are to be considered as upper medium grade obligations. Factors giving security to principal and interest are considered adequate, but elements may be present which may suggest a susceptibility to impairment some time in the future.

Baa.   Bonds which are rated Baa are considered as medium grade obligations; that is, they are neither highly protected nor poorly secured interest payments and principal security appears adequate for the present, but certain protective elements may be lacking or may be characteristically unreliable over any great length of time. Such bonds lack outstanding investment characteristics and, in fact, have speculative characteristics as well.

Ba.   Bonds which are rated Ba are judged to have speculative elements; their future cannot be considered as well assured. Often the protection of interest and principal payments may be very moderate and thereby not well safeguarded during both good and bad times over the future. Uncertainty of position characterizes bonds in this class.

B.   Bonds which are rated B generally lack characteristics of the desirable investment. Assurance of interest and principal payments or of maintenance of other terms of the contract over any long period of time may be small.

Caa.   Bonds which are rated Caa are of poor standing. Such issues may be in default, or there may be present elements of danger with respect to principal or interest.

Ca.   Bonds which are rated Ca represent obligations which are speculative in a high degree. Such issues are often in default or have other marked shortcomings.

C.   Bonds which are rated C are the lowest-rated class of bonds, and issues so rated can be regarded as having extremely poor prospects of ever attaining any real investment standing.

As seen above, gradations of investment quality are indicated by rating symbols, each symbol representing a group in which the quality characteristics are broadly the same. It should also be noted that Moody's applies numerical modifiers 1, 2, and 3 in each generic rating classification from Aa through B in its corporate bond rating system. The modifier 1 indicates that the security ranks in the higher end of its generic rating category; the modifier 2 indicates a mid-range ranking; and the modifier 3 indicates that the issue ranks in the lower end of its generic rating category.[23]

Standard and Poor's Rating System

Standard and Poor's began rating securities in 1941. It was formed from the merger of Poor's Publishing Company and Standard Statistics Company. In most of its publications, Standard and Poor's mentions the following considerations as the basis of its ratings:

a. Likelihood of default—capacity and willingness of the obligor as to the timely payment of interest and repayment of principal in accordance in the terms of the obligation.

b. Nature and provisions of the obligation.

c. Protection afforded by, and relative position of, the obligation in the event of a bankruptcy, reorganization, or other arrangement under the laws of bankruptcy and other laws affecting creditors' rights.

The key to Standard and Poor's rating system is as follows:

AAA. Debt rated AAA has the highest rating assigned by Standard and Poor's. Capacity to pay interest and repay principal is extremely strong.

AA. Debt rated AA has a very strong capacity to pay interest and repay principal and differs from the highest rated issues only in small degree.

A. Debt rated A has a strong capacity to pay interest and repay principal, although it is somewhat more susceptible to the adverse effects of changes in circumstances and economic conditions than debt in higher rated categories.

BBB. Debt rated BBB is regarded as having an adequate capacity to pay interest and repay principal. Whereas it normally exhibits adequate protection parameters, adverse economic conditions or changing circumstances are more likely to lead to a weakened capacity to pay interest and repay principal for debt in this category than in higher rated categories.

BB, B, CCC, CC.   Debt in this category is regarded, on balance, as predominantly speculative with respect to capacity to pay interest and repay principal in accordance with the terms of the obligation. BB indicates the lowest degree of speculation and CC the highest degree of speculation. While such debt will likely have some quality and protective characteristics, these are outweighed by large uncertainties or major risk exposures to adverse conditions.

C.   This rating is reserved for income bonds on which no interest is being paid.

D.   Debt rated D is in default, and payment of interest and/or repayment of principal is in arrears.

It should be noted that the ratings from AA to B may be modified by the addition of a plus or minus sign to show relative standing with the major rating categories. Standard and Poor's may also assign a provisional rating indicated by the letter *P*. It is defined as follows.

A provisional rating assumes the successful completion of the project being financed by the debt being rated and indicates that payment of debt service requirements is largely or entirely dependent upon the successful and timely completion of the project. This rating, however, while addressing credit quality subsequent to completion of the project, makes no comment on the likelihood of, or the risk of default upon failure of, such completion. The investor should exercise his own judgement with respect to such likelihood and risk.[24]

Besides their 20 letter-coded ratings for fixed income securities, ranging from triple-A for the best credits to D for issues in default, Standard and Poor's publishes a *Credit Watch* list that tells the investment community that Standard and Poor may raise or lower a rating. The list specifies whether a credit being "watched" is likely to go up or down by describing their status as positive or negative, or describes the situation as "developing." The list is available weekly as part of Standard and Poor's publication *Credit Week*.[25] In general Standard and Poor's manages to get a final decision on a *Credit Watch*-listed firm within 90 days.[26] The list should not be interpreted as a "Credit Crutch" list but merely as a signal to the market that Standard and Poor's may be about to change a rating. Besides Standard and Poor's, two Chicago firms produce credit watch lists. One is compiled by the investment analysts at Duff and Phelps Inc. and the other by the fixed income experts in the trust department at Harris Trust and Savings Bank.[27]

IMPORTANCE OF BOND RATINGS

A bond rating is an important economic event with potential implications.

First, a bond rating is intended to be an indicator of the probability of default or loss of market value which may be experienced by a firm facing degrees of financial difficulties. The rating agencies adopt a conservative view of ratings as the minimum level of overall bond quality that a firm can expect to maintain given the present conditions. For example, *Moody's Bond Record* notes: "Since ratings involve a judgement about the future, on the one hand, and since they are used by investors as a means of protection, on the other, the effort is made when assigning ratings, to look at 'worst' potentialities in the 'visible' future rather than solely at the past record and the status of the present."[28] Thus bond ratings may be interpreted as a signal of bond investment quality.

Second, the ratings are particularly useful because they have been found to be good predictors of bond defaults. Hickman conducted an analysis of the experiences of corporate bond ratings during the period 1900–1943.[29] An important result is presented in the following data showing the percentage of bonds in each rating category at the time of offering which subsequently defaulted:

RATING CATEGORY	DEFAULT RATE (in percentages)
I (Aaa)	5.9
II (Aa)	6.0
III (A)	13.4
IV (Baa)	19.1
V-IX (Ba-C)	42.4

Thus during the more than 40 years covered, only 6 percent of the bonds in the top two rating categories defaulted, while the rate was twice as high in the third category, three times as high in the fourth category, and 40 percent in the last speculative category defaulted. Hickman also found rating agencies able to predict default losses. This impressive agencies' accuracy in ranking issues by probability of default was reconfirmed by Harold for the period 1929–35.[30] Similarly, Burrell found that the proportions of corporate bonds whose income was interrupted and whose market values suffered relatively greater declines were inversely related to bond ratings.[31] All this empirical evidence points to the usefulness of the corporate bond ratings as measures of the probability of default and as predictors of the magnitude of the losses at default.[32]

Third, the ratings are useful because they have been found to be highly correlated with bond yields to maturity. The lower the bond rating, the higher the average yield to maturity in that rating group. Exhibit 1.1 shows the yield average by rating for industrial, public utilities, and municipal bonds in each of the *Moody's* top four rating groups over the 1972–1981 period. While the correlation is a fact, the causation is not evident. One explanation is that the rating determines to a certain extent the interest rate the issuer must pay on the bond.[33] Another explanation may be that both bond yield and bond ratings are determined by the same underlying economic factors in general and default rate in particular. In fact the empirical studies on the influence of bond ratings on bond returns and bond yields is conflicting. On one hand studies by Rubinfeld,[34] Katz,[35] and Grier and Katz[36] show an influence, while on the other hand studies by Hettenhouse and Sartoris[37] indicate no observable influence. West[38] closes the debate by indicating that there is an influence on bond yields and that the primary reason for the nexus between ratings and yields is the use of the former as a tool of financial regulation.

Fourth, the systematic risk of a security, β, indicates how the return for a given security varies with the market. A beta greater than one indicates that the return of that security increased (decreased) at a higher rate than the market return. Thus β is considered to be a measure of the non-diversifiable risk that common stock investors face for individual equity securities. Corporate bond ratings, as seen earlier, are also measures of investment quality and risk. Both measures should be related. In fact, both measures were found to be consistent across firms examined.[39]

Fifth, the corporate bond rating may have a market impact,

EXHIBIT 1.1 YIELD AVERAGES BY RATINGS

YEARS	INDUSTRIALS				PUBLIC UTILITIES				MUNICIPALS			
	Aaa	Aa	A	Baa	Aaa	Aa	A	Baa	Aaa	Aa	A	Baa
1972	6.97	7.11	7.36	7.99	7.46	7.60	7.72	8.17	5.04	5.19	5.38	5.60
1973	7.78	7.40	7.63	8.07	7.60	7.72	7.84	8.17	4.95	5.09	5.29	5.47
1974	8.42	8.64	8.90	9.14	8.71	9.04	9.50	9.84	5.89	6.04	6.30	6.53
1975	8.61	8.90	9.21	10.26	9.03	9.44	10.09	10.96	6.42	6.77	7.37	7.62
1976	8.23	8.59	8.88	9.67	8.63	8.92	9.29	9.82	5.65	6.12	7.17	7.49
1977	7.86	8.04	8.36	8.87	8.19	8.43	8.61	9.06	5.20	5.39	5.86	6.12
1978	8.58	8.74	8.94	9.35	8.87	9.10	9.29	9.62	5.52	5.68	5.99	6.27
1979	9.39	9.65	9.91	10.42	9.86	10.22	10.49	10.96	5.89	6.12	6.34	6.72
1980	11.57	11.99	12.44	13.39	12.30	13.00	13.34	13.95	7.84	8.06	8.44	9.00
1981	13.70	14.19	14.62	15.48	14.64	15.30	15.95	16.60	10.42	10.89	11.31	11.75

SOURCE: Moody's Investors Service, Inc., *Moody's Corporate Bond Yield Averages by Ratings* (New York: Moody's, 1982) and *Moody's Municipal Bond Yield Averages by Rating* (New York: Moody's, 1982).

although the impact may be anticipated by the market. Evidence seems to indicate that the rate-changing lag, which is the difference between the market's realization of new information and the agency's response in terms of a rating change, is at least six months for bonds[40] and 15–18 months for common stocks.[41] There seems to be also conflicting evidence on the market reaction to a rating change. While Weinstein shows that there is little response to a rating change, Griffin and Sanvicente report that firms experiencing a rating change show significantly different common stock behavior less than 12 months prior to the rating change compared with that of a control sample, with the added result that abnormal price changes for downgrades were significantly negative in the month the changes in rating were announced.[42] Griffin concludes as follows:

These results are consistent with the proposition that the rating process obtains the release of what otherwise might remain private information. Limited evidence of security price movement after the announcement has been reported, though upward or downward drifts in security prices following announcement can only be considered anomalies in light of evidence on market efficiency.[43]

Sixth, the bond ratings are definitely useful to borrowers, investors, bond dealers and underwriters, and bank and insurance companies. Borrowers whose obligations are rated if they pay a fee have their interest cost determined by the rating they receive.[44] Investors rely on ratings to measure both credit soundness and relative market value of the bond. Bond dealers and underwriters rely on ratings as an assessment and marketing mechanism when seeking to match borrowers and investors. Finally, most banks and insurance companies rely on rating when evaluating the riskiness of their bond portfolios.[45]

BOND RATINGS PROCESS

NATURE OF THE BOND RATING PROCESS

The bond rating process does not differ very much from one rating agency to another. All rating agencies charge a fee for the corporate long-term rating services. For example, the fee for long-term obligation rating by Standard and Poor's depends on the time expended in the determination of the rating and ranges from $500 to $15,000. In general the rating process includes most of the following steps:[46]

1. The issuer approaches the rating agency and requests the rating of its long term obligation. Sometimes the issuer wants to know what the rating may be if he were to do a public financing or what the rating on old issue may be if he were to issue additional long term debt.

2. The issuer is requested to complete various rating request forms.

3. The rating agency assigns an analytical team to the issue.

4. The team proceeds with the gathering, collection, and analysis of all relevant internal and external information. The team may require a meeting with the issuer's management to resolve any question or concern. In the case of Standard and Poor's, the potential issuers give a formal presentation which details:

> The company's 5 year historical operating record, including income statements, balance sheets, and sources and application of funds analysis (this same information, including underlying assumptions, is projected 5 years into the future).
>
> Comparisons with similar companies.
>
> Analysis of capital spending.
>
> Financing alternatives, if not readily determinable from the data presented.
>
> Other key factors the issuer may believe will impact on the rating.[47]

The team may also visit the issuer's facilities to allow the issuer to make an on-site presentation and to get a better feel of the issuer's operations.

5. The analytical team makes a thorough presentation to the rating committee. In the case of Standard and Poor's, the discussion covers generally the following topics:

> Proposed issue and terms of the indenture.
>
> Capitalization.
>
> Nature of the company's business and history.
>
> Management.

Earnings and cash flow history and forecast.

Financing plans.

Ratio analysis, including accounting factors.

Rating history, if applicable.

Rating recommendation, including major considerations.[48]

6. The issuer is notified of the decision. At that point the issuer may elect not to appeal the decision and the rating is released to the market. If the issuer elects to appeal the decision and present additional information to the rating committee, the case is reopened and more discussion and a new vote take place to either confirm or modify the rating.

The rating process does not stop at this stage. The new rating is entered into the on-going monitoring and surveillance systems of the rating agencies.

The steps outlined in this section are not engraved in gold. The rating agencies are constantly looking for methods to improve the process, with the objective of determining consistent rating criteria. For example, Standard and Poor's has a rating criteria committee whose objective is the determination of consistent rating criteria. This committee is divided into various subcommittees working in areas such as:

Meaning of ratings: a philosophical overview.

General approach to analyzing risk and protection.

Evaluating diversification.

Evaluating acts of God/acts of man.

General policies and approach to evaluating security and credit supports.

Joint and several obligations.

Project financings.

Accounting aspects of ratings.

Financial statement analysis.[49]

Needless to say, rating policies are in constant change and up-grading.[50]

THE BOND RATING FOLKLORE

The folklore surrounding the bond rating process is a result of both the importance of bond rating and the mystery and secrecy surrounding the same process. As more and more gets known about the bond rating process questions start to arise about their role and impact which may affect their long-term future. Some of the folklore and the resulting questions are examined next.

First, the decision to give a low rating to a bond may mean the bond would not be marketable. It amounts to the rating agencies making the final decision on which companies would be raising money in the market. Anthony Broy, for example, mentions that if "S&P should rate a municipality B—defined as 'investment characteristics are virtually nonexistent,' the ratee would soon be in need of either a government bailout or divine intervention."[51] Questions may arise about the legitimacy of such power.

Second, companies dissatisfied with their ratings may "appeal" the decision. The rating agencies are always willing to provide a rehearing for more information and argument. To get a better rating, investment bankers, corporate financial officers, and state and city officials may have to bring more information and may have to work up a presentation for the agencies, including slide presentations, motion pictures, samples of products and scale models of operations, in the hope of putting on a good show and raising the ratings. Cultivating the rating agency may become a central folklore of the rating process or, as referred to by Irwin Ross, "the rating game."[52] As Ross puts it, "the investment banker may even put inexperienced clients through a dress rehearsal of the act. After the rating is announced, many executives, even those whose companies are not issuing new debt, will meet with the agencies at least once a year to fill them in on developments—the idea being to maintain the rating if it is good, or to upgrade it if possible."[53] Questions may arise about the necessity and even the absurdity of cultivating the bond raters at the expense of improving the quality of the bond. One example in point: on November 9, 1974, Standard and Poor's assigned a BBB rating on the preferred stock issue of Iowa-Illinois Gas and Electric Company. The company protested and presented new information leading Standard and Poor's to raise the rating to A.

Third, it is rather obvious that to get a good rating or avoid a bad rating, company officials have to work with the raters and listen to their suggestions. The suggestions may include agreeing to more restrictive covenants, to a cutback in the size of an issue, to a speeded-up debt repayment schedule, or even to a modification of their financing plans. This may constitute a direct interference in the management of companies by individuals who may not be very familiar with the strengths and weaknesses of these companies. Altering the financial plans of companies is equivalent to altering the production and investment plans and even the nature of the companies' activities. One can only hope that they are right in assigning their ratings. As Ross puts it again, "Even the raters concede that they have no objective criteria for determining whether they are doing an accurate job. On occasion they make the argument that the market validates their opinion. This is partly true— certainly the market would not go along if the agencies gave a triple-A rating to a triple b-company. But on close calls—say, between an A and an AA—the agencies' decision largely *determines* the market action. Which is, of course, why the agencies are so important."[54] Again, questions arise on the role the rating agencies should be playing in devising or changing companies' financial plans and consequently their investment and production plans.

Fourth, how should rating differences between rating agencies be interpreted? Standard and Poor's and Moody's are assumed to have the same information on companies but come sometimes to different conclusions on the ratings of some corporate bonds. Ross again mentions the case of International Paper bringing out $150 million of sinking-fund debentures, with Moody's upgrading the company from A to Aa and Standard and Poor's downgrading it from AA to AA-.[55] Could it be that the rating agencies are using different information, different formulas? Is it a clear case of judgment fallibility? Or could it be that the rating agencies can be clearly wrong on one particular complex case? McNamee and Gibson pointed to the ratings of Bankers Trust as a clear case where bank bond ratings were wrong.[56] They state:

Bankers Trust New York Corp. is a case in point. Both Moody's and Fitch give this major bank holding company—it's seventh largest—their highest rating, AAA. We put it in Group IV, our lowest quality category. Why?

Because we read their published statements with care, then did a lot of arithmetic and abided by the results. Specifically, here is how Bankers Trust New York Corp. ranked on our tests, which we applied to a group of sixty-six bank holding companies:

> On four tests of capital adequacy, Bankers ranked 63rd, 61st, 63rd, and 63rd.
>
> On profitability, Bankers ranked 55th and 57th.
>
> On loan quality, Bankers ranked 46th and 48th.
>
> On investment portfolio equity, Bankers ranked 64th, 56th, 62nd, and 59th.
>
> On leverage, Bankers ranked 30th and 56th.[57]

Again, questions may arise about the different ratings given by the rating agencies and about the accuracy of their ratings. To avoid these situations, the rating agencies may have to move to computer modeling of the rating process. Consider for example the following statement made by Brenton W. Harries, President of Standard and Poor's Corporation:

On the other hand, as you well know, ratings are not changed willy-nilly, month to month or year to year. Once we set a rating, we try to be absolutely certain that it is going to hold for a number of years, hopefully, for the average life of the security. There are times, when, as in the Penn Central case, we had to change the rating twice in 18 months. This was certainly predictive of the direction in which that company was moving. Sometimes you miss these situations and you can rarely catch a fraud situation completely. But we do try to be predictive. I want to do more in the area of computer models to project financial performance.[58]

But to their credit, and despite the potential lack of accuracy in some cases, no one has ever accused the rating agencies of being anything but objective and honest.

Fifth, the rating agencies pore over a great deal of information about the companies they are rating. They also get in touch with the companies' competitors and other trade sources. They visit some of the companies' facilities, factories and buildings. They examine the covenants of the indenture and all the financial information on property protection, financial resources, and future earning power. In general the top management is expected to meet with the bond rating committee. In short the rating agencies do a thorough job of evaluating the investment quality of the bonds

they intend to rate. Some observers agree and others disagree with
this assessment of the rating agencies' work. Those who disagree
may be represented by the following statement made by a spokes-
man of Data General Corp., Westboro, Massachusetts, after its
first $60 million sinking-fund debenture was rated BBB by Standard
and Poor's and Baa by Moody's:

We have no particular quarrel over the rating, nor the procedure of evaluation. . . . But their analyses seemed to be somewhat superficial as far as
their knowledge of our industry and our marketplace goes, and perhaps
they didn't do as thorough a job as they could have.[59]

Those who agree may be represented by the following statement
made by an associate treasurer at Monsanto Co., St. Louis, after
floating a $200 million bond issue:

There's obviously the potential for companies to be treated in a somewhat
arbitrary manner by the rating agencies, but our company management
had ample opportunity to tell our story and get our point across.[60]

EXPLANATION AND PREDICTION OF BOND RATINGS

NEED FOR A BOND RATING THEORY AND MODEL

Bond ratings are intended to convey a signal about the investment quality of bonds in general and various degrees of assurances
that the issuers will be able to fulfill their obligations. They are very
important to both issuers and investors for evident reasons. Thus,
both issuers and investors may want to be better prepared and be
able to explain and/or predict a given bond rating. The explanation
and/or the prediction of bond ratings rests on the formulation of a
proper theory of bond ratings that specifies the diagnostic cues that
may enter in the bond rating process and of a reliable bond ratings
prediction model that provides adequate signals about the rating
assigned a given issue. Both the theory and the model are the main
objectives of the rest of the book.

APPROACH TO BE USED

To be able to specify a relevant theory and model of bond predictions and to learn from the contributions and limitations of related

research efforts, a four-part approach will be used. In Chapter 2 the importance of financial analysis to the bond rating process will be presented with an emphasis on determining the financial variables and diagnostic accounting ratios that may constitute adequate determinants of the industrial bond ratings. In Chapter 3 the relevant research on the prediction of industrial bond ratings will be presented. The various models published in the accounting, financial and economic literature will be discussed and evaluated in terms of their contributions and limitations. In Chapter 4 an industrial bond ratings model resting on a theoretical and economic rationale will be presented. Both the validation and predictive ability of the model will be discussed and verified. Finally, in Chapter 5 the bond rating model will be further explained in terms of procedures of implementation.

CONCLUSIONS

As seen in this chapter, debt financing can go from the simplest to the most complex capital structure. Given this diversity and the need to provide the market with adequate information on the investment quality of bond financing, various rating agencies perform the difficult task of assigning ratings of investment quality to industrial and other bonds. These ratings play a major role for both the issuers and the investors who need a better explanation of the nature of these ratings, which is the objective of this chapter, and a better explanation and prediction of a bond rating model, which is the objective of the remaining chapters.

NOTES

1. Publicly issued debt obligations must comply with the requirements of the Trust Indenture Act of 1939 (TIA). Among other things, it imposes certain standards of conduct on the trustee. Charged with protecting the rights of debtholders under an indenture, the trustee, generally a bank, is often also a significant creditor of the corporate obligor and has its own interest in the firm. The sensitive conflict of interest is examined by Frederica R. Obrzut, "The Trust Indenture Act of 1939: The Corporate Trustee as Creditor," *UCLA Law Review*, 24 (1976), pp. 131–59.

2. These covenants are specified in bond contracts reviewed in an American Bar Foundation compendium entitled *Commentaries on Indentures* and reported by C. W. Smith, Jr. and J. B. Warner, "On Financial

Contracting: An Analysis of Bond Covenants," *Journal of Financial Economics* (June 1979), pp. 117–62. Similar examples of covenants were also reported by Elliot L. Atamian, "Negotiating the Restrictive Covenants of Loan Agreements Associated with the Private Placement of Corporate Debt Securities," *The University of Washington Business Review* (October 1964), pp. 56–72.

3. Abner Kalay, "Toward a Theory of Corporate Dividend Policy," Ph.D. diss. (University of Rochester, Rochester, N.Y., 1979). Kalay reports that every firm in a sample of 150 randomly selected firms had a covenant restricting the payment of dividends.

4. R. Leftwich, "Evidence on the Impact of Mandatory Changes in Accounting Principles on Corporate Loan Agreements, *Journal of Accounting and Economics* (March 1981), p. 6.

5. Robert W. Johnson, "Subordinated Debentures: Debt That Serves as Equity," *The Journal of Finance* (March 1955), pp. 1–16. He praised the advantages of subordination as follows:

It appears that these debentures may be prudently issued by a company which could tolerate additional fixed charges against income and additional debt in relation to net working capital but could not, under customary standards, increase the ratio of superior debt to net worth. Since they are hybrid securities in some respects, if subordinated debentures are to remain useful and to gain further stature, corporations must cling to those features which characterise a creditor obligation and issue only those amounts which can be safely supported (p. 16).

6. Harold Bierman, Jr. and Bowman Brown, "Why Corporations Should Consider Income Bonds," *Financial Executive* (October 1967), p. 76.

7. Frank A. Halford, "Income Bonds," *Financial Analysts Journal* (January–February 1964), p. 73.

8. Sidney M. Robbins, "A Bigger Role for Income Bonds," *Harvard Business Review* (November–December 1955), p. 114. In the same article Robbins mentions that besides the contingent interest charge freeing the corporation from meeting fixed payments, the income bonds may include features such as long maturities, capital funds, sinking funds, cumulative privileges, and rules for determining when interest must be paid that could make them attractive to both investors and management.

9. A growing trend is emerging favorable to the issuance of an "income indexed" bond which are income bonds indexed to the price level. The rationale for making them income indexed bonds rather than price-level indexed bonds is to protect the firms against the possibility that their earnings may fail to correlate with general nation-wide inflation. For more information, see Robert Haney Scott, "Why Doesn't Business Float Indexed Bonds?" *Business Economics* (September 1979), pp. 19–22.

10. Nathan Kahn, "Corporate Motivation for Convertible Bond Debt

Exchanges," *Journal of Accounting, Auditing and Finance* (Summer 1982), p. 327. In the same article Kahn examined a sample of firms resorting to the discounted convertible debt exchanges and found four distinct types of conversion changes:

New bonds are convertible at a lower conversion price.

New bonds are not convertible, but bondholder receives shares of common stock.

New bonds are not convertible, but bondholder receives warrants to purchase stock.

New bonds are not convertible, and no stock or warrants offered.

11. Rodney Johnson and Richard Klein, "Corporate Motives in Repurchases of Discounted Bonds," *Financial Management* (Autumn 1974), pp. 44-49. In this article they demonstrated that repurchases in excess of current sinking fund requirements cannot be justified on a discounted cash flow basis unless the issuing firm is anticipating future reductions in interest rates.

12. G. Pye uses the following reasoning for the claim that callable bonds will most likely be purchased by short-term lenders:

Long term lenders face the risk of receiving lower yields to maturity if their bonds are called. There seems to be no particular source of gain on other securities they might be holding that would offset such losses. Therefore, the call option will increase the variability of net return on their portfolio and so its cost to them will be somewhat greater than its expected value. On the other hand, short term lenders in holding callables give up a lottery of possible capital gains for a certain payment. If lower interest rates in the near future are associated with unemployment and reduced profit expectations, gains on the bonds will offset losses on any stocks in their portfolios. However, lower interest rates need not be associated with reduced profit expectations. If they are not, lower interest rates will mean higher, not lower, stock prices. Unless lower interest rates are highly associated with lower stock prices, the call option will reduce the variability of the net return for the short-term lender. The cost of the option for him will then be somewhat less than its expected value.

From G. Pye, "The Valuation of the Call Option of a Bond," *Journal of Political Economy* (April 1966), p. 203.

13. This points to the intuitive idea that a call privilege is a vendible good, subject to negotiation and reciprocal compensation rather than government regulation. This point is particularly made in the article by Willis J. Winn and Arleigh Hess, Jr., "The Value of the Call Privilege," *The Journal of Finance* (May 1959), pp. 182-95. Their argument is summarized as follows:

Whether the market places a value on the unrestricted call privilege or on a call provision which incorporates the compensating arrangement, the very act of evaluation would focus attention on the factors which affect the value of the redemption right and would lead issuers and investors to think of the privilege as a vendible good.

This attitude may dispense with some of the controversy over the justification of callability and over government regulation of this privilege. Finally, it might lead to some new method of dealing with the call privilege which would be more satisfactory to all parties concerned. (p. 195)

14. *The Wall Street Journal,* in an article entitled "Wary that Greenbacks Won't Outlast Inflation, the Timid Turn to Commodity-Backed Bonds" published on February 9, 1981, mentions that "dozens of companies are now said to be studying the idea."

15. Eduardo S. Schwartz, "The Pricing of Commodity-Linked Bonds," *The Journal of Finance* (May 1982), p. 525.

16. D. Lessard, "Risk Efficient External Financing for Commodity Producing Developing Countries: A Progress Report," Paper (Cambridge, Mass.: MIT, 1979); "Commodity-linked Bonds from Less-Developed Countries: An Investment Opportunity," Paper (Cambridge, Mass.: MIT, 1977); "Risk Efficient External Financing Strategies for Commodity Producing Countries," Paper (Cambridge, Mass.: MIT, 1977).

17. Moody's Investors Service, Inc., *Pitfalls in Issuing Municipal Bonds*

18. Standard and Poor's, *Credit Week* (April 12, 1982), p. 1561.

19. Gilbert Harold, *Bond Ratings as an Investment Guide* (New York: Ronald Press, 1938), pp. 9–13.

20. Marilyn Much, "The Rating Game: When Baa Spells bah," *Industry Week* (January 8, 1979), p. 45.

21. Irwin Ross, "Higher Stakes in the Bond-Rating Game," *Fortune* (April 1976), p. 134.

22. Some banks elect to assign their own ratings. For example, the Research Section at Harris Bank (Chicago) assigns their own ratings to municipal bonds on the basis of the following rating guide:

Investment Grade							Non-Investment Grade
9 8	7 6	5	4 3	2 1			0
Excellent	Very good	Good	Moderate	Adequate			Speculative

23. Moody's Investors Service, Inc., *Moody's Bond Survey* (April 26, 1982), p. 2181.

24. Standard and Poor's, *Credit Week* (April 12, 1982), p. 1561.

25. *Credit Week* sells separately for approximately $695 a year.

26. Bill Barnhart, "S&P Credit Watch Keeps an Eye on Debt Issues," *Chicago Tribune* (April 7, 1982), Section 3, p. 3.

27. The Trust Department of Harris Bank provides a Fixed Income Portfolio Service (FIPS) to subscribers which consists of a credit watch list for list of domestic issues using the following categories:

Category 1 for those firms considered underrated by Standard and Poor's.

Category 2 for those issues where Harris is in agreement with Standard and

Poor's. A+ modifier is used for strong agreement. A− modifier is used for mild agreement.

Category 3 for those issues considered overrated by Standard and Poor's.

28. Moody's Investors Service, Inc., *Moody's Bond Record* (July 1976), p. 1.

29. W. Braddock Hickman, *Corporate Bond Quality and Investor Experience* (Princeton: Princeton University Press, for the National Bureau of Economic Research, 1958), pp. 139–210.

30. Gilbert Harold, *Bond Ratings as an Investment Guide* (New York: The Ronald Press, 1938), pp. 93–106; 141–46.

31. O. K. Burrell, *A Study of Investment Mortality* (Eugene: University of Oregon: Bureau of Business Research, School of Business Administration, May 1947), pp. 10–11.

32. It is wise to know that a different interpretation of this evidence, with less favorable implications for the rating agencies' capabilities, is presented in J. S. Ang and K. A. Patel, "Bond Rating Methods: Comparison and Validation," *Journal of Finance* (May 1975), p. 633.

33. R. M. Goodman, "Municipal Bond Rating Testimony," *Financial Analysts Journal* (May–June, 1968), pp. 59–65.

34. D. Rubinfeld, "Credit Ratings and the Market for General Obligation Municipal Bonds," *National Tax Journal* 26 (1973), pp. 17–27.

35. S. Katz, "The Price Adjustment Process of Bonds to Rating Reclassifications: A Test of Bond Market Efficiency," *Journal of Finance* (May 1974), pp. 551–561.

36. P. Grier and S. Katz, "The Differential Effects of Bond Ratings Changes Among Industrial and Public Utility Bonds by Maturity," *Journal of Business* (April 1976), pp. 226–239.

37. George W. Hettenhouse and William L. Sartoris, "An Analysis of the Informational Value of Bond-Rating Changes," *Quarterly Review of Economics and Business* (Summer 1976), pp. 65–78.

38. Richard R. West, "Bond Ratings, Bond Yields and Financial Regulation: Some Findings," *Journal of Law and Economics* (April 1973), p. 168.

39. Carl J. Schwendiman and George E. Pinches, "An Analysis of Alternative Measures of Investment Risk," *The Journal of Finance* (March 1975), p. 199. The study found, however, that significant results exist only between relatively extreme values. In any case the results may imply that β could be an important variable to predict corporate bond ratings.

40. Mark I. Weinstein, "The Effect of a Rating Change Announcement on Bond Price," *Journal of Financial Economics* (December 1977), pp. 329–50.

41. G. E. Pinches and J. C. Singleton, "The Adjustment of Stock Prices to Bond Rating Changes," *The Journal of Finance* (March 1978), pp. 29–44.

42. Weinstein, "The Effect of a Rating Change Announcement."

43. P. A. Griffin and A. Z. Sanvicente, "Common Stock Returns and Rating Changes: A Methodological Comparison," *The Journal of Finance* (March 1982), pp. 103–20.

44. It is, however, more and more frequent that some corporations with mediocre credit ratings are using a back-door passage to long-term fixed rate debt through interest rate swaps. In the simplest form of interest swap, the corporation with mediocre credit rating borrows from the bank at a floating rate, usually at a margin over London interbank-offered rate (LIBOR). The corporation with good credit rating issues a fixed rate bond. The bank then matches the two, which exchange interest rate flows in a manner that leaves the corporation with the mediocre rating paying the fixed rate on the bond plus the margin over LIBOR on its loan; the corporation with good rating pays only LIBOR and saves the spread over the interbank rate it would have normally paid.

45. Failure to rely on the rating may create problems for the banks. For example, in July 1982, Continental Illinois National Bank & Trust of Chicago was sued in Federal District Court by a stockholder alleging that the bank engaged in "fraudulent, reckless and negligent" conduct in making $1.8 billion in bad loans to the failed Penn Square Banks and other businesses. The stockholder alleged the bank approved major loans "in violation of traditional operating procedures and frequently with inadequate local documentation."

46. Paul A. Griffin, "Usefulness to Investors and Creditors of Information Provided by Financial Reporting" (Financial Accounting Standards Board, Stamford, Conn. 1982), p. 149.

47. For more information see *Standard and Poor's Rating Guide, Corporate Bonds, Commercial Paper, Municipal Bonds, International Securities* (New York: McGraw-Hill Book Co., 1979), p. 19.

48. Ibid., p. 17.

49. Ibid., p. 18.

50. For example, in April 1982 Standard and Poor's announced the procedures it will follow for rating debt and certain equity securities registered under the SEC's new temporary shelf registration rule. This SEC rule (Rule 415) as a part of a nine-month deregulation experiment, permits a company whose stock is widely held to file one registration statement detailing its long-term plan for securities sales and waiting for the right market conditions before selling securities. The procedures announced by Standard and Poor's consist of a) arranging a meeting with the issue at the time the issuer files shelf registration, b) assessing the issuers affairs to determine the relationship of the securities registered to the company's financial plans, and

c) issuing a preliminary rating on the debt and preferred stock issues included in the shelf registration.

51. Ibid., p. 13.

52. Anthony Broy, "How Good are the Bond Rating Agencies?" *Financial World* (September 1, 1976), p. 11.

53. Irwin Ross, "Higher Stakes in the Bond-Rating Game," *Fortune* (April 1976), p. 133.

54. Ibid., p. 133.

55. Ibid., p. 142.

56. George C. McNamee and Edward J. Gibson, "Bank Bond Ratings are Wrong—Look at Bankers Trust," *The Bankers Magazine* (Winter 1977), p. 12.

57. Ibid., p. 12.

58. John J. Clark with Brenton W. Harries, "Some Recent Trends in Municipal and Corporate Securites Markets: An Interview with Brenton W. Harries, President of Standard and Poor's Corporation," *Financial Management* (Spring 1976), p. 16.

59. "The Men Who Make Treasurers Tremble," *Forbes* (September 1, 1970), p. 20.

60. Marilyn Much, "The Rating Game: When Baa Spells Bah," *Industry Week* (January 8, 1979), p. 47.

BIBLIOGRAPHY

Abdel-Khalik, A. Rashad, Robert B. Thompson, and Robert E. Taylor, "The Impact of Reporting Leases off the Balance Sheet on Bond Risk Premiums: Two Exploratory Studies." In *Economic Consequences of Financial Accounting Standards* (Research Report), pp. 103–57. Stamford, Conn.: FASB, July 1978.

Altman, Edward I. and Paul S. Tubiana, "The Multi-Firm Bond Issue: A Fund Raising Financial Instrument." *Financial Management* (Summer 1981), pp. 23–33.

Bierman, Harold, Jr., and Bowman Brown, "Why Corporations Should Consider Income Bonds." *Financial Executive* (October 1967), pp. 55–68.

Black, F., and J. Cox, "Valuing Corporate Securities: Some Effects of Bond Indenture Provisions." *Journal of Finance* (May 1976), pp. 352-67.

Bloch, Ernest, "Pricing a Corporate Bond Issue: A Look Behind the Scenes." In *Essays in Money and Credit*, pp. 72-76. New York: Federal Reserve Bank of New York, 1964.

Broy, Anthony, "How Good are the Bond Rating Agencies." *Financial World* (September 1, 1976), pp. 11-15.

Burrell, O. K., *A Study of Investment Mortality*. Eugene: University of Oregon: Bureau of Business Research, School of Business Administration, May 1947.

Cohan, A. B., *Yields on Corporate Debt Directly Placed*. National Bureau of Economic Research, Number 84, General Series. New York: Columbia University Press, 1967.

Douglas-Hamilton, Margaret H., "Creditor Liabilities Resulting from Improper Interference with the Management of a Financially Troubled Debtor." *Business Lawyer* 31 (1975), pp. 343-65.

Everett, Edward, "Subordinate Debt-Nature and Enforcement." *Business Lawyer* (July 1965), pp. 953-87.

Fogelson, James H., "The Impact of Changes in Accounting Principles on Restrictive Covenants in Credit Agreements and Indentures." *Business Lawyer* 73 (1978), pp. 769-87.

Gamble, George O., "An Application of Current Value Theory to Accounting for Investments in Bonds." *Journal of Accounting, Auditing and Finance* (Summer 1982), pp. 320-26.

Goodman, R. M., "Municipal Bond Rating Testimony." *Financial Analysts Journal* (May-June 1968), pp. 59-65.

Grier, P. and S. Katz, "The Differential Effects of Bond Rating Changes Among Industrial and Public Utility Bonds by Maturity." *Journal of Business* (April 1976), pp. 226-39.

Griffin, P. A. and A. Z. Sanvicente, "Common Stock Returns and Rating Changes: A Methodological Comparison." *The Journal of Finance* (March 1982), pp. 103-120.

Halford, Frank A., "Income Bonds." *Financial Analysts Journal* (January-February 1964), pp. 73-79.

Hettenhouse, George W. and William L. Sartoris, "An Analysis of the Informational Value of Bond-Rating Changes." *Quarterly Review of Economics and Business* (Summer 1976), pp. 65-77.

Holthausen, Robert W., "Evidence on the Effect of Bond Covenants and Management Compensation Contracts on the Choice of Accounting Techniques." *Journal of Accounting and Economics* (March 1981), pp. 73-109.

"How They'll Rate Your Company's Bonds." *Business Management* (March 1966), pp. 38-79.

Jen, Frank C., "The Value of the Deferred Call Privilege." *National Review* (March 1966), pp. 369-78.

Johnson, Rodney, and Richard Klein, "Corporate Motives in Repurchases of Discounted Bonds." *Financial Management* (Autumn 1974), pp. 44–49.

Johnson, Robert W., "Subordinated Debentures: Debt That Serves as Equity." *Journal of Finance* (March 1955), pp. 1–16.

Kahn, Nathan, "Corporate Motivation for Convertible Bond Debt Exchanges." *Journal of Accounting, Auditing and Finance* (Summer 1982), pp. 327–37.

Katz, S., "The Price Adjustment Process of Bonds to Rating Reclassifications: A Test of Bond Market Efficiency." *Journal of Finance* (May 1974), pp. 551–61.

Kennedy, Joseph C., *Corporate Trust Administration*, New York: New York University Press, 1961.

Leftwich, R., "Private Determination of Accounting Methods in Corporate Bond Indentures." (Graduate School of Management Dissertation Proposal, University of Rochester, Rochester, N.Y., 1978).

Leftwich, R., Richard, "Evidence on the Impact of Mandatory Changes in Accounting Principles on Corporate Loan Agreements." *Journal of Accounting and Economics* (March 1981), pp. 4–36.

Lindbeck, A., *The "New" Theory of Credit Control in the United States*. New York: Almquist and Winsell, 1959.

Lindvall, J. R., "New Issue Corporate Bonds, Seasoned Market Efficiency, and Yield Spreads," *Journal of Finance* (September 1977), pp. 1057–67.

McNamee, George C. and Edward J. Gibson, "Bank Board Ratings are Wrong—Look at Bankers Trust." *The Bankers Magazine* (Winter 1977), pp. 11–12.

Much, Marilyn, "The Rating Game: When Baa Spells Bah." *Industry Week* (January 8, 1979), pp. 44–47.

Obrzut, Frederica R., "The Trust Indenture Act of 1939: The Corporate Trustee as Creditor." *UCLA Law Review*, 24 (1976), pp. 131–59.

Pye, G., "Gauging the Default Premium." *Financial Analysts Journal* (January–February 1974), pp. 49–52.

Reilly, R. K. and M. D. Joehnk, "The Association Between Market Determined Risk Measures for Bonds and Bond Ratings." *Journal of Finance* (December 1976), pp. 1387–1404.

Report of the Twentieth Century Fund Task Force on Municipal Bond Credit Ratings. *The Rating Game*. New York: Twentieth Century Fund, 1974.

Pinches, G. E., and J. C. Singleton, "The Adjustment of Stock Prices to Bond Rating Changes." *The Journal of Finance* (March 1978), pp. 29–44.

Robbins, Sidney M., "A Bigger Role for Income Bonds," *Harvard Business Review* (November–December 1955), pp. 100–14.

Rodgers, Churchill, "The Corporate Trust Indenture Project." *Business Lawyer* 20 (1965), pp. 551–71.

Ross, Irwin, "Higher Stakes in the Bond-Rating Game." *Fortune* (April 1976), pp. 133–42.

Rubinfeld, D., "Credit Ratings and the Market for General Obligation Municipal Bonds." *National Tax Journal* 26 (1973), pp. 17–27.

Schwartz, Eduardo S., "The Pricing of Commodity-Linked Bonds." *The Journal of Finance* (May 1982), pp. 525–39.

Schwendiman, Carl J. and George E. Pinches, "An Analysis of Alternative Measures of Investment Risk." *The Journal of Finance* (March 1975), pp. 193–200.

Scott, Robert Haney, "Why Doesn't Business Float Indexed Bonds?" *Business Economics* (September 1979), pp. 19–22.

Shapiro, Harvey, "How Corporations are Trying to Improve their Credit Ratings." *Institutional Investor* (January 1976), pp. 47–52.

Sherwood, H. C., *How Corporate and Municipal Debt Is Rated*, New York: Wiley, 1976.

Smith, C. W., Jr., and J. B. Warner, "On Financial Contracting: An Analysis of Bond Covenants." *Journal of Financial Economics* (June 1979), pp. 117–62.

"The Men Who Make Treasurers Tremble." *Forbes* (September 1, 1970), pp. 19–20.

Weinstein, Mark I., "The Effect of a Rating Change Announcement on Bond Price." *Journal of Financial Economics* (December 1977), pp. 329–50.

West, Richard R., "Bond Ratings, Bond Yields and Financial Regulation: Some Findings." *Journal of Law and Economics* (April 1973), pp. 159–68.

Winn, Willis J., and Arleigh Hess, Jr., "The Value of the Call Privilege." *Journal of Finance* (May 1959), pp. 182–95.

Zingbarg, Edward, "The Private Placement Loan Agreement." *Financial Analyst Journal* (July/August 1975), pp. 33–52.

2

FINANCIAL ANALYSIS AND BOND RATINGS

INTRODUCTION TO FINANCIAL ANALYSIS

Financial analysis is an information processing system used to provide relevant information for decision making. The main source of information is the published financial statements. Basically, various accounts from the published financial statements are evaluated in relation to each other to form performance indicators which are then compared to "established" standards. These performance indicators are better known as ratios and constitute the main tool of conventional financial analysis. Some of these ratios are particularly relevant to an evaluation of bonds and to the assignment of bond ratings. Before examining some of these ratios and given the importance of published financial statements as a source of information, this chapter will first elaborate on the format and content of financial statements.

FINANCIAL STATEMENTS AND ACCOUNTING DATA

The financial statements included in the annual reports generally include a balance sheet, an income statement, a statement of changes in the financial position, notes to the financial statements, a reconciliation of retained earnings, an auditor's opinion, and supplementary information on the effects of changing prices. These reports are discussed next. To help familiarize the reader with these reports, Appendix A presents the financial statements of a well known American company for the year ending December 31, 1981.[1]

THE BALANCE SHEET

The balance sheet, or statement of financial position, expresses the financial position of a firm at the end of the accounting period, a moment in time. More precisely, it presents both the assets of a firm and claims on those assets (liabilities and owners' equity) at a point in time. Two major questions of interest to the reader are, first: which resources of a firm are recognized as assets and which claims against the firm's assets are reorganized as liabilities? Second: What valuations are placed on these assets and liabilities?

Assets

Four characteristics must be met for a resource (other than cases) to be recognized as an asset: (1) the resource must, singly or in combination with other resources, contribute directly or indirectly to future net cash inflows (or to obviating future net cash outflows); (2) the enterprise must be able to obtain the benefit from the resource and control the access of others to it; (3) the transaction or event giving rise to the enterprise's claim to or control of the benefit must already have occurred; and (4) the future benefit must be quantifiable or measurable in units of money.[2]

The assets are broken down into further, more specific categories by order of decreasing liquidity.

Current assets is "used to designate cash and other assets or resources commonly identified as those that are reasonably expected to be realized in cash or sold or consumed during the normal operating cycle of the business."[3] Current assets consist generally of cash, marketable securities held as short term investments, accounts and notes receivables net of allowance for uncollectible accounts, inventories of merchandise, raw materials, supplies, work in process and finished goods, and prepared operating costs.

Investments is used to designate the investments in securities of other firms to be held for a long term and whose financial statements have not been consolidated with the parent or investor firm. Long-term investment of 50 percent of the voting stock of a corporation (subsidiary) calls for consolidation of the financial statements of the subsidiary with the parent firm.

Property, plant and equipment designates the long-lived assets, generally termed fixed assets, acquired for long-term use rather than resale, generally include land, buildings, machinery and equipment, and various equipment. With the exception of land, these assets are carried at original cost less accumulated depreciation.

Intangible assets designates resources that lack physical existence and includes copyrights, patents, trademarks, goodwill, organization costs, franchises, lease holds and similar items.[4]

Liabilities

Four characteristics must be met before an obligation is recognized as a liability: (1) the obligation must involve a probable future sacrifice of resources—a future transfer of cash, goods, or services (or a foregoing of a future cash receipt); (2) the obligation must be one of the specific enterprise; (3) the transaction or event giving rise to the enterprise's obligation must already have occurred; and (4) the amount of the obligation and the time of its settlement must be measurable with reasonable accuracy.[5]

The liabilities are further broken down in specific categories.

Current liabilities is "used principally to designate obligations whose liquidation is reasonably expected to require the use of existing resources properly classified as current assets, or the creation of other current liabilities."[6] It includes accounts payables, notes payables, accrued expenses, accrued taxes, and the current portion of long-term debt.

Long-term liabilities designates obligations having a due date or maturities longer than a year. It includes bonds, mortgages, long-term leases, deferred income taxes, and deferred pension obligations.

Owner's Equity

Owner's equity represents the ownership interests in the firm and includes what was originally invested by them and whatever earnings are "plowed back" in the firm. It includes (1) capital stock, common or preferred, which is the portion of the capital specified in the articles of incorporation at par value;[7] (2) additional paid-in capital, which is the portion paid in excess of the stated or par value; and (3) retained earnings, which represents earnings undistributed and "plowed back" into the firm.

Valuation of Assets and Liabilities

There are four possible valuation methods: (1) acquisition cost or historical cost, which is the amount of cash or other payment made by the firm when it acquired specific assets; (2) current entry value or replacement cost, which is the amount of cash or equivalent necessary to replace the asset by a "similar" asset; (3) current exit value or net realizable value, which is the amount assumed to be realized if the assets were sold in an orderly fashion; and (4) capitalized value, which is present value of future cash flows which can be generated by the asset.

Unfortunately not one single valuation base is used to value all the assets and liabilities. All four valuation bases are used by generally accepted accounting principles. Exhibit 2.1 presents a summary of valuation methods for various assets and liabilities. This situation presents quite an intellectual challenge to those investors who are not versed into the complexities and idiosyncracies of accounting valuations.

THE INCOME STATEMENT

The income statement presents a measure of the financial performance of a firm over an accounting period. The net income is equal to the revenues and gains minus expenses and losses. Let's examine each of these elements of the income statement.

Revenues

Revenues measure the inflow of net assets resulting from the sales of goods or services. Revenue may be recognized at the time of sale when (1) most of the services to be provided have been performed and (2) some measurable consideration has been received. Revenue may be recognized during the period of production for certain long-term contracts and special order merchandise. Revenue also may be recognized at the time of cash collection for installment sales of merchandise, real estate or franchises.

Expenses

Expenses measure the outflow of net assets that have been used to generate the revenues. They are therefore recognized in the same period the revenues have been generated.[8] Expenses are composed of cost of goods sold, selling, and administrative expenses. The

EXHIBIT 2.1   VALUATION BASES UNDER GENERALLY
              ACCEPTED ACCOUNTING PRINCIPLES

ACCOUNTS	VALUATION BASE
Cash	Face or current exchange value (current cash equivalent)
Marketable securities	The portfolio is valued at lower of cost or market (current exit value)
Accounts and notes receivable	Short-term accounts are valued at current cash equivalent, long-term accounts at the present value of the future cash flows (discounted at the historical market interest rate on date of issue)
Inventories	Lower of cost or market (current entry value)
Investments	Investments in bonds are valued at the present value of the future cash flows. Investments in stocks are valued at lower of cost or market where there is no significant influence and using the equity method where there is "significant influence"
Land	Acquisition cost
Depreciable assets	Acquisition cost (net of accumulated depreciation)
Patents, goodwill and intangibles	Stated at the amount payable if they are to be paid within the next year, if not, stated at the present value of future cash flows
Nonmonetary liabilities	If arising from transactions where revenues have already been recognized (warranties on product sold), they are stated at the estimated future cost of the warranty services; if arising from advances from customers for future goods or services, they are stated at the amount of cash received

value of the cost of goods sold depends on the cost flow assumptions either First-in First-out (FIFO), Last-in First-out (LIFO) or Weighted Average. Under the FIFO method, the cost of goods sold is valued at the cost of the earliest units acquired. Under the LIFO method, the cost of goods sold is valued at the cost of the latest units acquired. Under the weighted average method, the cost of goods sold is valued at the average of the costs of all goods available for sale use during the period. There is an important implication to the cost-flow assumptions. FIFO results in lower cost of goods sold and higher income than LIFO where prices are rising. This LIFO results in a cost of goods sold figure that is close to current values and in lower cash outlays for income taxes.[9]

Format and Classification Within the Income Statement

In general, the income statement contains the following categories:

a. *Income from Continuing Operations:* It is equal to the revenues and gains from the operating areas of the business firm minus the corresponding expenses and losses.

b. *Income, Gains and Losses from Discontinued Operations:* This section includes the income, gains and losses resulting from the disposal of a segment of the firm.[10]

c. *Extraordinary Gains and Losses:* This section includes all activities termed extraordinary if they meet all three of the following criteria: (1) unusual in nature, (2) infrequent in occurrence, and (3) material in amount.[11]

d. *Adjustment for Accounting Changes:* This section includes four types of accounting changes, namely, (1) change in accounting estimate, (2) change in accounting principle, (3) change in reporting entity, and (4) correction of errors in prior years' financial statements. According to APB Opinion No. 20, these changes are to be reflected in the accounts and reported on the financial statements retroactively for a change in accounting entity, prospectively for a change in accounting estimate, and generally, currently for a change in accounting principle.[12]

Earnings per Share

APB Opinion No. 15 recommends that earnings per share be included in the body of the income statement before receiving an auditor's unqualified opinion.[13] Most firms have a complex capital structure which includes convertible bonds or convertible preferred stock. To warn about the dilutive effect of such a situation, a dual presentation of primary and fully diluted earnings per share is required. Primary earnings per share represents the earnings applicable to each share of outstanding common stock and common stock equivalent. Common stock equivalents are securities which are likely to be converted into, or exchanged for, common stock instead of their own periodic cash yields over time. Fully diluted earnings per share represent the earnings applicable to each share if besides outstanding common stock all options, warrants, and convertible securities were exchanged for common stock.

THE STATEMENT OF CHANGES IN FINANCIAL POSITION

The statement of changes in financial position presents the inflows (sources) and outflows (uses) of funds for the accounting period. "Funds" are defined generally as working capital (current assets minus current liabilities). Other definitions of funds include cash only; cash and marketable securities; or cash, marketable securities, and accounts receivables net of current liabilities. Whatever the definition of funds, the statement of changes in financial position includes both the sources and uses of funds. They are as follows:

1. *Sources: From operations:* equal to income from continuing operations plus all the expenses not requiring an outflow of funds.

2. *Sources: Proceeds from Issuing Noncurrent Debt and Capital Stock:* equal to funds generated from the issuance of stock and from long-term borrowing.

3. *Sources: Proceeds from the Sale of Net Current Assets:* equal to funds generated from the sale of buildings, equipment, land and other non-current assets.

4. *Uses: For Distributions to Owners:* equal to the dividends distributed to both common and preferred shareholders.

5. *Uses: For Redemption of Long-term Debt or Capital Stock:* equal to the funds used for retiring non-current debt and acquiring capital stock. (Treasury stock)

6. *Uses: For Acquisition of Non-current Assets:* equal to the funds used for the purchase of land, machinery and equipment and other non-current assets.

NOTES TO THE FINANCIAL STATEMENTS AND OTHER ITEMS
IN THE ANNUAL REPORTS

Notes to the Financial Statements

Given the complexity of the three major financial statements, the balance sheet, income statement, and statement of changes in the financial position, additional information may be needed to guide the annual report user toward a better understanding of the accounting data. This additional information forms the major part of the notes to the financial statements. Examples of notes are shown in the Annual Reports in Appendix A. A high fluency in the accounting language is needed to comprehend the information conveyed by the notes.

Reconciliation of Retained Earnings

This section is used to reconcile the beginning and ending balances in retained earnings.

Auditor's Opinion

This is an important section of the annual report used to express the opinion of the independent certified public accountant on the financial statements, supporting schedules and notes. The four types of opinion which may result from an independent audit of financial statements are:

1. *Unqualified opinion:* when the auditor states that the financial statements "presents fairly" the position and activities of the firm.
2. *Qualified opinion:* when the auditor may feel that the financial statements "presents fairly" the position and activities of the firm, but cannot make one or more of the statements necessary for an unqualified opinion. A qualified opinion is conveyed by the use of "except for" or "subject to" statement in the audit report. "Except for" is used to convey an objection about the financial statements being presented.[14] "Subject to" is used to convey a contingency, uncertainty, or unresolved situations that may affect the financial statements.[15]
3. *Disclaimer of opinion:* when the auditor has been so limited, or there is a serious and material departures from GAAP, and as a result, the finanmerely an inability to give an opinion.
4. *Adverse opinion:* when the auditor feels that the audit has shown some

serious and material departures from GAAP, and as a result, the financial statements do not present fairly the position and activities of the firm.

Supplementary Information on the Effects of Changing Prices

The Financial Accounting Standards Board (FASB) Statement No. 33 "Financial Reporting and Changing Prices" requires that the company provide supplementary information concerning the effects of inflation on its financial statements. Required disclosures include selected financial information on a constant dollar basis (reflecting the effects of general inflation) as computed by use of the Consumer Price Index for All Urban Consumers (CPI), and on a current cost basis (reflecting specific price changes of goods and services). The FASB has provided flexibility and encouraged experimentation within the guidelines of the statement. Accordingly, users of annual reports should exercise discretion when considering the supplementary information on the effects of changing prices.

ROLE OF FINANCIAL STATEMENT ANALYSIS

The question of the role of financial statement analysis is important considering the theoretical and empirical evidence supporting the efficiency of the capital market. It is generally assumed that the securities market is efficient. A perfectly efficient market is in continuous equilibrium, so the intrinsic values of securities vibrate randomly and market prices always equal underlying intrinsic values at every instant in time.[16] Applied to the securities market, this assumption implies that market prices "fully reflect" all publicly available information and, by implication, market prices react instantaneously and without bias to new information. Of the three levels of market efficiency, the semi-strong form is the most relevant to the role of financial statement analysis.[17] The semi-strong form of the efficient market hypothesis states that the equilibrium-expected returns (prices) "fully reflect" all publicly available information. In other words, no trading rule based on available information may be used to earn an excess return. The semi-strong form is most relevant to accounting because publicly available information includes financial statements. Tests of the semi-strong hypothesis were concerned with the speed with which prices adjusted to specific kinds of events. Some of the events examined were stock splits, announcement of annual earnings, large secondary offering of common stocks, new issues of stocks, announcements of changes in the discount rate, and stock dividends. The results again support the efficient market hypothesis in the sense that prices adjust rather quickly after the first public announcement of information. Which brings to question again the role of financial analysis in such an efficient capital market. There is definitively a role for financial analysis in such an efficient market.

First, the first role results from the two findings that first, accounting information and stock price movements are significantly associated, even when the effects of other information (e.g. dividend announcements) are taken into account, and second, accounting information appears to be able to assist in the assessment of prospective return and risk. Both findings imply that financial statements analysis may assist to make intelligent investment decisions.

Second, for the first role to be possible, the financial statement analysis must be expertly and quickly done.

Third, a final role of financial statement analysis is to explain and predict economic events that may affect the firm and that are not reflected in some capital market framework. Examples include bond ratings, bankruptcy, take over, and so forth. . . . The likelihood of these events requires a careful analysis of the financial, operating and extraordinary dimensions of the affairs of the firm.

FINANCIAL RATIO ANALYSIS

USEFULNESS OF RATIO ANALYSIS

Financial analysis is a methodology designed to provide data for decision-makers. It is intended to be flexible enough to assist different users in their decision. Financial analysis rests entirely on the use of financial ratios. Financial ratios are more convenient to interpret than the financial statement accounts. This convenience is possible because the financial ratios represent "significant relationships" between various items in the financial statements. These financial ratios are then compared to established standard ratios for the firm or other firms in the industry. If the comparison is with similar ratios of the firm over a certain number of years, the analysis is referred to as time-series analysis. If the comparison is with similar ratios of other firms over a certain number of years, the analysis is referred to as cross-sectional analysis. Whatever the type of analysis chosen, ratio analysis is intended to evaluate important financial aspects of the firm that depict its financial strengths. Examples include liquidity, leverage, profitability and turnover dimensions. Some of the types of ratios used to measure these dimensions are presented next. They are classified into four major categories: (1) the firm's ability to meet its short-term obligations; (2) the capital structure of the firm and its ability to meet its long-term obligations; (3) the profitability and efficiency resulting from the use of capital; and (4) the efficiency resulting from the operational use of its assets.

LIQUIDITY RATIOS

Liquidity ratios are used to assess the ability of the firm to meet its short-term financial obligations when and as they fall due. These ratios are of prime interest to short-term lenders.

Current Ratio

The current ratio may be expressed as:

$$\frac{\text{current assets}}{\text{current liabilities}}$$

Current assets are composed mainly of cash, short-term marketable securities, accounts receivable, inventories, and prepaid expenses. Current liabilities are composed mainly of accounts payable, dividends, tax payable, and short-term bank loans. The current ratio has been considered for a long time as a good indicator of the firm's liquidity.[18] It is, however, susceptible to "window dressing": that is, susceptible to manipulation intended to approximate a "desirable" current ratio.

Quick (Acid-Test) Ratio

The Quick ratio may be expressed as:

$$\frac{\text{quick assets}}{\text{current liabilities}}$$

Quick assets are composed of cash, short-term marketable securities and receivables. The quick ratio is intended to be a focus on immediate liquidity. Both the quick ratio and the current ratios have been criticized for failure to incorporate information about the timing and magnitude of future cash flows.[19]

Defensive Interval Measure

The defense interval measure was presented as a better replacement of both the current ratio and the quick ratio:

$$\frac{\text{total defensive assets}}{\text{projected daily operating expenditures}}$$

The total defensive assets have been appropriately defined as follows:

Defensive assets include cash, short-term marketable securities and accounts receivable. Inventories are not included in the total, nor are current liabilities deducted from the total. The denominator includes all projected operating costs requiring the use of defensive assets. Ideally, this would be based on the cash budget for the next year or shorter period. Since this information is unlikely to be available to external analysts, the total of operating expenses on the income statement for the prior period will usually serve as a basis for calculating the projected expenditures. The adjustments must be made to the total expense figure on that statement:

  (1) Depreciation, deferred taxes and other expenses that do not utilize defensive assets must be subtracted.
  (2) Adjustments should be made for known changes in planned operations.[20]

Other measures of liquidity based on a fund flow concept include: a) the ratio of net working capital to funds provided by operations[21]; b) the ratio of funds provided from operations to current debt[22]; and c) a liquidity index based on projected fund flows.[23] Each of these fund flow based ratios reflects the idea that liquidity depends on the ability of liquid assets and cash inflows to cover the cash outflow by a material margin.

A measure of future liquidity may be expressed as follows: the five-year cash flow as a percentage of five-year growth needs is equal to the five-year sum of: (1) net income available for common stockholders plus (2) depreciation and amortization plus (3) income from discontinued operations and extraordinary items net of taxes, divided by the five-year sum of (1) capital expenditures plus (2) changes in inventories during most recent five years plus (3) common dividends.

LEVERAGE/CAPITAL STRUCTURE RATIOS

Leverage ratios are used to assess the long-term solvency risk of the firm, that is, its ability to meet interest and principal payments on long-term obligations as they become due. These ratios are of prime interest to long-term lenders and bond holders.

Debt to Equity Ratios

There are two possible debt to equity ratios:

$$\text{(a) long-term debt to equity} = \frac{\text{long-term debt}}{\text{shareholders' equity}}$$

$$\text{(b) total debt to equity} = \frac{\text{current liabilities} + \text{long term debt}}{\text{shareholders' equity}}$$

Both debt equity ratios press the degree of leverage in the capital structure of the firm. They are also used as a measure of the financial risk associated with the common stocks of the firm.[24]

Times Interest Earned Ratio

The times interest earned ratio may be expressed as:

$$\frac{\text{net income (from continuing operations)} \atop \text{before interest and income taxes}}{\text{interest expense}}$$

or:

$$\frac{\text{net income plus total interest} \atop \text{(adjusted by tax rate)}}{\text{interest expense (adjusted by tax rate)} \atop + \text{ preferred dividend requirement}}$$

PROFITABILITY RATIOS

The profitability ratios portray the ability of the firm to efficiently use the capital committed by stockholders and lenders to generate revenues in excess of expenses. These ratios are consequently of interest to both stockholders and bondholders.

Rate of Return on Assets

The rate of return on assets, also lessen as the rate of return on investment (ROI) is computed as follows:

$$ROI = \frac{\text{net income + interest expense net of income tax savings + minority interest in earnings}}{\text{average total assets}}$$

This ratio measures the efficient use of the assets by the firm to generate earnings. One way of explaining the changes in ROI over time is to disaggregate the ratio as follows:

$$ROI = \text{Profit Margin Ratio} \times \text{Assets Turnover Ratio}$$

or

$$ROI = \frac{\text{net income + interest expense net of income savings + minority interest in earnings}}{\text{sales}} = \frac{\text{sales}}{\text{average total assets}}$$

where the profit margin ratio reflects the firm's ability to control the level of costs corresponding to the sales realized, and the assets turnover ratio corresponds to the ability to generate sales from the assets used. The improving ROI may be realized either by improving the profit margin ratio or the assets turnover ratio or by improving both.

Return on Equity

The return on equity is computed as:

$$\frac{\text{income available for common stockholders}}{\text{common stockholders' equity}}$$

This ratio indicates how efficiently the capital supplied by the common stockholders was employed within the firm.

Other examples of profitability ratios used by some analysts includes the expense to revenue ratio, the operating income ratio ([sales-cost of goods sold-selling and administrative expenses]/

sales), the earnings per share (presented earlier), the price-earnings ratio (market price of a common stock/earnings per share), the dividends to net income or pay out ratio, and the operating income to operating assets ratio.

TURNOVER RATIOS

Turnover or efficiency ratios are intended to convey various aspects of operational efficiency. They are generally computed on the basis of a sales figure in the numerator and the balance of an asset in the denominator. The previously mentioned total assets turnover ratio is one example of turnover ratios. Other examples include the following ratios:

Inventory Turnover

The inventory turnover is computed as:

$$\frac{\text{cost of goods sold}}{\text{average inventory}}$$

It is used as an indicator of operational efficiency.

Accounts Receivable Turnover

The accounts receivable turnover is computed as:

$$\frac{\text{sales}}{\text{average (net) accounts receivable}}$$

By dividing the accounts receivable turnover by 360 days, one also obtains the average collection period for accounts receivable. It is an indicator of the efficiency in the collection efforts of accounts receivable.

Plant Assets Turnover

The plant assets turnover is computed as:

$$\frac{\text{sales}}{\text{average plant assets}}$$

It is used as a measure of the relationship between sales and the plant assets used by the firm for its operations.

ADJUSTMENTS TO FINANCIAL STATEMENTS

Ratio analysis depends to a great extent on data provided by the published financial statements and notes. Because these data may be computed differently from one firm to another due to the choice of different accounting techniques, the analyst may be required to adjust the financial statements to make the ratios from different firms and/or industries comparable. In what follows, some of the most important adjustments are presented.

Comprehensive Income

The first type of adjustment may be to insure that the computation of income and the classification of recurring and nonrecurring items on income statements are similar. This task may become easier with the eventual adoption of some of the recommendations of the FASB exposure draft on *Reporting Income, Cash Flows, and Financial Position of Business Enterprises.* Among the useful recommendations are the adoption of the term "comprehensive income" to represent the enterprise's total net income from all sources and of the disclosure of the following components of comprehensive income: (a) income from continuing central operations (that is, the basic business and primary source of comprehensive income); (b) income from discontinued operations; (c) income from peripheral or incidental transactions (such as, results of activities that are unusual in nature); and (d) income from price changes, or holding gains and losses (applicable to either a historical cost or current value accounting system).

Inventory Flow Assumption

The second type of adjustment is that resulting from the restatement of ratios of different firms to either a FIFO or LIFO flow assumption to make them comparable. This is important since the use of FIFO may generate a higher profit and hence may show a different rate of return on assets than under LIFO. This adjustment is much easier by the IRS regulations issued in early 1981, permitting virtually all types of supplemental LIFO disclosures, in footnotes and in special reports, as long as the disclosures accompany the primary presentation of income on a LIFO basis and they are clearly identified as supplementary to or an explanation of the LIFO presentation.

Depreciation Policy

The third type of adjustment results from the use of an accelerated depreciation method for tax and the straight line method for book purposes. The choice of different depreciation techniques for tax and book purposes results in the recognition of deferred income taxes in the balance sheet. The analyst may want to convert the depreciation charges to either the accelerated depreciation charges recognized for taxes or the straight line charges reorganized for book purposes to achieve some comparability from one firm to another.

Deferred Income Taxes

Timing differences arises from four sources as follows: (1) revenues included in pretax book income earlier than recognized for tax purposes, (2) revenues included in taxable income earlier than recognized for tax purposes, (3) expenses subtracted earlier in determining pretax book income than deducted in determining taxable income, and (4) expenses deducted earlier in determining taxable income than subtracted in determining pretax book income. APB Opinion No. 11 requires that comprehensive allocation be followed and that the deferral method be used "since it provides the most useful and practical approach to interperiod tax allocation and the presentation of income taxes in the financial statements."[25] The deferral method requires that the income taxes saved currently because book income exceeds taxable income be set up as a deferred credit in the balance sheet.[26] As a result, the computation of some ratios (ROI and debt equity ratios) would be different from the same ratios computed by firms not deferring taxes. As a result, adjustments may have to be made by the analyst to obtain uniform data for making comparisons.

Use of "Defeasance" Techniques

The adjustments illustrated earlier are some examples of the numerous transformations that can be made to accounting data to make them comparable between firms. The types of adjustments are dictated by the information provided in the financial statements and in the notes regarding the accounting policies exposed by each firm. Given, however, the interest in this book with debt evaluation and rating, a special adjustment is reported here that is needed to offset the use of defeasance technique. Defeasance was used by firms to reduce debt on their balance sheet and to increase their reported income. The method takes several forms. In one variation a company acquires government securities at a discount and places them in a trust, promising to use the future income from the securities to pay off the interest and principal due on its own debt securities as they mature. The company eliminates the debt from its balance sheet. The company also recognizes a profit because the discounted government securities cost less than the cost of redeeming the company's debt at face value. Fortunately, the SEC issued a release in August 1982 in which it stated that the companies using defeasance techniques should follow a tentative conclusion by the FASB that debt should not be considered as extinguished and that no gain or loss should be recognized, unless the debtor has no further legal obligation with respect to the debt.

SHORTCOMINGS IN FINANCIAL RATIO ANALYSIS

Most of the ratios useful for an effective financial analysis are summarized in Exhibit 2.2. Before using them, however, the rater and/or the analyst should be aware of their limitations.

First, financial statements serve as the primary source of data for the computations of ratios. Given, however, the flexibility in choosing among various generally accepted accounting principles, the ratios among firms may not be comparable unless appropriate adjustments are made to the financial statements. Moreover, comprehensive financial rates analysis is constrained by the lack of standard accepted computational rules. With the exception of the computations of earnings per share, the regulatory agencies have refrained from enacting or suggesting specific guidelines. As a result there is no consensus on the computational methodology of the ratios.[27]

Second, ratio analysis rests on a proper definition of income, especially when income is required in the computation of the ratio. There is actually a big gap between the economic definition of income and the accounting income as based on a historical cost valuation.[28] Economic income was appropriately defined by Hicks.[29] Basically, he defined a person's personal income as "the maximum amount he can consume during a week, and still *expect* to be as well-off at the end of the week as he was at the beginning."[30]

EXHIBIT 2.2 SUMMARY OF MAIN FINANCIAL RATIOS

RATIO	NUMERATOR	DENOMINATOR
1. Current	Current assets	Current liabilities
2. Quick	Quick assets	Current liabilities
3. Defensive interval measure	Total defensive assets	Projected daily operating expenditures
4. Long-term debt to equity	Long-term debt	Shareholders' equity
5. Total debt to equity	Current liabilities + long-term debt	Shareholders' equity
6. Times interest earned	Net income (from continuing operations) before interest and taxes	Interest expense
7. Times interest earned	Net income + total interest expense (adjusted by tax rate)	Interest expense (adjusted by tax rate) + preferred dividend requirement
8. Rate of return on assets	Net income + interest expense net of income tax savings + minority interest in earnings	Average total assets

EXHIBIT 2.2—*Continued*

RATIO	NUMERATOR	DENOMINATOR
9. Return on equity	Income available for common stockholders	Common stockholders' equity
10. Inventory turnover	Cost of goods sold	Average inventory
11. Accounts receivable turnover	Sales	Average (net) accounts receivable
12. Plant assets turnover	Sales	Average plant assets
13. Five-year cash flow as percentage of five-year growth needs	Five-year sum of (1) net income available for common stockholders + (2) depreciation and amortization + (3) income from discontinued operations and extraordinary items net of taxes	Five-year sum of (1) capital expenditures, + (2) change in inventories during most recent five years + (3) common dividends

This definition has become the basis of many discussions on the concept of income. One problem raised by such a definition, however, is the lack of consensus or the interpretation of the term "as well-off." The most accepted interpretation is that of capital maintenance, in which case the "Hicksian" income is the maximum amount that may be consumed in a given period and still maintain the capital intact.

There are actually four concepts of capital maintenance: (1) financial capital measured in units of money—money maintenance—which is the concept used to compute accounting income; (2) financial capital measured in units of the same purchasing power—general purchasing power money maintenance—which is the concept used to compute accounting income adjusted for changes in the general price level; (3) physical capital measured in units of money—productive capacity maintenance—which is the concept used to compute current income; (4) physical capital measured in units of the same purchasing power—general purchasing power productive capacity maintenance—which is the concept used to compute current income adjusted for changes in the general price level.

Which of these incomes is a good surrogate of economic income and should be used in the computation of ratios? The theoretical and sound answer is in favor of the current income adjusted for changes in the general price level.[31] FASB Statement No. 33 goes one step forward to help the computation of such figure by requiring the presentation of both general price level and specific price level information.

Third, ratios are generally used to control for the systematic effects of size on the variables under examination. However, Lev and Sunder showed that the ratio form adequately controls for size only under highly restrictive conditions.[32] They sound an important warning: "When these conditions are not met, size is not adequately controlled for, and more seriously, the amount of bias varies with size; it is large for small firms and relatively small for large firms. Given these problems, the use of ratio analysis in financial analysis and research should be accompanied by a theoretical justification and an empirical analysis of the degree to which the data meet the ratio assumptions. In the likely case of deviations from these assumptions, an analysis of the sensitivity of findings to these deviations from should be conducted."[33] The second major issue examined in the article is the choice of the size variable where the choice should be justified on theoretical grounds or "information should be provided on the degree of substitutability of the different measures, and the sensitivity of the findings to alternative measures."[34]

Finally, ratio analysis relies mostly on the comparison of the specific ratios of a specific firm with an industry average. Knowledge of the industry's average and standard deviations is crucial for inferences based on ratio analysis. However, not only measures of dispersion of the ratio distribution are rarely communicated to users, but also the findings are that, in general, financial ratios are not normally distributed and that skewness exists.[35] To approximate normality some transformation of financial ratios may be necessary. Examples of possible transformations include the logarithmic and the power and square root transformations.

FINANCIAL ANALYSIS AND THE EVALUATION OF BONDS

USEFULNESS OF FINANCIAL ANALYSIS IN THE BOND RATING PROCESS

As stated earlier, the bond rating is a statement about the debtor's situation and the probability that he will be able to meet coupon or principal payments. Thus, to the rater or the bond analyst the primary responsibility is to determine the probability that the firm (or other issues) will be able to meet coupon and/or principal payments. Evidently this task requires a thorough examination of accounting data and the use of the techniques of financial analysis. More specifically the rater or the bond analyst will have to compute enough financial ratios to assess the following conditions: (a) the firm's ability to meet its short-term obligations, (b) the capital structure of the firm and its ability to meet its long-term obligations, (c) the profitability and efficiency resulting from the use of capital, and (d) the efficiency resulting from the operational use of its assets. While most of the ratios identified earlier can be helpful to assess the four conditions, the rater and/or the bond analyst may have to carry the analysis further for a comprehensive evaluation of the bond. Such a comprehensive evaluation may require the examination of the following factors.

Bond Yields

Three bond yield concepts may be of interest, namely the current yield, the yield to maturity and the yield to average life. They are computed as follows:

The current yield of a bond is the dollar coupon rate of the bond divided by the current market price. Suppose an XYZ bond sells on the market at $900. It has a 9 percent coupon (interest paid annually), a $1,000 par value and five years to maturity. The current yield of the bond is:

$$\frac{\$90}{\$900} = 10\%$$

The yield to maturity is the interest rate for which the present value of the face value of the bond over the number of years to maturity plus the present value of an annuity of the coupon rate in dollars over the number of years to maturity equal the market value of the bond. Applied to the XYZ bond example the yield to maturity is the rate of interest that makes

Present value of $1,000, five years hence + Present value of a five-year annuity of $90 = $900

or using a short-cut formula, the yield to maturity is:

$$\frac{\$90 + \dfrac{1,000-900}{5}}{\dfrac{1,000+900}{2}} = 11.57\%$$

Raters and bond analysts may prefer to compute the yield to average life of the bond, rather than the yield to maturity, when a lot-drawing sinking fund is used to pay off the issue.[36] The main difference between the yield to maturity and the yield to average life results from the substitution of the expected life of the bond for the maturity of the bond. Let's go back to the XYZ bond example and suppose that the XYZ company planned for sinking fund payments

equal to 20 percent of the issue coming due over each of the next
five years. The average life of the XYZ bond is given by:

YEAR	PROBABILITY	AVERAGE LIFE
1	.2	.2
2	.2	.4
3	.2	.6
4	.2	.8
5	.2	1.0
		3.0 years

The yield to average life is then computed as:

$$\frac{\$90 + \dfrac{1,000 - 900}{3}}{\dfrac{1,000 + 900}{2}} = 12.98\%$$

In general, the rater or the analyst will not use the short-cut formula
mentioned for the various yield calculations but instead will rely on
a bond table such as shown in Exhibits 2.3 and 2.4. For example,
the rater or the bond analyst looks up the yield on, say, a $7\frac{3}{4}$ percent coupon issue due in 19 years and six months, selling at 102.54,
and finds the right yield of 7.50 in Exhibit 2.3. Similarly the rater or
the bond analyst looks up the yield on an 8 percent coupon issue
due in 20 years and selling at 82.8409 and finds the right yield to be
10 percent in Exhibit 2.4.

The Industry

The industry within which the firm operates is an important factor for both the raters and the analyst. For one thing there are certain ratios which are specific to each industry and should be considered for the evaluation of bonds in addition to the conventional
ratios identified earlier. There are numerous examples.

For the airlines, a load factor is important. They are two types of
load ratios, namely the passenger load factor, which is the percentage of seats occupied during a year, and the break-even passenger
load, which is the percentage of occupied seats necessary for the
coverage of total costs. Profits increase when the passenger board
factor exceeds the break-even passenger load. The airlines rely also
on efficiency ratios. These ratios include among others the average

EXHIBIT 2.3   BOND TABLE: 7¾%

YEARS and MONTHS

Yield	18-6	19-0	19-6	20-0	20-6	21-0	21-6	22-0
4.00	148.69	149.58	150.44	151.29	152.12	152.94	153.74	154.52
4.20	145.35	146.15	146.94	147.72	148.47	149.21	149.94	150.65
4.40	142.10	142.84	143.55	144.25	144.94	145.61	146.27	146.91
4.60	138.96	139.62	140.27	140.90	141.52	142.13	142.72	143.30
4.80	135.90	136.50	137.09	137.66	138.22	138.76	139.29	139.81
5.00	132.94	133.48	134.00	134.52	135.02	135.50	135.98	136.44
5.20	130.07	130.55	131.02	131.47	131.92	132.35	132.78	133.19
5.40	127.28	127.71	128.12	128.53	128.92	129.30	129.68	130.04
5.60	124.57	124.95	125.32	125.67	126.02	126.36	126.68	127.00
5.80	121.95	122.28	122.59	122.91	123.21	123.50	123.79	124.06
6.00	119.40	119.68	119.96	120.23	120.49	120.74	120.98	121.22
6.10	118.15	118.41	118.67	118.92	119.16	119.39	119.62	119.84
6.20	116.92	117.16	117.40	117.63	117.85	118.06	118.27	118.48
6.30	115.71	115.93	116.15	116.36	116.56	116.76	116.95	117.14
6.40	114.52	114.72	114.92	115.11	115.30	115.48	115.65	115.82
6.50	113.34	113.53	113.71	113.88	114.05	114.21	114.37	114.52
6.60	112.18	112.35	112.51	112.67	112.82	112.97	113.11	113.25
6.70	111.04	111.19	111.34	111.48	111.61	111.74	111.87	111.99
6.80	109.92	110.05	110.18	110.30	110.42	110.54	110.65	110.76
6.90	108.81	108.92	109.04	109.15	109.25	109.35	109.45	109.55
7.00	107.71	107.82	107.91	108.01	108.10	108.19	108.27	108.36
7.10	106.64	106.72	106.81	106.89	106.96	107.04	107.11	107.18
7.20	105.57	105.65	105.72	105.78	105.85	105.91	105.97	106.03
7.30	104.53	104.59	104.64	104.70	104.75	104.80	104.84	104.89
7.40	103.50	103.54	103.58	103.62	103.66	103.70	103.74	103.77
7.50	102.48	102.51	102.54	102.57	102.60	102.62	102.65	102.67
7.60	101.48	101.50	101.51	101.53	101.55	101.56	101.58	101.59
7.70	100.49	100.49	100.50	100.51	100.51	100.52	100.52	100.53
7.80	99.51	99.51	99.50	99.50	99.49	99.49	99.48	99.48
7.90	98.55	98.54	98.52	98.50	98.49	98.47	98.46	98.45
8.00	97.61	97.58	97.55	97.53	97.50	97.48	97.45	97.43
8.10	96.67	96.63	96.60	96.56	96.53	96.49	96.46	96.43
8.20	95.75	95.70	95.66	95.61	95.57	95.53	95.49	95.45
8.30	94.85	94.79	94.73	94.68	94.62	94.57	94.53	94.48
8.40	93.95	93.88	93.82	93.75	93.69	93.64	93.58	93.53
8.50	93.07	92.99	92.92	92.85	92.78	92.71	92.65	92.59
8.60	92.20	92.11	92.03	91.95	91.88	91.80	91.73	91.67
8.70	91.34	91.25	91.16	91.07	90.99	90.91	90.83	90.76
8.80	90.49	90.39	90.29	90.20	90.11	90.02	89.94	89.86
8.90	89.66	89.55	89.44	89.34	89.25	89.15	89.07	88.98
9.00	88.84	88.72	88.61	88.50	88.40	88.30	88.20	88.11
9.10	88.02	87.90	87.78	87.67	87.56	87.45	87.35	87.26
9.20	87.22	87.09	86.97	86.85	86.73	86.62	86.52	86.42
9.30	86.43	86.30	86.16	86.04	85.92	85.80	85.69	85.59
9.40	85.66	85.51	85.37	85.24	85.12	85.00	84.88	84.77
9.50	84.89	84.74	84.59	84.46	84.33	84.20	84.08	83.97
9.60	84.13	83.97	83.83	83.68	83.55	83.42	83.30	83.18
9.70	83.38	83.22	83.07	82.92	82.78	82.65	82.52	82.40
9.80	82.64	82.48	82.32	82.17	82.02	81.89	81.76	81.63
9.90	81.92	81.75	81.58	81.43	81.28	81.14	81.00	80.87
10.00	81.20	81.02	80.86	80.70	80.54	80.40	80.26	80.13
10.20	79.79	79.61	79.43	79.26	79.11	78.95	78.81	78.67
10.40	78.42	78.23	78.05	77.87	77.71	77.55	77.40	77.26
10.60	77.09	76.89	76.70	76.52	76.35	76.19	76.03	75.88
10.80	75.79	75.59	75.39	75.20	75.03	74.86	74.70	74.55
11.00	74.53	74.32	74.12	73.93	73.74	73.57	73.41	73.26
11.20	73.30	73.08	72.88	72.68	72.50	72.32	72.15	72.00
11.40	72.10	71.88	71.67	71.47	71.28	71.10	70.93	70.78
11.60	70.93	70.71	70.49	70.29	70.10	69.92	69.75	69.59
11.80	69.79	69.56	69.35	69.14	68.95	68.77	68.60	68.43
12.00	68.68	68.45	68.23	68.03	67.83	67.65	67.47	67.31

EXHIBIT 2.4   BOND TABLE: 8%

Market Yield Percent per Year Compounded Semiannually	Years to Maturity							
	$^1/_2$	5	10	15	19$^1/_2$	20	30	40
5.0	101.463	113.128	123.384	131.396	137.096	137.654	146.363	151.678
5.5	101.217	110.800	119.034	125.312	129.675	130.098	136.528	140.266
6.0	100.971	108.530	114.877	119.600	122.808	123.115	127.676	130.201
6.5	100.726	106.317	110.905	114.236	116.448	116.656	119.690	121.291
7.0	100.483	104.158	107.106	109.196	110.551	110.678	112.472	113.374
7.1	100.435	103.733	106.367	108.225	109.424	109.536	111.113	111.898
7.2	100.386	103.310	105.634	107.266	108.314	108.411	109.780	110.455
7.3	100.338	102.889	104.908	106.318	107.220	107.303	108.473	109.044
7.4	100.289	102.470	104.188	105.382	106.142	106.212	107.191	107.665
7.5	100.241	102.053	103.474	104.457	105.080	105.138	105.934	106.316
7.6	100.193	101.638	102.767	103.544	104.034	104.079	104.702	104.997
7.7	100.144	101.226	102.066	102.642	103.003	103.036	103.492	103.706
7.8	100.096	100.815	101.371	101.750	101.987	102.009	102.306	102.444
7.9	100.048	100.407	100.683	100.870	100.986	100.997	101.142.	101.209
8.0	100	100	100	100	100	100	100	100
8.1	99.9519	99.5955	99.3235	99.1406	99.0279	99.0177	98.8794	98.8170
8.2	99.9039	99.1929	98.6529	98.2916	98.0699	98.0498	97.7798	97.6589
8.3	99.8560	98.7924	97.9882	97.4528	97.1257	97.0962	96.7006	96.5253
8.4	99.8081	98.3938	97.3294	96.6240	96.1951	96.1566	95.6414	95.4152
8.5	99.7602	97.9973	96.6764	95.8052	95.2780	95.2307	94.6018	94.3282
8.6	99.7124	97.6027	96.0291	94.9962	94.3739	94.3183	93.5812	93.2636
8.7	99.6646	97.2100	95.3875	94.1969	93.4829	93.4191	92.5792	92.2208
8.8	99.6169	96.8193	94.7514	93.4071	92.6045	92.5331	91.5955	91.1992
8.9	99.5692	96.4305	94.1210	92.6266	91.7387	91.6598	90.6295	90.1982
9.0	99.5215	96.0436	93.4960	91.8555	90.8851	90.7992	89.6810	89.2173
9.5	99.2840	94.1378	90.4520	88.1347	86.7949	86.6777	85.1858	84.5961
10.0	99.0476	92.2783	87.5378	84.6275	82.9830	82.8409	81.0707	80.4035
10.5	98.8123	90.4639	84.7472	81.3201	79.4271	79.2656	77.2956	76.5876
11.0	98.5782	88.6935	82.0744	78.1994	76.1070	75.9308	73.8252	73.1036

length of trip, the average miles per plane departure, the revenues per passenger mile and the average number of hours each plane is in the air.

For railroads, three ratios are important, namely the maintenance ratio, which is the ratio of maintenance expenditures over total operating revenues; the transportation ratio, which is the ratio of transportation expenses over total operating revenues; and the net ton-miles per train hour.

For the banks, the important ratios include the capital-to-deposits ratio, the risk-assets-to-capital ratios, the net-loan-losses-to-net-operating-income ratio, and the loans-to-deposits ratio.

For life insurance companies, the rates and the analyst may look at the mortality ratio, which is the ratio of actual mortality to forecasted mortality, and the interest ratio, which is the actual ROI to standard ROI. The key factor is to insure that the legal reserves set aside out of premiums are being invested efficiently.

Besides these specific ratios, the rater or the analyst may be interested in those factors of the industry which may give a reasonable indication of what the general course of an industry is likely to be in the ensuing years, namely the position in the economy (capital goods, consumer durables, or consumer nondurable sectors), life cycle of the industry (growth, stable, or declining phase), competitive nature (nature and intensity of the competition), labor situation (strength of the unions), supply factors (control of or dependence on sources), volatility (stable dependent on external events), and major vulnerabilities.

Management

Management is an important rating factor of interest to both the rater and the analyst. Management may be the key to a company's success in the industry. Most of the ratios presented earlier may be used to evaluate management's policies in running the company. To a certain extent the accounting data may be used as a surrogate of management's performance in planning and executing plans, in pursuing its financial and operating policies, in managing the current accounts, in choosing the capital structure and in reaching profit and growth targets. The contribution of management to the company's success may ultimately have to be quantified and internalized in the financial statements using the evolving "human asset accounting." But before this new form of accounting gains more popularity and acceptance, face to face meetings with management may be the best approach for both raters and analysts to appraise the "human" potential of the firm. A non-inclusive list of the possible questions management may have to answer include the following:

What are management's policies and goals?
What funds will management have to raise externally to achieve its goals?

In this connection, what are management's cash-flow projections for the next 5 years?

What are management's plans for the immediate future?

Has management provided for unforeseen events?

What is the company's philosophy about acquisitions?

What are its new product plans?

What is the company spending on research and development?

What is the company's advertising program?[37]

USEFULNESS OF FINANCIAL ANALYSIS IN THE EXPLANATION
AND PREDICTION OF BOND RATINGS

Multivariate Analysis

The preceding analyses are all of a univariate nature, that is, the ratios are examined one at a time. Given the number of relevant ratios, the analysis may become cumbersome since some of these ratios may be redundant to the issue in operation. An analysis based on a multivariate rather than univariate model would avoid the interdependencies among various ratios and the ambiguous inferences resulting from conflicting signals. A multivariate analysis would rely on few "diagnostic" ratios and avoid the redundancy in the use of similar ratios in a univariate analysis.[38] The main characteristic of the multivariate analysis is the simultaneous inclusion of several diagnostic ratios in the analysis. Basically, the multivariate analysis will consist of (a) choosing the "diagnostic ratios" to be included in the model and (b) deciding on the type of mathematical relationship among the variables.

Predictive Ability of Ratios and Choice of Diagnostic Ratios

The choice of diagnostic or relevant ratios to the explanation and prediction of bond ratings and to be included in a multivariate model rests on their predictive ability. Predictive ability means that the choice among different accounting ratios to be included in the model should depend on each ratio's ability to predict events of interest to users. More specifically, "the measure with the greatest predictive power with respect to a given event is considered to be the 'best' method for that particular purpose."[39] The criterion of "predictive ability" follows from the emphasis on "relevance" as the primary criterion of financial reporting.[40] Relevant data, therefore, are characterized by an ability to predict future events. The criterion of predictive ability is also well accepted in the natural and physical sciences as a method of choosing among competing hypotheses. Beaver et al.,[41] by showing that alternative accounting measures have the properties of competing hypotheses, rationalized the use of predictive ability in accounting. An obvious advantage of the predictive approach is that it allows us empirically to evaluate alternative accounting measurements and to make a clear choice on the basis of a discriminatory criterion. A growing body of empirical accounting research has evolved from the predictive ability approach. Two streams may be identified: one concerned with the ability of accounting data to explain and predict economic events, and the other with the ability of accounting data to explain and predict market reaction to disclosure. The concern in this book is with the first stream, and more precisely with the ability of accounting data to explain and predict bond ratings. The research on the ability of accounting data to explain and predict bond ratings using a multivariate model is extensive and varied. In the next chapter many of these empirical bond rating models will be presented.

CONCLUSIONS

Financial analysis rests on an adequate use of information from the published financial statements. Therefore, a good grasp of some of the accounting patterns and idiosyncrasies governing the preparation of published financial statements is necessary to make the financial ratios relevant to users. With respect to bond evaluation and rating univariate ratios, analysis may bring some answers and indications about the financial strength of a firm. However, the information content of diagnostic ratios is better enhanced when used in a multivariate model. Such multivariate models composed of diagnostic ratios would be more helpful and less cumbersome for bond ratings than univariate analysis. In the following chapters more will be said about these multivariate models, their construction and implementation.

NOTES

1. These statements are presented just as an illustration and not as an example of what should be expected from conventional statements.

2. Financial Accounting Standards Board, *Statement of Financial Concepts No. 3* (December 1980), paragraphs 17 and 20.

3. *Accounting Research Bulletin No. 43*, AICPA (1953), chap. 3A.

4. A precise definition is lacking. For example, *Accounting Principles Board Opinion No. 17* is devoted entirely to intangibles but never defines the term.

5. Financial Accounting Standards Board, Statement of Financial Concepts No. 3, paragraphs 17 and 29.

6. *Accounting Research Bulletin No. 43*, AICPA (1953), chap. 3A.

7. While common shares have only a residual claim, preferred shares are granted special privileges entitling their holder to dividends at a certain rate that must be paid before dividends to common shareholders. Preferred shares may be participating, which entitles their holders to also participate in the distribution of the residual left to common shareholders. They may be convertible, which entitles their owner to convert them into a specified amount of common shares at specified times. Most preferred dividends are cumulative, entitling their holder to eventually receive all postponed dividends. Finally, most preferred shares are callable, which entitles the corporation to reacquire them at specified prices.

8. The accounting principle governing this treatment is the matching principle. Basically, it holds that expenses should be recognized in the same period as the associated revenues. That is, revenues are recognized in a given period according to the realization principle and then the related expenses are recognized. The association is best accomplished when it reflects the "cause and effect" relationship between cost and revenues. Operationally, it consists of a two-stage process of accounting for expenses. First, costs are capitalized as assets representing bundles of service potential or benefits. Second, these assets are written off as expenses to recognize the proportion of the asset's service potential that has expired in the generation of revenues during the period.

9. It seems however, that for some companies, FIFO accounting makes more sense. M. H. Granof and D. G. Short asked the controllers of 380 corporations that have not adopted LIFO why they haven't. They found that most non-LIFO companies are *not* incurring a tax penalty. Other reasons included the following:

a.   FIFO is preferable for those firms using tax loss or tax credit forwards.

b.   LIFO prevents these companies from taking advantage of the "lower of cost or market."

c.   A company may now report the results of a subsidiary in its financial statements based on any inventory method, even though the subsidiary used LIFO to compute taxable income. The court of appeals held that Insilco Corporation did not violate the LIFO conformity requirement when, as a parent corporation, it issued consolidated financial statements in which inventories were priced at an average cost method, even though the consolidated inventories included the inventories of three subsidiaries that reported to the parent on a LIFO basis.

d. Various drawbacks of LIFO could outweigh possible tax benefits. For more information see, Granof, M. H., and D. G. Short, "For Some Companies, FIFO Accounting Makes Sense," *The Wall Street Journal*, August 30, 1982, p. 10.

10. Accounting Principles Board, *Opinion No. 30* (1973, paragraph 15), recommends the recognition of the net income, gains and losses (net of income tax effects), at the measurement date if it is a loss and at the time of realization if it is a gain. This treatment follows the well known *conservatism principle* which recommends recognizing losses as soon as possible and postponing the recognition of gains until realization.

11. Accounting Principles Board, *Opinion No. 30* (1973); Financial Accounting Standard Board, *Statement of Financial Accounting Standards No. 4* (1975).

12. Accounting Principles Board, *Opinion No. 20* (1970).

13. Accounting Principles Board, *Opinion No. 15* (May 1969).

14. "Except for" is used if: (1) the scope of the audit has been limited, (2) the financial statements contain a departure from GAAP, (3) GAAP were not consistently applied.

15. The Canadian Institute of Chartered Accountants dropped the "subject to" opinion requirement effective November 1980.

16. P. Samuelson, "Proof that Properly Discounted Present Values of Assets Vibrate Randomly," *Bell Journal of Economics and Management Science* (Autumn 1973), pp. 369–74.

17. E. Fama, "Efficient Capital Markets: A Review of Theory and Empirical Work," *Journal of Finance* (May 1970), pp. 383–447. Fama also presented the weak and strong forms of the efficient market hypothesis. The weak form of the efficient market hypothesis states that the equilibrium-expected returns (prices) "fully reflect" the sequence of past returns (prices). In other words, historical price and volume data for securities contain no information that may be used to earn a profit superior to a simple "buy-and-hold" strategy. This form of the hypothesis began with the theory that price changes follow a true "random walk." This school, though, is naturally challenged by "technical analysts" or "chartists," who believe that their rules based on past information can earn greater-than-normal profits. Filter rules, serial correlation, and run tests have tested the weak form of the efficient market hypothesis. The results support the hypothesis, particularly for returns longer than a day. The strong form of the efficient market hypothesis states that the equilibrium-expected returns (prices) fully reflect

all information (not just publicly available information). In other words, no trading rule based on any information including inside information may be used to earn an excess return. Evidence on the strong form of the efficient market hypothesis is not conclusive. While one study was able to show that mutual funds do not have any superior consistent performance over time, given a presumed access to special information, another study argued for the possibility of superior returns, given an access to specialists' look.

18. R. A. Foulke, *Practical Financial Statement Analysis*, 6th Edition (New York: McGraw-Hill, 1968).

19. J. E. Walter, "Determination of Technical Solvency," *Journal of Business* (January 1957), pp. 30–43; K. W. Lemke, "The Evaluation of Liquidity: An Analytical Study," *Journal of Accounting Research* (Spring 1970), pp. 47–77.

20. S. Davidson, G. H. Sorter, and H. Kalle, "Measuring the Defensive Position of a Firm," *Financial Analyst Journal* (January-February 1964). p. 23.

21. H. Bierman, Jr., "Measuring Financial Liquidity," *The Accounting Review* (October 1960), pp. 628–32.

22. J. E. Walter, "Determination of Technical Solvency," *Journal of Business* (January 1957), pp. 30–43.

23. K. W. Lemke, "The Evaluation of Liquidity: An Analytical Study," *Journal of Accounting Research* (Spring 1970), pp. 47–77.

24. Financial risk is generally defined in terms of the volatility of the earning streams that accrue to common stockholders. In general, the higher the proportion of debt in the capital structure, the higher the volatility of earnings and the higher the financial risk of the firm.

25. Accounting Principles Board, *Opinion No. 11* (1967), paragraph 34.

26. Edward E. Williams and M. Chapman Findlay III, *Investment Analysis* (Englewood Cliffs, N.J.: Prentice-Hall, Inc., 1974), p. 154.

27. Although there is a lack of consensus on how the financial ratios should be computed, empirical evidence seems to show that there is agreement on which ratios are important. For more information see Charles H. Gibson, "How Industry Perceives Financial Ratios," *Management Accountants* (April 1982), pp. 13–19.

28. Ahmed Belkaoui, *Accounting Theory* (San Diego, Calif.: Harcourt Brace Jovanovich Inc., 1981), p. 143.

29. The accounting income is operationally defined as the difference between the realized revenues arising from the transactions of the period and the corresponding historical costs. It suffers from the following limitations: (a) it fails to recognize unrealized increases in values of assets held in a given period because of the application of the historical cost and the realization principles; (b) it relies on the historical cost principle, making comparability difficult, given the different acceptable methods of computing

"cost" (for example, the different inventory costing methods) and the different acceptable methods of cost allocation generally deemed arbitrary and incorrigible; and (c) it relies on the historical cost principle which may give the impression to users that the balance sheet represents an approximation of value rather than merely a statement of unallocated cost balances. Besides, the emphasis on an income determination led to a resolution of controversial issues based on their impact on the income statement, thereby creating in the balance sheet a mixture of items that are quite hard to define, for example, deferred tax allocation debits and credits.

30. J. R. Hicks, *Value and Capital,* End Ed. (Oxford: Clarendon Press, 1946) p. 172. Hick's "week" refers to a specified period of time rather than a week.

31. Ahmed Belkaoui, *Accounting Theory* (San Diego, Calif.: Harcourt Brace Jovanovich, Inc., 1981), p. 143.

32. They stated that a ratio is an adequate instrument for size control when the variable under examination, y, is strictly proportional to the size of the operations. For more information see B. Lev and S. Sunder, "Methodological Issues in the Use of Financial Ratios," *Journal of Accounting and Economics* (December 1979), p. 190.

33. Ibid., pp. 193-34.

34. Ibid., p. 198.

35. Paul Barnes shows that where financial ratios are non-normally distributed, the comparison of a financial ratio with an industry average is likely to misinform. However, he also shows that where financial ratios are input to certain statistical models (regression and multiple discriminant analysis) normality is irrelevant. Paul Barnes, "Methodological Implications of Non-Normally Distributed Financial Ratios," *The Journal of Business Finance and Accounting* (Spring 1982), pp. 51–62.

36. Standard and Poor's Ratings Guide (New York: McGraw-Hill Book Company, 1979), p. 28.

37. Hugh C. Sherwood, *How Corporate and Municipal Debt is Rated* (New York: John Wiley & Sons, 1976), p. 36.

38. The diagnosticity of a ratio is the degree of importance or relevance it has to the true state of the world. In the context of the prediction of an economic event, a ratio is diagnostic if it serves to predict the particular event. Accordingly, given a diagnostic ratio, any additional ratio implying the same referent dimension(s) or object(s) and also statistically correlated to it is a redundant ratio.

39. W. H. Beaver, J. W. Kennelly, and W. M. Voss, "Predictive Ability as a Criterion for the Evaluation of Accounting Data," *The Accounting Review* (October 1968), p. 675.

40. American Accounting Association, *A Statement of Basic Accounting Theory* (New York: AAA, 1966), Chapter 3.

41. Beaver et al., "Predictive Ability," p. 676.

BIBLIOGRAPHY

Abdel-Khalik, A. Rashad, "The Efficient Market Hypothesis and Accounting Data: A Point of View." *The Accounting Review* (October 1978), pp. 791-93.

Ashton, R. H., "The Predictive Ability Criterion and User-Prediction Models." *The Accounting Review* (October 1974), pp. 719-32.

Barnes, Paul, "Methodological Implications of Non-Normally Distributed Financial Ratios." *Journal of Business Finance and Accounting* (Spring 1982), pp. 51-62.

Beaver, William H., J. W. Kennelly, and W. M. Voss, "Predictive Ability as a Criterion for the Evaluation of Accounting Data." *The Accounting Review* (October 1968), pp. 675-83.

Belkaoui, Ahmed, *Accounting Theory*. San Diego, Calif.: Harcourt Brace Jovanovich, 1981.

———. *Théorie Comptable*. Quebec, Les Presses de l'Université du Québec, 1981.

Berstein, L. A., "In Defense of Fundamental Investment Analysis." *Financial Analyst Journal* (January-February 1975), pp. 57-61.

Bierman, H., Jr., "Measuring Financial Liquidity." *The Accounting Review* (October 1960), pp. 628-32.

Bird, R. G., and A. G. McHugh, "Financial Ratios: An Empirical Study," *Journal of Business Finance and Accounting* (Spring 1977), pp. 29-45.

Davidson, S., G. H. Sorter, and H. Kalle, "Measuring the Defensive Position of a Firm," *Financial Analyst Journal* (January-February 1964), pp. 23-29.

Deakin, E. B., III, "Distributions of Financial Accounting Ratios: Some Empirical Evidence," *The Accounting Review* (January 1976), pp. 90-96.

Fama, E., "Efficient Capital Markets: A Review of Theory and Empirical Work." *Journal of Finance* (May 1970), pp. 383-447.

Foster, G., *Financial Statement Analysis*. Englewood Cliffs, N.J.: Prentice-Hall, Inc., 9178.

Foulke, R. A., *Practical Financial Statement Analysis*, 6th Edition. New York: McGraw-Hill, 1968.

Gibson, Charles H., "How Industry Perceives Financial Ratios." *Management Accountant* (April 1982), pp. 13-19.

Granof, M. H. and D. G. Short, "For Some Companies, FIFO Accounting Makes Sense." *The Wall Street Journal*, August 30, 1982, p. 10.

Griffin, Paul A., *Usefulness to Investors and Creditors of Information Provided by Financial Reporting: A Review of Empirical Accounting Research*. Stamford, Conn.: FASB, 1981.

Gupta, M. C., and R. J. Huefner, "A Cluster Analysis Study of Financial
    Ratios and Industry Characteristics." *Journal of Accounting
    Research* (Spring 1972), pp. 77–95.

Horrigan, J. O., "A Short History of Financial Ratios Analysis." *The
    Accounting Review* (April 1968), pp. 284–94.

Lasman, Daniel A., and Roman L. Weil, "Adjusting the Debt-Equity
    Ratio." *Financial Analysts Journal* (September/October 1978), pp.
    49–58.

Lemke, K. W., "The Evaluation of Liquidity: An Analytical Study." *Jour-
    nal of Accounting Research* (Spring 1970), pp. 47–77.

Lev, B., and Shyam Sunder, "Methodological Issues in the Use of Financial
    Ratios." *Journal of Accounting and Economics* (December 1979),
    pp. 187–210.

Lev, B., *Financial Statement Analysis: A New Approach.* Englewood
    Cliffs, N.J.: Prentice-Hall, Inc., 1974.

Lev, B., "Industry Average as Targets for Financial Ratios." *Journal of
    Accounting Research* (Autumn 1969) pp. 290–99.

Mecimore, C. D., "Classifying and Selecting Financial Ratios." *Manage-
    ment Accounting* (February 1968), pp. 11–17.

Nelson, A. T., "Capitalizing Leases: The Effect on Financial Ratios." *Jour-
    nal of Accountancy* (July 1963), pp. 49–58.

Pinches, G. E., K. A. Mingo, and J. M. Caruthers, "The Stability of Finan-
    cial Patterns in Industrial Organizations." *Journal of Finance* (April
    1973), pp. 389–396.

Sherwood, Hugh C., *How Corporate and Municipal Debt is Rated.* New
    York: John Wiley & Sons, 1976.

Sorter, G., and G. Benston, "Appraising the Defensive Position of a Firm:
    The Interval Measure." *The Accounting Review* (October 1960),
    pp. 633–40.

Walter, J. E., "Determination of Technical Solvency." *Journal of Business*
    (January 1957), pp. 30–43.

Whittington, G., "Some Basic Properties of Accounting Ratios." *Journal of
    Business Finance and Accounting* (Summer 1980), pp. 219–232.

Williams, Edward E., and M. Chapman Findlay III, *Investment Analysis,*
    Englewood Cliffs, N.J.: Prentice-Hall, Inc., 1974.

3

PREDICTING CORPORATE BOND RATINGS: A SURVEY

INTRODUCTION

We have stated in the first two chapters the importance of bond ratings to the financial community and the need for adequate prediction models. Before presenting our model in chapter 4, it is important to survey the various attempts made in the literature to develop bond rating models using various financial variables and various statistical approaches. The financial variables as presented later differ from one study to another and are basically not supported by any theoretical model linking the financial variables to the bond ratings. The statistical approaches used include regression analysis, dichotomous probability functions, multiple discriminant analysis, and multivariate probit analysis. Given this diversity in the choice of financial variables and statistical approaches to the formulation of a bond rating prediction model, the existing research studies are evaluated in terms of their contribution and limitations.

EARLY RESEARCH

Four studies considering bond quality and bond ratings open the door to research on bond rating prediction models. These studies include (1) Gilbert Harold Study,[1] (2) W. Braddock Hickman Study,[2] (3) Atkinson and Simpson Study,[3] and (4) Lawrence Fisher Study.[4]

HAROLD'S STUDY

Gilbert Harold compared the performance of agency-rated corporate bonds from 1929 through 1936. Based on a sample of 363 bonds rated by Poor, Fitch, Moody and Standard, he examined the yield and default records of each class of these bonds. He concluded that the difference in the ratings assigned to the same bond by different rating agencies should cause the prudent investor to reconsider the bases of bond ratings.

HICKMAN'S STUDY

Hickman's study was carried out under the direction of the National Bureau of Economic Research. The field of investigation was the universe of straight corporate bonds offered from 1900 through 1943, including those outstanding on January 1, 1900. Nine prospective measures of bond quality including industry; agency rating; legal status in Maine, Massachusetts, and New York; market rating; times-charges-earned ratio; ratio of net income to gross income; lien position; size of issue; and asset size of obligor were compared with four measures of investor experience (or retrospective measures of bond quality) including default rate, promised yield, realized yield, and loss rate. Of interest to this book are the findings first, that agency ratings, market ratings, legal lists, and other selected indicators of prospective bond quality proved useful guides in ranking bond offerings and outstandings in order of the risk of subsequent default; second, that a list of bonds meeting a fixed market rating standard was less stable than lists selected by agency ratings or legal status; and third, that the errors in rating corporate bonds can be traced principally to the business cycle and the difficulty of forecasting business trends. Another important finding was first, that during the period 1900 through 1943 the record of the rating agencies was remarkably good by showing a consistent inverse relationship between the bond ratings and default rates; and second, the capital loss on default, as measured by the difference between par value and the market value at default, was inversely related to the ratings.

ATKINSON AND SIMPSON'S STUDY

Atkinson and Simpson's study extended Hickman's study into
the post-World War II era, with some modifications. Applying
standard measures such as agency ratings, earnings coverage,
security, and market rating, they compared postwar with prewar
corporate-bond quality. The results of the study indicate defaults
of bonds outstanding decreased from an average prewar 1.7 percent to a postwar average of less than 0.1 percent.

Each of the studies examined—Harold's, Hickman's and Atkinson and Simpson's—does not advance the understanding of the
bond rating process and/or prediction, given that they were mainly
concerned with the question of how default records and yields were
related to bond ratings.

FISHER'S STUDY

Fisher examined empirically the factors that may explain differences in corporate bond yields. To eliminate nonfirm specific factors, he used risk premiums rather than yields to maturity as the
dependent variable. He defined the risk premium of a bond as the
difference between the market yield to maturity and the corresponding pure rate of interest, where the latter was defined as the
market yield on a riskless bond maturing on the same day as the
bond under consideration. He also hypothesized that the risk
premium on corporate bonds is determined by both the default risk
and the marketability risk. The following variables were used as
proxies for default risk:

X_1 = *Earnings variability,* measured as the coefficient of variation on
       earnings after tax of the most recent nine years.

X_2 = *Reliability in meeting obligations,* the length of time since the latest
       of the following events occurred: the firm was founded, the firm
       emerged from bankruptcy, or a compromise was made in which
       creditors settled for less than 100 percent of their claims.

X_3 = *Leverage,* measured as the ratio of market value of the firm's equity
       to the par value of its debt.

The marketability risk was measured by the total value of the firm's bonds (X_4), based on the assumption that the smaller the amount of bonds outstanding, the less frequently they would be traded and hence "thinner" and less perfect is their market. A multiple regression technique was used to test the hypothesis. Various regressions were run cross-sectionally for 71 firms in 1927, 45 firms in 1932, 89 firms in 1937, 73 firms in 1949, and 88 firms in 1953. The regression run on all the 366 bonds yielded the following estimated coefficients of the basic equation:

$$Y_i = .987 + .307X_1 - .253X_2 - .537X_3 - .275X_4; \quad (R^2 = .75)$$
$$ (.032) \quad (.036) \quad (.031) \quad (.021)$$

where Y_i is the risk premium of corporate bond i and X_1 through X_4 are the logarithms of the four independent variables identified earlier. The R^2 of .75 indicates the good explanatory power of the model. The model was not, however, tested on a control group. Moreover, the choice of the variable did not rest on an explicit theory of bond pricing under certainty.

STUDIES USING REGRESSION ANALYSIS

To use regression analysis to develop a bond ratings prediction model, define y_i as the bond ratings assigned to a firm i, let $X_{1i} \ldots X_{ki}$ be the values of the financial variables that influence the bond ratings. Assuming the relationship between the dependent variable Y_i and the independent variables is additive and linear, the bond ratings model may be stated as follows:

$$y_i = a_0 + a_1X_{1i} + a_2X_{2i} + \ldots + a_kX_{ki} + e_i$$
$$E(e_i) = 0$$

The model assumes that the bond ratings of a given firm Y_i are a linear function of the financial variables X's. To test the validity of the model the estimates of the parameters $a_0, \ldots, a_i$ are obtained from an experimental sample. The calculated equation is then applied to data from a control sample of firms to test the predictive ability of the model. Such is the model used in the next two studies.

HORRIGAN'S STUDY

In his study, James Horrigan described a study of the power of accounting data to predict bond ratings.[5] The study included two phases.

In the first phase, Horrigan regressed the ratings of a sample of corporate bond issues on 15 financial ratios. The sample included 201 corporations with Moody's ratings and 151 corporations with Standard and Poor's ratings, which did not change during the 1959–64 period. The 15 financial ratios came from the following categories: (1) short-term liquidity, (2) long-term liquidity, (3) short-term capital turnover, (4) long-term capital turnover, (5) profit margin, and (6) return on investment. In addition, a dummy variable (0.1) for subordination status was included in the model. Before conducting the first stage of the study, Horrigan formulated a series of hypotheses about the expected relationship between each ratio category and bond ratings. Subject to constraints related to their intercorrelations, the ratios having the highest correlations with ratings were selected as the most promising variables to be included in the regression analysis. Six variables were finally chosen: (1) subordination, (2) total assets, (3) ratios of working capital over sale, (4) net worth over total debt, (5) sales to net worth, and (6) net operating profit to sales.

In the second phase, Horrigan regressed the ratings of a new sample of corporate bond issues on the six variables obtained in the first phase. The new sample included 70 and 60 firms receiving new ratings from Moody's and Standard and Poor's, respectively, during the period 1961–64, and 27 and 58 firms whose ratings were changed by Moody's and Standard and Poor's during the same period. A rating scale based on the regression results was able to predict 58 percent of the Moody's new ratings and 52 percent of the Standard and Poor's ratings, and 54 percent of Moody's changed ratings and 57 percent of Standard and Poor's changed ratings. The firms misclassified were all in the adjacent categories.

WEST'S STUDY

West was critical of Horrigan's methodology and suggested that a somewhat different approach, making less use of accounting data, may be more predictive.[6] West was particularly concerned by the general lack of theory underlying Horrigan's hypotheses and suggested that a model used by Lawrence Fisher[7] to determine risk premium on corporate bonds may perform better than Horrigan's model, given that (1) the Fisher model was theoretically and empirically supported, and (2) the risk premium is a better surrogate for default risk than are bond ratings.

Using the same five cross sections of data used by Fisher (1927, 1932, 1937, 1949, 1953), excluding firms whose bonds were not rated or whose bonds had unique features and including only firms having Moody's ratings, he regressed the logarithms of the coded ratings on the logarithms of the independent variables of earnings variability, period of solvency, equity to debt ratio, and bonds outstandings. The model correctly predicted 62 percent of Moody's for the 1953 cross section and 60 percent for the 1961 cross section. Compared to Horrigan's model, the Fisher/West's model improved R^2 by only 5 percent and prediction accuracy by only 2 percent. Given the ease of calculation of Horrigan's model, it is still of more significance. As West concluded:

> To be sure, both the theoretical foundation and empirical quality of the Fisher model appear to be somewhat superior to Horrigan's. But on the critical matter of predictive accuracy, the model was not much better than Horrigan's. Since the two perform about equally well in this regard, the easier calculations of Horrigan's model may be the more reasonable criterion to follow in choosing between them.[8]

STUDIES USING DICHOTOMOUS PROBABILITY FUNCTIONS

To use the dichotomous probability function to develop a bond ratings prediction model, define y_i as the probability that a bond issued by a firm i will be given the higher of two ratings. Let $X_{1i} \ldots X_{ki}$ be the values of the financial variables that influence the bond ratings. Assuming the relationship between Y_i and the independent variables X's is additive and linear, the bond ratings model may be stated as follows:

$$Y_i = a_0 + a_1 X_{1i} + \ldots + a_k X_{ki} + e_i$$
$$E(e_i) = 0$$

The model assumes that the conditional probability of a bond having the higher of a pair of ratings is a function of the variables X's. To test the validity of the model, the estimates of the parameters $a_0, \ldots, a_i$ are obtained from observations on an experimental sample of firms. The obtained equation is then applied to data from a control sample of firms to test the predictive ability of the model. Such is the model used by the next study.

POGUE AND SOLDOVSKY'S STUDY

Pogue and Soldovsky used a linear probability model to determine the probability of group membership in one group of the pair of bonds.[9] The explanatory variables used in the regression included the following variables all expressed as a six-year mean: long-term debt over a percentage of total capitalization as a measure of leverage; after-tax net income over a percentage of net total assets as a measure of profitability and its coefficient of variation as a measure of earnings instability; net total assets as a measure of size, after-tax sum of net income plus interest over interest charges as a measure of earnings coverage; and a dummy variable to distinguish the broad industry effect. The dependent variables were either one of the following: probability of Aaa rather than Baa rating, probability of Aaa rather than the Aa rating, probability of Aa rather than A rating, and probability of A rather than Baa rating. Separate regressions were run for each pair of successive ratings on data course years 1961–66 and the results were used to rate twenty industrial bonds, twenty utility bonds and thirteen railroad bonds. Their model was able to predict correctly fifty out of fifty-three bonds in the experimental sample and eight out of ten bonds in the holdout sample from the same period 1961–66.

Pogue and Soldovsky also found that the probability of a bond having the higher of a pair of ratings is inversely related to the leverage and earnings instability of the issuing firm and is directly related to the firm's size and profitability, with leverage and profitability having the most significant influence on corporate bond ratings.

STUDIES USING MULTIPLE DISCRIMINANT ANALYSIS

Multiple discriminant analysis is a multivariable statistical tool used by the researcher to classify observations (firms in these studies) into a priori groups (Standard and Poor's or Moody's rating categories) on the basis of a set of independent variables (financial variables). For a two-group case, multiple discriminant analysis computes the discriminant coefficients which have the property of providing the "best" linear function distinguishing between the Two group variance of the Z_i scores to the pooled within group variance of the Z_i scores. The discriminant function is of the form:

$$Z_i = A_0 + A_1X_j + A_2X_{2j} + A_3X_{3j} + \ldots + A_kX_{kj}$$

where:

Z_i = the i variable firm's discriminate score
A_j = the discriminate coefficient for the j variable

In the two-group case, if Z_i exceeds some critical value of Z, the i variable observation belongs to group one. If Z_i is less than the critical value Z, the observation belongs to group two.

To use the multiple discriminant analysis to develop a bond ratings prediction model, the following steps are used: (1) develop discriminant functions for the bond rating categories on the basis of an experimental or estimation sample; (2) classify forms in the experimental sample; (3) examine the validity of the discriminant function on a control or validation sample.

PINCHES AND MINGO'S STUDIES

Pinches and Mingo selected for their first study all industrial bonds rated B or above listed in the new issue section of *Moody's Bond Survey* from January 1, 1967, to December 31, 1968.[10] A sample of 180 corporate bonds ranging from B to Aa was randomly subdivided into 132 firms comprising an estimation sample and 48 firms comprising a holdout (validation) sample.

The first stage of the analysis consisted of collecting or calculating 35 financial variables to be potentially used in the discriminant model.

The second stage consisted of a factor analysis of the 35 financial variables in order to: (1) gain a better understanding of the regularity and order in the data; and (2) identify basically independent dimensions of the data. The factor analysis reflected the data into seven factors which appeared to represent: (1) size, (2) financial

leverage, (3) long-term capital intensiveness, (4) return on investment, (5) short-term capital intensiveness, (6) earnings stability,
and (7) debt and debt coverage stability. Five of these dimensions
were considered, and the variable most highly correlated with each
of the five dimensions was chosen to be included in the discriminant function.

The third stage consisted of determining the best multiple discriminant analysis model (MDA). The MDA model that performed
best incorporated six variables: X_1 = subordination, X_2 = years of
consecutive dividends, X_3 = issue size, X_4 = net income + interest/
interest: five-year mean, X_5 = long-term debt/total assets, and
X_6 = net income/total assets. Subordination was represented by a
dichotomous (0–1) variable.

The fourth stage consists of applying the model to classify the
firms from the estimation sample. The classification matrix is
shown in Exhibit 3.1. The total hit rate of the model is obtained by
summing the main diagonal entries which is 92 out of 132 bonds or
69.70 percent. The numbers between parentheses in the exhibit represent the hit rate for each ratings category. Notice that it differs
from one category to another.

The fifth stage consists of applying the model to classify the firms
from the control sample. The classification matrix is shown in
Exhibit 3.1. While the fourth stage was an explanatory stage, the
fifth stage is a predictive one. The hit rate was 31 out of 48 bonds
(65.48 percent). The ratings misclassified were within one rating
higher or lower than the actual rating. There are, however, great
differences in each rating's category—Aa (25 percent), A (100 percent), Baa (0 percent), Ba (88 percent) and B (67 percent). The
MDA model was ineffective in explaining in the estimating sample
and in predicting in the holdout sample the Baa rating category.
This was attributed to the failure of the variables included in the
MDA model to discriminate between Baa and adjacent rating categories.

Because of the poor performance of the model for Baa bonds and
because the Baa rating has become generally accepted in the investment community as the cutoff between investment and non-invest-
ment grade bonds, Pinches and Mingo conducted another study to
examine the role of subordination in the prediction of bond
ratings.[11] More precisely, they conducted two separate multiquad-

EXHIBIT 3.1   PINCHES AND MINGO'S CLASSIFICATION TABLES

1. ESTIMATING SAMPLE

		Actual Ratings					
		Aa	A	Baa	Ba	B	Total
Predicted Ratings	Aa	10 (71.42%)	4	0	0	0	14
	A	2	22 (84.61%)	0	2	0	26
	Baa	0	8	4 (16%)	13	0	25
	Ba	0	0	0	39 (88.63%)	5	44
	B	0	0	0	6	17 (15.55%)	23
							132

II. HOLDOUT SAMPLE

	Aa	A	Baa	Ba	B	Total
Aa	1 (25%)	3	0	0	0	4
A	0	9 (100%)	0	0	0	9
Baa	0	2	0 (0%)	7	0	9
Ba	0	1	0	15 (88.2%)	1	17
B	0	0	0	3	6 (66.66%)	9
						48

EXHIBIT 3.2 COMPARATIVE RESULTS OF TWO MULTIPLE DISCRIMINANT MODELS

| MOODY'S RATINGS | NUMBER OF BONDS | 1ST PINCHES AND MINGO'S STUDY | 2ND PINCHES AND MINGO'S STUDY |
| | | Six Variable Linear Classification | Separate Five Variable Quadratic Classification |
		Hit Rate	Hit Rate
Aa	14	78.6	71.4
A	24	91.7	83.3
Baa	25	12.0	48.0
Ba	44	90.9	88.6
B	23	73.9	73.9
Total	130	71.5	75.4

ratic discriminant analyses—one for nonsubordinated bonds rated Aa, A, and Baa and one for subordinated bonds rated Baa, Ba, and B. The improvement in the total and individual hit rates is shown in Exhibit 3.2.

ANG AND PATEL'S STUDY

Ang and Patel were interested in determining whether the statistical models or the agencies' ratings are superior.[12]

In a first phase, they compared four statistical bond rating methods and two "naive" prediction models on their ability to duplicate the Moody's. The four bond rating methods were Horrigan's, West's, Pogue and Soldovsky's, and Pinches and Mingo's. The results showed a consistent pattern in which Pogue and Soldovsky's model ranked first, Pinches and Mingo's second, West's third, Horrigan's fourth, and the naive models fifth and sixth. In short, the results indicate that the statistical models explain some part of the rating process.

In a second phase, Ang and Patel compared Moody's actual ratings, along with the predicted ratings obtained by the four statistical models and the two naive models, to ex-post measures of bond default and loss rate on investment yield (the difference between the realized yield and the promised yield). The results showed that various bond rating methods were only able to perform better than the naive models when the lead time was short. Over longer lead times, the difference between all methods was insignificant. What was surprising, however, was the fact that in two of the five years examined, both the Pogue and Soldovsky and the Pinches and Mingo models outperformed Moody's. It seems that the agency ratings may not be consistent, which leads to the following advice:

Since a bond rating is not a good indication of long-run risk of financial loss, investors and institutions with relatively long planning horizons should not use it as a guideline to investment. Rather, they should diversify across all rating groups or even concentrate on lower rating bonds if the analyst is confident that the probability of the firm being solvent in the next few years is high.[13]

BELKAOUI'S STUDY

In his prediction model, Belkaoui avoided the diversity of approaches used in earlier studies, attributable mainly to the lack of explicit and testable statements of what a bond rating represents and used an economic rationale for the choice of the variables to be included in the model.[14] The model used firm-, market-, and indenture-related variables. The firm-related variables included (1) the total size of the firm, (2) the total size of the debt, (3) the long-term capital intensiveness, (4) the short-term capital intensiveness, (5) the total liquidity, the (6) the debt coverage. The market-related variable included a measure of investor's expectations. Finally, the indenture-related variable included a subordination measure. The randomly selected sample of 275 industrial corporate bonds included bonds rated B or above by Standard and Poor's during 1978. The total sample was also divided randomly into an experimental sample of 160 and a control sample of 97. As shown in Exhibits 3.3 and 3.4, the discriminant model incorporating the eight variables correctly predicted 62.8 percent of the ratings in an experimental sample and 65.9 percent of the ratings in a control sample. Examination of the relative importance of the eight variables indicated that, on a univariate basis, subordination is the most important variable. However, in a multivariate context, subordination status became less important, while the current ratio became the most important variable, followed closely by the fixed charge coverage ratio.

STUDIES USING MULTIVARIATE PROFIT ANALYSIS

KAPLAN AND URWITZ'S STUDY

Kaplan and Urwitz criticized the previous regression models because they treated the dependent variable (bond rating) as if it were on an interval scale and criticized multiple discriminant models because they treated bond ratings as classifying bonds into separate categories.[15] To exploit the ordinal nature of bond ratings, they used the multivariate profit analysis proposed by McKelvey and Zavoina[16] to rate 120 outstanding or "seasoned" industrial corporate bonds and 207 new issues. The new issue sample was split

*EXHIBIT 3.3 CLASSIFICATION OF EXPERIMENTAL
SAMPLE BONDS IN BELKAOUI'S STUDY*

| ACTUAL RATING | PREDICTED RATING | | | | | | PERCENTAGE CORRECT |
	AAA	AA	A	BBB	BB	B	
AAA	12	7	1	0	0	0	60.00
AA	0	21	9	0	0	0	70.00
A	1	4	21	4	0	0	70.00
BBB	0	0	11	11	8	0	36.66
BB	0	0	1	4	20	5	66.66
B	0	0	0	0	5	15	75.00
Total							65.50

*EXHIBIT 3.4 CLASSIFICATION OF CONTROL SAMPLE
BONDS IN BELKAOUI'S STUDY*

| ACTUAL RATING | PREDICTED RATING | | | | | | PERCENTAGE CORRECT |
	AAA	AA	A	BBB	BB	B	
AAA	2	1	1	0	0	0	50
AA	1	11	4	1	0	0	64
A	0	2	24	0	8	1	68
BBB	0	3	1	7	0	0	63
BB	0	0	0	1	9	6	56
B	0	0	0	0	3	11	78
Total							65.9

up randomly into an estimation sample of 140 issues and a holdout sample of 67 issues. The following financial ratios and variables were chosen as possible independent variables:

1. Interest coverage ratios: cash flow before interest and taxes/interest charges; cash flow before interest and taxes/total debt
2. Capitalization (leverage) ratios: long-term debt/total assets; long-term debt/net worth

3. Profitability ratio: net income/total assets
4. Size variables: total assets; size of bond issue
5. Stability variables: coefficient of variation of total assets; coefficient of variation of net income
6. Subordination status: 0–1 dummy variable

Both accounting and market betas and the standard errors of the residuals used to estimate them were also used as independent variables. When compared to the ordinary least square regression model, Kaplan and Urwitz found that contrary to their expectations, the regression model performs slightly better than the probit model. The regression model correctly predicted 71 percent of the ratings compared to 68 percent for profit. Their final conclusion was that the regression model seems robust and does not bias the equations.

EVALUATION OF EXISTING RESEARCH

The research surveyed in this chapter tried, in a first stage, to develop a bond ratings model from an experimental sample of bond ratings on the basis of a selected list of accounting and financial variables and using either regression, dichotomous probability function, multiple discriminant, or multivariate probit analysis. In a second stage, the obtained model was applied to a holdout sample to test the predictive ability of the model. Despite the general success of these models, there are some unresolved problems which may limit their usefulness.

First, with the exception of Belkaoui's study, these models suffer from the lack of an explicit and testable statement of what a bond rating represents and the absence of an "economic rationale" for the variable to be included. As stated by Foster: "One has more confidence that variables will possess some predictive value when there is such a rationale for their inclusion."[17]

Second, all the models did not account for the differences among the companies, in their accounting for long-term leases; given that these studies preceded FASB standard #13, they must have included both companies capitalizing or expensing long-term leases. To avoid the question of whether the choice of the accounting method for leases influences the assigned ratings of bonds, the studies should have controlled for the accounting methods used.

Third, the studies using the regression models have treated the dependent variable of the bond rating as if it were on an interval scale. They assumed that the underlying dependent variable default risk has been categorized into equally spaced discrete variables. The assumption is that the risk differential between an AAA and an AA bond is the same as between a BB and B bond. Because bonds convey ordinal information (an AAA bond is more secure than an AA bond which is more secure than an A bond, and so on), the multiple discriminant and the multivariate profit models are more appropriate. However, as seen in the Kaplan and Urwitz study, the regression model seemed more robust than the multivariate profit model, which leaves the multiple discriminant model as the most appropriate.

Fourth, all the studies confused ex-ante predictive power with ex-post discrimination. When a given discriminant model is developed on the basis of a sample A_1 and tested on a time-coincident sample A_2, the authors claimed predictive success but have actually only demonstrated ex-post discriminant success.[18] Testing on A_2 implies only that the inference about the importance of the independent variables in the discriminant function is warranted. Prediction requires inter-temporal validation. Ex-ante prediction means using the discriminant model developed on the basis of A_1 from time dimension t on a sample B from time dimension $t+1$.

CONCLUSIONS

From the above discussions it appears that the limitations of the previous studies are to be corrected before developing a bond rating prediction model. The prediction model presented in the next two chapters will avoid some of the pitfalls mentioned in this chapter. First, it will rely on a theoretical model for the choice of the independent variables. Second, it will rely on multiple discriminant analysis to develop the multiple discriminant functions. Third, it will proceed with both a validation and an examination of the predictive power of the model.

NOTES

1. Gilbert Harold, *Bond Ratings as Investment Guide* (New York: Ronald Press, 1938).

2. W. Braddock Hickman, *Corporate Bonds, Quality and Investment Performance* (Princeton, N.J.: Princeton University Press, 1958).

3. Thomas A. Atkinson and Elizabeth T. Simpson, *Trends in Corporate Bond Quality* (New York: National Bureau of Economic Research, 1967).

4. Lawrence Fisher, "Determinants of Risk Premium on Corporate Bonds," *Journal of Political Economy* (June 1959), pp. 217–237.

5. James O. Horrigan, "The Determination of Long-Term Credit Standing with Financial Ratios," *Empirical Research in Accounting: Selected Studies, 1966*, Supplement to Vol. 4, *Journal of Accounting Research*, pp. 44–62.

6. Richard R. West, "Discussion," *Ibid.*, pp. 67–71.

7. _____, "An Alternative Approach to Predicting Corporate Bond Ratings," *Journal of Accounting Research* (Spring 1970), pp. 118–127.

8. Ibid., p. 125.

9. Thomas F. Pogue and Robert M. Soldovsky, "What is in a Bond Rating?" *Journal of Financial and Quantitative Analysis* (June 1969), pp. 201–228.

10. George E. Pinches and Kent A. Mingo, "A Multivariate Analysis of Industrial Bond Ratings," *The Journal of Finance* (March 1973), pp. 1–18.

11. George E. Pinches and Kent A. Mingo, "The Role of Subordination and Industrial Bond Ratings," *The Journal of Finance* (March 1975), pp. 201–206.

12. James S. Ang and Kiritkumar A. Patel, "Bond Rating Methods: Comparison and Validation," *The Journal of Finance* (May 1978), pp. 631–640.

13. Ibid., p. 640.

14. Ahmed Belkaoui, "Industrial Bond Ratings: A New Look," *Financial Management* (Autumn 1980), pp. 44–51.

15. Robert S. Kaplan and Gabriel Urwitz, "Statistical Models of Bond Ratings: A Methodological Inquiry," *The Journal of Business* 52, no. 2 (1979), pp. 231–61.

16. R. McKelvey and W. Zavoina, "A Statistical Model for the Analysis of Ordinal Level Dependent Variables," *Journal of Mathematical Sociology* 4 (Summer 1975), pp. 103–20.

17. George Foster, *Financial Statement Analysis* (Englewood Cliffs, N.J.: Prentice-Hall, Inc., 1978), p. 443.

18. Maurice O. Joy and John O. Toffelson, "On the Financial Application of Discriminant Analysis," *Journal of Financial and Quantitative Analysis* (December 1975), p. 728.

BIBLIOGRAPHY

Altman, Edward I. "Financial Ratios, Discriminant Analysis and the Prediction of Corporate Bankruptcy." *The Journal of Finance* (September 1968), pp. 589–609.

Altman, E. I. and S. Katz. "Statistical Bond Rating Classification Using Financial and Accounting Data." In Michael Schiff and George Sorter (eds.), *Proceedings of the Conference on Topical Research in Accounting.* New York: New York University, 1976, pp. 205–39.

Ang, James S. and Kiritkumar A. Patel. "Bond Rating Methods: Comparison and Validation." *The Journal of Finance* (May 1978), pp. 631–640.

Atkinson, Thomas A. and Elizabeth T. Simpson. *Trends in Corporate Bond Quality.* New York: National Bureau of Economic Research, 1967.

Belkaoui, Ahmed. "Industrial Bond Ratings: A New Look." *Financial Management* (Autumn 1980), pp. 44–51.

Fisher, Lawrence. "Determinants of Risk Premium on Corporate Bonds." *Journal of Political Economy* (June 1959), pp. 217–237.

Frank, R. E., W. F. Massy, and G. D. Morrison. "Bias in Multiple Discriminant Analysis." *Journal of Marketing Research* (August 1965), pp. 250–258.

Harold, Gilbert. *Bond Ratings as Investment Guide.* New York: Ronald Press, 1938.

Hickman, W. Braddock. *Corporate Bonds, Quality and Investment Performance.* Princeton, N.J.: Princeton University Press, 1958.

Horrigan, James O. "The Determination of Long-Term Credit Standing with Financial Ratios." *Empirical Research in Accounting: Selected Studies, 1966,* Supplement to vol. 4. *Journal of Accounting Research,* pp. 44–62.

Joy, Maurice O. and John O. Toffelson. "On the Financial Application of Discriminant Analysis." *Journal of Financial and Quantitative Analysis* (December 1975), pp. 723–738.

Kaplan, Robert S. and Gabriel Urwitz. "Statistical Models of Bond Ratings: A Methodological Inquiry." *The Journal of Business,* vol. 52, no. 2 (1979), pp. 231–61.

McKelvey, R. and W. Zavoina. "A Statistical Model for the Analysis of Ordinal Level Dependent Variables." *Journal of Mathematical Sociology* 4 (Summer 1975), pp. 103–20.

Pinches, George E. and Kent A. Mingo. "A Multivariate Analysis of Industrial Bond Ratings." *The Journal of Finance* (March 1973), pp. 1–18.

_____. "The Role of Subordination and Industrial Bond Ratings." *The Journal of Finance* (March 1975), pp. 201–206.

Pogue, Thomas F. and Robert M. Soldovsky. "What is in a Bond Rating?" *Journal of Financial and Quantitative Analysis* (June 1969), pp. 201–228.

West, Richard R. "An Alternative Approach to Predicting Corporate Bond Ratings." *Journal of Accounting Research* (Spring 1970), pp. 118–127.

4

INDUSTRIAL BOND RATINGS: A PREDICTION MODEL

INTRODUCTION

The best known measures of prospective bond quality are the bond ratings assigned by the three rating agencies: Moody's, Standard and Poor's, and Fitch. Their ratings provide a judgment of the investment quality of a long-term obligation and a measure of default risk. Accordingly, they may affect the interest rate an organization pays on its bond. Although each rating agency has defined the meaning of its ratings, the agencies have not explicitly specified the process they use to arrive at these ratings. Given the importance of ratings, various authors have attempted to explain and predict them based on the financial and/or statistical characteristics of the bonds and issuing firms. These rating prediction studies were reviewed in the previous chapter. Although the models derived do an adequate job of capturing the human judgments of bond raters, they suffer from (a) a diversity of approaches used in selecting independent variables for the regression, discriminant, or multivariate probit models; (b) a lack of an "economic rationale" underlying the choice of these variables;[1] (c) a failure to account for the differences among the companies in their accounting for long-term leases; and (d) the confusion of ex-ante predictive power with ex-post discrimination. Consequently this study will correct for the above limitations to develop a multiple discriminant bond rating model.

ECONOMIC RATIONALE[2]

A bond rating is primarily a judgment of the investment quality of a long-term obligation of a firm. It reflects the raters' expectations and estimates of the relevant characteristics of the quality of the investment. To capture the determinants of bond ratings, these characteristics of the investment quality must be identified and rationalized on an economic basis.

The investment quality of a bond is determined by the interaction among three general variables: firm-, market-, and indenture-related variables.

The firm-related variables depict the ability of the firm to provide adequate protection for the bond holders. This ability depends on both size and coverage factors. The size factor allows rating of the bonds in terms of the security it provides. The security itself is a function of the command over total resources the firm has. Going from the most aggregate to the least aggregate expression, the command over total resources depends on: (1) the total size of the firm, (2) the total size of the debt, (3) the long-term capital intensiveness, and (4) the short-term capital intensiveness. Thus, variables expressing each of these determinants of the size factor should be included in a bond rating model.

The coverage factor allows rating of bonds in terms of the ability of the firm to service the financial changes. Thus, while the size factor is concerned with stock considerations, the coverage factor is concerned with flow considerations. The ability of the firm to service the financial charges of its debt is itself a function of the flow of financial resources. Going from the most aggregate to the least aggregate, the flow of financial resources depends on (1) the total actual liquidity of the firm, (2) the debt coverage and (3) the future liquidity of the firm. Thus, variables expressing each of these determinants of the coverage factor should be included in any bond rating model.

The market-related variables depict the ability of the firm to create a favorable market response to all its securities. They reflect the investors' expectations in the aggregate about the firm's performance. Thus, variables expressing measures of investors' expectations about the firm's profitability should be included in any bond rating model.

The indenture-related variables depict the relevant covenants and terms of the indenture that is the basic legal document constituting the contract between the bond holders and the bond issuer. They are deemed very important in bond rating.[3] In spite of the possible difficulties of operationalizing them, variables expressing relevant covenants of the indenture should also be included in any bond rating model.

DEVELOPMENT OF THE MODEL

METHOD

To avoid the limitations of the studies surveyed in chapter 3, the following methodology will be used:

First, the bond rating model will be based on a multiple discriminant model. Because bonds convey ordinal information (an AAA bond is more secured than an AA bond which is more secure than an A bond, etc. . . .) the multiple discriminant and the multivariate probit models are more appropriate than the regression model. And as seen in the Kaplan and Urwitz study,[4] the regression model seems more robust than the multivariate probit model which leaves the multiple discriminant model as the most appropriate.

Second, to avoid confusing between tests of validation or classification efficiency and tests of prediction the following steps will be used:[5]

The first step is to "fit" a discriminant function over a sample of firms A_1 from data collected in 1981. This sample is the analysis sample.

The second step is to use the linear discriminant function obtained in the first step to classify firms of a time-coincident holdout or validation sample A_2. This sample A_2 of firms with data collected in 1981 is the validation sample. As mentioned in chapter 3, this step has been confused in other studies with prediction. Ex-post discrimination may provide a useful foundation for explanation of the past, but it does not provide sufficient evidence for concluding that the future can be predicted.[6]

Assuming successful ex-post discrimination, the explanatory significance of the financial variables (independent variables) is investigated using both samples A_1 and A_2 from 1981 data. That is, the samples are recombined to form an estimating sample and a new linear discriminant model for the total 1981 sample is estimated. This involves merely a reestimation of the coefficients and not a search for variables.

The next step is to use the linear discriminant model, obtained as just explained, to classify sample B observations from another year and in this case from 1980. As stated correctly: "Prediction thus requires intertemporal validation whereas explanation requires only cross validation."[7]

Both cross-validation (the second step) and intertemporal validation (preceding paragraph) will yield a classification matrix showing the hit rate for the model. Similarly to all the previous studies cited in chapter 3, the success of the predictions will be measured by the hit rate, that is, the percentage of industrial bonds correctly classified.

SAMPLES SELECTION

As explained in the preceding sections, four randomly selected samples of industrial bonds rated B or above by Standard and Poor's will be used.[8]

1. An analysis sample of 266 industrial bonds rated B or above by Standard and Poor's in 1981.

2. A validation sample of 115 industrial bonds rated B or above by Standard and Poor's in 1981.

3. An estimating sample of 381 industrial bonds rated B or above by Standard and Poor's in 1981. The estimating sample is a combination of the analysis and validation samples. The year 1981 was used to insure that all firms represented have a uniform accounting treatment of financial leases following the Financial Accounting Standard Board Statement 13 "Accounting for leases" effective since 1976.

4. A control sample of 388 industrial bonds rated B or above by Standard and Poor's in 1980.[9]

Exhibit 4.1 provides a brief summary of the exact composition of the total sample. Thirty-seven industries were represented in each of the samples (aerospace, airlines, appliances, automotive, beverages, building materials, chemicals, conglomerates, containers, drugs, electrical and electronics, food processing, food and lodging, general machinery, instruments, leisure time industries, metals and mining, miscellaneous manufacturing, natural resources [fuel], office equipment and computers, oil service and supply, paper, personal care products, publishing, radio and TV broadcasting, railroads, real estate and housing, retailing [food], retailing [nonfood], service industries, special machinery, steel, textiles and apparel, tire and rubber, tobacco, trucking, utilities). The lists of industrial bonds used in each sample are shown in Appendixes B and C.

VARIABLES IN THE MULTIPLE DISCRIMINANT MODEL

Nine variables were selected to be included in the multiple discriminant model as representative of the factors identified in the economic rationale section.

X_1 = *Total assets.* Included as representative of the total size of the firm.

X_2 = *Total debt.* Included as a measure of the total indebtedness of the firm.

X_3 = *Long-term debt/total invested capital.* Included as a measure of the long-term capital intensiveness of the firm. By invested capital is meant the sum of the total debt, preferred stock and common equity (which includes common stocks, capital surplus, and retained earnings).

X_4 = *Short-term debt/total invested capital.* Included as a measure of the short-term capital intensiveness of the firm.

X_5 = *Current assets/current liabilities.* Included as a measure of the total liquidity of the firm.

X_6 = *Fixed charge coverage ratio:* Net income plus total interest expense (adjusted by tax rate)/interest expense (adjusted by tax rate) plus preferred dividend requirement. Included as a measure of debt coverage.

X_7 = *Five-year cash flow as percentage of five-year growth needs.* Five-year sum of (1) net income available for common stockholders, plus (2) depreciation and amortization, plus (3) income from discontinued operations and extraordinary items net of taxes divided by five-

EXHIBIT 4.1   SAMPLE SIZE OF INDUSTRIAL CORPORATE BONDS

RATINGS	ANALYSIS SAMPLE 1981		VALIDATION SAMPLE 1981		ESTIMATING SAMPLE 1981		CONTROL SAMPLE 1980	
	Numbers	%	Numbers	%	Numbers	%	Numbers	%
AAA	13	4.88	6	5.21	19	4.98	20	5.15
AA	51	19.17	17	14.78	68	17.84	99	25.51
A	112	42.10	35	30.43	147	38.58	140	36.08
BBB	51	19.17	30	26.08	81	21.25	50	12.88
BB	9	3.38	20	17.39	29	7.61	40	10.30
B	30	11.27	7	6.08	37	9.71	39	10.05
Total	266	100	115	100	381	100	388	100

year sum of (1) capital expenditures, plus (2) change in inventories during most recent five years (except utilities), plus (3) common dividends. Included as a measure of future liquidity.

X_8 = *Stock price/common equity per share.* Included as a measure of investors' expectations.

X_9 = *Subordination* (0-1). Included as a measure of the most relevant covenant in the indenture.

These nine variables are in general different from the variables used in previous corporate industrial bond rating models. Exhibit 4.2 presents a comparative analysis of the variables used in these studies. Most of the variables and factors used in this study are absent in the other models due mainly to the absence of an economic rationale in their choice of variables. For example, measures of investors' expectations and short-term capital intensiveness are used in only two models (this study and Kaplan and Urwitz's); short-term capital intensiveness only is used in this study; actual liquidity is used in only two models (this study and Horrigan's); future liquidity only is used in this study; only long-term capital intensiveness is used in all the models.

DISCRIMINANT ANALYSIS RESULTS ON THE ANALYSIS SAMPLE

The overall discriminating power of the model using the analysis sample was accomplished by testing for differences in the group centroids. The overall F value for the model $F = 20.25$ ($p < .001$) permits rejection of the null hypothesis that the differences in the group centroids of the six bond rating groups was zero. This result justifies an examination of the discriminating power of each of the nine independent variables. Exhibit 4.3 presents the means and univariate F ratios for all nine variables by bond rating groups. All the variables were significant. From a univariate point of view and on the basis of the magnitude of the F ratio, it may be stated that subordination status is the most important variable followed by short-term debt over invested capital, total assets, fixed change coverage ratio, total debt, long-term debt over total invested capital, stock price over book value, and five-year cash flow over five-year growth needs.

EXHIBIT 4.2   COMPARATIVE ANALYSIS OF VARIABLES USED IN BOND RATING MODELS

RATIO	THIS STUDY	HORRIGAN	WEST	PINCHES AND MINGO	KAPLAN AND URWITZ
1. Total size of the firm	Total assets	Total assets	Not used	Not used	Total assets
2. Total size of the debt	Total debt	Not used	Bonds outstanding	Not used	Not used
3. Long-term capital intensiveness	Long-term debt as a percentage of total invested capital	Net worth over total debt	Debt equity ratio	Long-term debt over total assets	a. Long-term debt over total assets b. Long-term debt over net worth
4. Short-term capital intensiveness	Short-term debt as a percentage of total invested capital	Not used	Not used	Not used	Not used
5. Actual liquidity	Current ratio	Working capital over sales	Not used	Not used	Not used
6. Debt coverage	Fixed charge coverage ratio	Not used	Not used	Five-year mean of net income plus interest charge over interest charge	a. Cash flow before interest and taxes over interest b. Cash flow

before interest
and taxes over
total debt

#	Factor					
7.	Future liquidity	Five-year cash flow as a percentage of five-year growth needs.	Not used	Not used	Not used	Not used
8.	Investors' expectations	Stock price as a percentage of book value	Not used	Not used	Not used	Accounting and market betas
9.	Indenture provision	Subordination status	Subordination status	Not used	Subordination status	Subordination status
10.	Others	Not used	Sales over net worth	Period of solving	Years of consecutive dividends	Net income over total assets
11.	Others	Not used	Net operating profit	Nine-year earnings	Net income over total assets	Coefficient of variations of total assets
12.	Others	Not used	Not used	Not used	Issue size	Issue size
13.	Others	Not used	Not used	Not used	Not used	Coefficient of variations of net income

EXHIBIT 4.3 VARIABLE MEANS AND TEST OF SIGNIFICANCE (ANALYSIS SAMPLE)*

VARIABLE	BOND RATING						F**
	AAA	AA	A	BBB	BB	B	
X_1	18433.72	5447.61	2056.82	2263.99	716.43	609.71	29.48
X_2	5655.25	1143.26	533.93	757.16	257.67	277.62	8.01
X_3	15.50	20.40	29.33	37.77	37.59	48.81	6.92
X_4	5.33	9.00	4.35	8.93	4.45	6.03	31.21
X_5	1.65	1.60	1.92	1.61	1.98	1.89	2.92
X_6	19.76	8.75	6.93	4.70	5.91	3.79	14.38
X_7	88.19	83.03	82.26	72.36	58.42	69.55	2.88
X_8	132.28	149.13	108.62	89.74	200.37	148.40	5.90
X_9	1.00	1.00	0.99	0.80	0.11	0.00	157.55

* $\alpha = 9.260$.
** All the F are significant at the 0.05 level of significance.

The independent variables were examined for multi-collinearity. Exhibit 4.4 shows the correlation matrix for all the variables. The intercorrelations (average $r = 0.0146$) are not judged large enough to produce a basis in the estimation of the parameters of the model.

A stepwise multiple discriminant analysis was used to determine the discriminant functions. The BMDP7M program was used for the task.[10] Exhibit 4.5 shows the obtained six functions. Based on Wilks' Lambda and its associated Chi square, the six functions were found to be significant. Exhibit 4.6 presents the pairs of values for the test of significance of the Mahalanobias distance between groups.[11] All the F values were significant, which permits one to reject the null hypothesis that the pairs of group centroids are equal at the .01 level.

To determine the relative importance of the variables in the model, four criteria were used.[12] The rank ordering of the nine variables according to the univariate F ratio, the forward and backward stepwise methods, and the scaled weighted method is shown in Exhibit 4.7. The univariate F ratio and the stepwise forward methods show subordination to be the most important and future liquidity ratio to be the least important. The stepwise backward method shows the long-term debt ratio to be the most important, followed by subordination, and the total assets to be the least important. Finally, the scale-weighted method shows the subordination to be the most important, followed by the current ratio, and the total debt to be the least important. Before evaluating the classification accuracy of the model, the equality of the covariance matrices among the six bond rating groups was tested, using box's M and its associated F test.[13] The resulting F value of 1.03 is not significant at the .05 level, resulting in the acceptance of the null hypothesis of equal covariance matrices and supporting the use of linear rather than quadratic classification rules. Similarly, we employed equal prior probabilities for classification, based on the belief that the distribution of bonds in the population is either unstable or unknown and that the main objective is evaluation of the importance of the variables included in the model without any consideration of prior probabilities.

Finally, the multiple discriminant model was used to classify the experimental group of bonds from which it was developed, based

EXHIBIT 4.4 CORRELATION COEFFICIENTS OVER THE NINE VARIABLES (ANALYSIS SAMPLE)

VARIABLE	X_1	X_2	X_3	X_4	X_5	X_6	X_7	X_8	X_9
X_1	1.000								
X_2	0.739	1.000							
X_3	−0.068	0.094	1.000						
X_4	0.078	0.002	−0.200	1.000					
X_5	−0.261	−0.202	−0.356	−0.216	1.000				
X_6	−0.030	−0.090	−0.534	−0.203	0.350	1.000			
X_7	0.044	−0.055	−0.346	0.046	0.316	0.304	1.000		
X_8	−0.054	−0.051	−0.048	0.007	0.128	0.291	−0.050	1.000	
X_9	0.206	0.069	−0.358	−0.008	−0.143	0.141	0.163	−0.226	1.000

EXHIBIT 4.5 DISCRIMINANT FUNCTIONS (ANALYSIS SAMPLE)

VARIABLE	BOND RATING					
	AAA	AA	A	BBB	BB	B
X_1	0.00091	0.00039	0.00025	0.00024	0.00026	0.00024
X_2	0.00028	-0.000020	-0.000022	-0.00009	-0.00015	-0.00024
X_3	0.48955	0.49510	0.59913	0.73027	0.75037	0.92494
X_4	0.68989	0.72489	0.65544	0.86627	0.73371	0.87970
X_5	7.69142	6.89274	8.15657	8.52282	9.35400	10.20789
X_6	1.03822	0.66162	0.64337	0.68019	0.54337	0.58578
X_7	0.02869	0.04225	0.04496	0.04496	0.04309	0.06080
X_8	0.01764	0.02030	0.01049	0.00378	0.01593	0.00386
X_9	28.47068	26.72795	25.09872	18.84681	0.38142	-4.60076
Constant	-48.13343	-34.42768	-36.42350	-35.75230	-129.57942	-38.46189

101

EXHIBIT 4.6   PAIRS OF F VALUES FOR THE TEST OF
             SIGNIFICANCE OF THE MAHALANOBIAS
             DISTANCE BETWEEN GROUPS (ANALYSIS
             SAMPLE)

GROUP	AAA	AA	A	BBB	BB
AA	13.81				
A	24.14	9.85			
BBB	29.25	19.31	11.91		
BB	29.46	24.36	21.30	12.28	
B	67.91	91.85	91.45	43.87	2.54

Degrees of freedom (9,252).

on the probability of group membership. The classification matrix
for the analysis sample is shown in Exhibit 4.8. The total number of
correctly classified bonds is obtained by summing the upper left-
lower right diagonal of the classification matrix in Exhibit 4.8. It
shows that the multiple discriminant analysis classified correctly
72.93 percent (194/266) of the firms. The model performs better for
some of the individual categories, AAA (76.92 percent), AA (74.51
percent), A (80.36 percent), BBB (54.90 percent), BB (66.67 percent), and B (73.33 percent).

VALIDATION

   As stated earlier, ex-post discrimination or cross-validation consists in classifying firms of a time-coincident holdout or validation
sample using the discriminant functions obtained from the analysis
sample. Another reason for validation is the need to check for possible biases due to sampling errors and search. Thus, the multiple
discriminant model obtained with the anlysis sample of 1981 was
used to classify firms from a validation sample of 1981. The classification results are shown in Exhibit 4.9. The model correctly rated

EXHIBIT 4.7 VARIABLE IMPORTANCE RANKED ACCORDING TO DIFFERENT CRITERIA

VARIABLE	UNIVARIATE F RATIO	STEPWISE FORWARD	STEPWISE BACKWARD	SCALE WEIGHTED
X_1	3	2	9	8
X_2	5	8	3	9
X_3	2	3	1	5
X_4	6	4	5	4
X_5	8	7	6	2
X_6	4	5	4	3
X_7	9	9	8	2
X_8	7	6	7	7
X_9	1	1	2	1

EXHIBIT 4.8   CLASSIFICATION TABLE (ANALYSIS SAMPLE)

FROM GROUP	NUMBER OF OBSERVATIONS (AND PERCENTAGES) CLASSIFIED INTO GROUPS						TOTAL
	AAA	AA	A	BBB	BB	B	
AAA	10 (76.92)	2 (15.38)	1 (7.69)	0 (0.00)	0 (0.00)	0 (0.00)	13 (100.00)
AA	6 (11.76)	38 (74.51)	7 (13.73)	0 (0.00)	0 (0.00)	0 (0.00)	51 (100.00)
A	1 (0.89)	10 (8.93)	90 (80.36)	10 (8.93)	1 (0.89)	0 (0.00)	112 (100.00)
BBB	1 (1.96)	1 (1.96)	12 (23.53)	28 (54.90)	6 (11.76)	3 (5.88)	51 (100.00)
BB	0 (0.00)	0 (0.00)	0 (0.00)	2 (22.22)	5 (66.67)	2 (22.22)	9 (100.00)
B	0 (0.00)	0 (0.00)	0 (0.00)	0 (0.00)	8 (26.67)	22 (73.33)	30 (100.00)

EXHIBIT 4.9 CLASSIFICATION TABLE (VALIDATION SAMPLE)

FROM GROUP	NUMBER OF OBSERVATIONS (AND PERCENTAGES) CLASSIFIED INTO GROUPS						TOTAL
	AAA	AA	A	BBB	BB	B	
AAA	2 (0.33)	4 (0.67)	0 (0.00)	0 (0.00)	0 (0.00)	0 (0.00)	6 (1.00)
AA	5 (0.29)	12 (0.71)	0 (0.00)	0 (0.00)	0 (0.00)	0 (0.00)	17 (1.00)
A	0 (0.00)	0 (0.00)	25 (0.71)	0 (0.00)	10 (0.28)	0 (0.00)	35 (1.00)
BBB	0 (0.00)	0 (0.00)	3 (0.10)	21 (0.70)	6 (0.20)	0 (0.00)	30 (1.00)
BB	0 (0.00)	0 (0.00)	0 (0.00)	4 (0.20)	13 (0.65)	3 (0.15)	20 (1.00)
B	0 (0.00)	0 (0.00)	0 (0.00)	0 (0.00)	2 (0.28)	5 (0.71)	7 (1.00)

67.8 percent of the firms in the validation sample. Using the Z statistic of Mosteller and Bush,[14] the null hypothesis that the results are due to chance is rejected, confirming the previous discriminating power results of the model. Exhibit 4.8 shows the hit rate for the nine categories. A final interesting result appearing in Exhibit 4.10 is the higher validation results presented by this study approach. As stated earlier, validation should not be confused with prediction. It merely provides sufficient evidence for concluding that the future can be predicted. Accordingly, in what follows, the discriminant model is reestimated on the basis of the total sample of 1981 (analysis plus validation samples) and then applied to a sample of 1980 to test its predictive ability.

ESTIMATING THE MODEL'S LINEAR DISCRIMINANT FUNCTIONS

Given the successful ex-post discrimination, the explanatory significance of the independent variables is investigated, using both the analysis and the validation sample from 1981. That is, the samples are recombined to form a total 1981 sample, and new linear discriminant functions are fitted. This step is merely a reestimation of the coefficients and not a new search for variables.

The overall discriminating power of the model based on the total 1981 sample was accomplished by testing for differences in the group centroids. The overall F value for the model of $F = 20.32$ ($p < .001$) permits rejection of the null hypothesis that the difference in the group centroids of the six bond rating groups was zero.

EXHIBIT 4.10   COMPARISON OF THE VALIDATION
                CLASSIFICATION

STUDY	% CORRECT VALIDATION SAMPLE
Pinches and Mingo	65 and 56
Horrigan	59
West	60
Belkaoui	65.9
This study	67.8

This result justifies again an examination of the discriminating power of each of the nine independent variables. Exhibit 4.11 presents the means and univariate F ratios for all nine variables by bond rating group.

All the variables were found to be significant. The nine independent variables were again examined for multicollinearity. Exhibit 4.12 shows the correlation matrix for all the variables. The intercorrelations (average $r = 0.021$) are not judged large enough to produce a bias in the estimation of the parameters of the model.

A stepwise discriminant analysis based on the BMDP7M program was again used to determine the discriminant functions. Exhibit 4.13 shows the multiple discriminant functions for each rating group. Based on Wilks' Lambda and its associated Chi square, the six functions were found to be significant. Exhibit 4.14 presents the pairs of F values for the test of significance of the Mahalanobias distance between groups. All the F values were significant, which permits one to reject again the null hypothesis that the pairs of group centroids are equal to the .01 level.

To determine the relative importance of the variables in the models, four criteria were again used. The rank ordering of the nine variables according to the univariate F ratio, the forward and backward stepwise methods, and the sealed weighted method is shown in Exhibit 4.15. Similarly to the analysis performed on the experimental sample, the rank ordering of the nine variables differs from one method to another. Before evaluating the classification accuracy of the model, the equality of the covariance matrices among the six bond rating groups was tested using box's M and its associated F test. The resulting F value of 1.05 is not significant at the 0.05 level, leading to the acceptance of the null hypothesis of equal covariance matrices and supporting the use of linear rather than quadratic classification rules. Similarly, we employed equal probabilities for classification.

Finally, the multiple discriminant model was used to classify the total estimating sample of bonds from which it was developed, based on the probability of group membership. The classification matrix for the estimating sample is shown in Exhibit 4.16. The total number of correctly classified bonds is obtained by summing the upper left-lower right diagonal of the classification matrix in Exhib-

EXHIBIT 4.11 VARIABLE MEANS AND TESTS OF SIGNIFICANCE (ESTIMATING SAMPLE)*

VARIABLE	BOND RATING						F VALUE
	AAA	AA	A	BBB	BB	B	
X_1	13632.415	5541.445	2100.367	1746.706	1084.565	696.059	25.164
X_2	4009.726	1097.522	554.030	581.456	367.962	987.135	7.359
X_3	13.963	18.954	28.224	37.165	41.775	47.856	50.471
X_4	5.952	8.414	4.419	7.816	6.324	5.808	6.250
X_5	1.778	1.564	1.962	1.781	1.962	1.856	2.214
X_6	17.589	10.817	7.099	4.720	4.100	3.775	15.943
X_7	89.373	85.539	81.278	76.912	63.765	67.348	3.302
X_8	144.494	147.080	110.247	102.406	155.813	141.427	4.132
X_9	0.947	0.985	0.911	0.617	0.344	0.054	58.732

$DF = 5,375$
F values significant at $\alpha = 0.05$

EXHIBIT 4.12   CORRELATION COEFFICIENTS OVER THE NINE VARIABLES (ESTIMATING SAMPLE)

VARIABLE	X_1	X_2	X_3	X_4	X_5	X_6	X_7	X_8	X_9
X_1	1.000								
X_2	0.603	1.000							
X_3	-0.137	0.063	1.000						
X_4	0.051	0.028	-0.155	1.000					
X_5	-0.259	-0.215	-0.271	-0.215	1.000				
X_6	0.102	-0.045	-0.513	-0.184	0.152	1.000			
X_7	0.020	-0.055	-0.361	0.042	0.284	0.251	1.000		
X_8	-0.088	-0.060	-0.022	-0.035	0.074	0.206	-0.0008	1.000	
X_9	0.206	0.108	-0.280	0.069	-0.079	0.008	0.101	-0.185	1.000

EXHIBIT 4.13   DISCRIMINANT FUNCTIONS (ESTIMATING SAMPLE)

VARIABLE	FUNCTIONS					
	AAA	AA	A	BBB	BB	B
X_1	0.000737	0.000431	0.000269	0.000250	0.000265	0.000242
X_2	0.000119	-0.000147	-0.000149	-0.000233	-0.000295	-0.000357
X_3	0.44234	0.48299	0.58069	0.71530	0.76589	0.85499
X_4	0.62823	0.67906	0.60516	0.79864	0.80544	0.84459
X_5	7.26898	6.80279	7.832642	8.35763	9.15411	9.24043
X_6	0.68425	0.54641	0.48850	0.50766	0.48010	0.49208
X_7	0.06102	0.06600	0.06777	0.07116	0.05952	0.06970
X_8	0.01802	0.01687	0.00809	0.00235	0.00705	0.00099
X_9	10.26302	9.76648	8.78782	4.27079	1.69732	-1.73660
Constant	-31.6004	-26.0425	-26.1304	-29.3824	-31.3397	-34.8229

F Statistic = 16.492

EXHIBIT 4.14   PAIRS OF F VALUES FOR THE TEST OF
SIGNIFICANCE OF THE MAHALANOBIAS
DISTANCE BETWEEN GROUPS
(ESTIMATING SAMPLE)

GROUP	AAA	AA	A	BBB	BB
AA	7.32				
A	19.86	13.79			
BBB	30.86	31.89	16.51		
BB	30.80	29.63	17.71	3.47	
B	48.50	59.90	44.72	13.45	2.51

$DF = 9,367$

it 4.16. It shows that the multiple discriminant analysis classified
correctly 67.19 percent (256/381) of the firms. The model performs
differently for the individual categories, AAA (47.37 percent), AA
(66 percent), A (80.27 percent), BBB (53 percent), BB (51 percent),
B (70.27 percent).

PREDICTION

Whereas explanation required only cross-validation, prediction
requires intertemporal validation. That is to say, the discriminant
model obtained from the total sample of 1981 must be used to classify a control sample of bonds from another year in order to test the
predictive ability of the model. The control sample chosen was a
sample of bonds from 1980. Thus, the multiple discriminant model
obtained from the total 1981 estimating sample (Exhibit 4.12) was
used to classify firms from the control sample of 1980. The classification or prediction results are shown in Exhibit 4.17. The model
correctly rated 63.65 percent of the firms in the control sample.
Using again the Z statistic of Mosteller and Bush, the null hypothesis that the results are due to chance is rejected, confirming the
previous discriminating power of the model (see chapter 4) and
establishing the predictive power of the model.

EXHIBIT 4.15 VARIABLE IMPORTANCE RANKED ACCORDING TO DIFFERENT CRITERIA (ESTIMATING SAMPLE)

VARIABLE	UNIVARIATE F RATIO	STEPWISE FORWARD	STEPWISE BACKWARD	SCALE WEIGHTED
X_1	3	3	3	8
X_2	5	8	4	9
X_3	2	2	2	5
X_4	6	4	7	4
X_5	9	6	9	2
X_6	4	7	5	3
X_7	8	9	6	6
X_8	7	5	8	7
X_9	1	1	1	1

EXHIBIT 4.16 CLASSIFICATION TABLE (ESTIMATING SAMPLE)

FROM GROUP	NUMBER OF OBSERVATIONS (AND PERCENTAGES) CLASSIFIED INTO GROUPS						TOTAL
	AAA	AA	A	BBB	BB	B	
AAA	9 (.47)	10 (.52)	0 (0.00)	0 (0.00)	0 (0.00)	0 (0.00)	19 (1.00)
AA	11 (0.16)	45 (0.66)	11 (0.16)	0 (0.00)	0 (0.00)	0 (0.00)	68 (1.00)
A	1 (0.0068)	13 (0.088)	118 (0.80)	9 (0.061)	5 (0.034)	1 (0.0068)	147 (1.00)
BBB	0 (0.00)	0 (0.00)	15 (0.18)	43 (0.53)	8 (0.098)	15 (0.18)	81 (1.00)
BB	0 (0.00)	0 (0.00)	0 (0.00)	7 (0.34)	15 (0.51)	7 (0.24)	29 (1.00)
B	0 (0.00)	0 (0.00)	1 (0.027)	4 (0.108)	6 (0.16)	26 (0.70)	37 (1.00)

EXHIBIT 4.17 CLASSIFICATION TABLE (CONTROL SAMPLE)

FROM GROUP	NUMBER OF OBSERVATIONS (AND PERCENTAGES) CLASSIFIED INTO GROUPS						TOTAL
	AAA	AA	A	BBB	BB	B	
AAA	9 (.45)	8 (.40)	3 (.15)	0 (0.00)	0 (0.00)	0 (0.00)	20 (1.00)
AA	7 (0.07)	62 (0.62)	30 (0.30)	0 (0.00)	0 (0.00)	0 (0.00)	99 (1.00)
A	0 (0.00)	31 (0.22)	99 (0.70)	10 (0.07)	0 (0.00)	0 (0.00)	140 (1.00)
BBB	0 (0.00)	0 (0.00)	12 (0.24)	35 (0.70)	3 (0.06)	0 (0.00)	50 (1.00)
BB	0 (0.00)	0 (0.00)	0 (0.00)	7 (0.17)	18 (0.45)	15 (0.37)	40 (1.00)
B	0 (0.00)	0 (0.00)	0 (0.00)	0 (0.00)	15 (0.38)	24 (0.61)	39 (1.00)

CONCLUSIONS

Based on the economic rationale, the discriminant analysis model developed in this study correctly rated 72.93 percent of the ratings in an analysis sample, 67 percent of the ratings in a validation sample, 67.19 percent of the ratings in a total estimating sample, and 63.65 percent of the ratings in a control sample. Both validation and predictive ability of the model were significant. Most misclassified firms were rated in adjacent categories to the true ratings. Such a model may be useful to the rating agencies themselves if it helps them to reduce inconsistencies among individual ratings, to form a preliminary rating of a bond, or to capture and evaluate the judgments of their raters. The model may be useful to investors when corporate bonds are not rated by Fitch, Moody's, and/or Standard & Poor's. Above all, the findings should be useful to those who pay to have bonds rated. Hence, managers may form an opinion of the eventual rating and take sound actions to improve some of the financial dimensions outlined in this study in order to achieve a better rating. The implementations of the model are briefly explained in the next chapter.

NOTES

1. George Foster, *Financial Statement Analysis* (Englewood Cliffs, N.J.: Prentice-Hall, Inc., 1978), p. 443. One exception is provided in Stewart C. Meyers, "Determinants of Corporate Borrowing," *Journal of Financial Economics* (November 1977), pp. 147–176. Myers argues that corporate borrowing is inversely related to the proportion of market value accounted for by "real opportunities or growth opportunities." These growth opportunities are contingent on discretionary future investment by the firm. So, issuing risky debt reduces the present market value of a firm holding growth opportunity by inducing a suboptimal investment strategy or by leading the firm and its creditor to bear the costs of avoiding the suboptimal strategy. However, as Myers admits, a general measure of this concept is difficult to derive from accounting data.

2. This economic rationale was first presented in Ahmed Belkaoui, "Industrial Bond Ratings: A New Look," *Financial Management* (Autumn 1980), pp. 45–46.

3. H. C. Sherwood, *How Corporate and Municipal Debt is Rated* (New York: John Wiley & Sons, Inc., 1976).

4. Robert S. Kaplan and Gabriel Urwitz, "Statistical Models of Bond

Ratings: A Methodological Inquiry," *The Journal of Business,* vol. 52, no. 2 (1979), pp. 231–61.

5. This procedure was suggested in O. Maurice Joy and John O. Tollefson, "On the Financial Applications of Discriminant Analysis," *Journal of Financial and Quantitative Analysis* (December 1975), pp. 726–27.

6. Ibid., p. 727.

7. Ibid., p. 728.

8. The C ratings were not included because of difficulties of insuring adequate and sufficient representation (and also to reduce the number of categories to manageable levels).

9. The reader may be interested in testing the model on a control sample of industrial bonds rated B or above in future years, whenever information on the independent variables in those years becomes available.

10. W. J. Dixon, *BMDP Statistical Software 1981* (Berkeley and Los Angeles: University of California Press, 1981).

11. B. J. Winer, *Statistical Principles in Experimental Design,* 2nd. Ed. (New York: McGraw-Hill Book Company, 1971), p. 845.

12. Robert A. Eisenbeis, Gary G. Gilbert, and Robert B. Avery, "Investigating the Relative Importance of Individual Variables and Variable Subsets in Discriminant Analysis," *Communications in Statistics* (September 1973), pp. 205–19.

13. William M. Cooley and P. R. Lohnes, *Multivariate Data Analysis* (New York: John Wiley & Sons, Inc., 1971).

14. F. Mosteller and R. R. Buch, "Selecting Quantitative Techniques," *Handbook of Social Psychology,* vol. I in G. Undzey, ed., (Reading, Mass.: Addison Wesley, 1954), pp. 289–334.

BIBLIOGRAPHY

Belkaoui, Ahmed. *Accounting Theory.* New York: Harcourt Brace Jovanvich, 1981.

———. "Industrial Bond Ratings: A New Look." *Financial Management* (Autumn 1980), pp. 44–51.

Cooley, William M. and P. R. Lohnes. *Multivariate Data Analysis.* New York: John Wiley & Sons, Inc., 1971.

Dixon, W. J. *BMDP Statistical Software 1981.* Berkeley and Los Angeles: University of California Press, 1981.

Eisenbeis, Robert A., Gary G. Gilbert, and Robert B. Avery. "Investigating the Relative Importance of Individual Variables and Variable Subsets in Discriminant Analysis." *Communications in Statistics* (September 1973), pp. 205–19.

Foster, George. *Financial Statement Analysis.* Englewood Cliffs, N.J.: Prentice-Hall, Inc., 1978.

Horrigan, J. O. "The Determinants of Long-Term Credit Standing with Financial Ratios." *Empirical Research in Accounting: Selected Studies,* 1966. Supplement to *Journal of Accounting Research* (1966), pp. 44–62.

Joy, O. Maurice and John O. Toffelson. "On the Financial Applications of Discriminant Analysis." *Journal of Financial and Quantitative Analysis* (December 1975), pp. 738-793.

Mosteller, F. and R. R. Bush. "Selecting Quantitative Techniques." *Handbook of Social Psychology,* vol. I in G. Undzey, ed. Reading, Mass.: Addison Wesley, 1954, pp. 289–334.

Pinches, G. E. and K. A. Mingo. "A Multivariate Analysis of Industrial Bond Ratings." *Journal of Finance* (March 1973), pp. 1–18.

West, R. R. "An Alternative Approach to Predicting Corporate Bond Ratings." *Journal of Accounting Research* (Spring 1970), pp. 118–127.

Winer, B. J. *Statistical Principles in Experimental Design.* End Ed. New York: McGraw-Hill Book Company, 1971.

5

BOND RATING PREDICTION: IMPLEMENTATIONS AND SUGGESTIONS

RECAPITULATION

As presented in chapter 1, debt financing goes from the simplest to the most complex capital structure. There are various types of industrial bonds varying as to the mode of interest payment, the nature of the claim, the type of guarantee and repayment. Given this diversity and the need to provide the market with adequate information on the investment quality of bond financing, various rating agencies perform the difficult task of assigning ratings of investment quality to industrial and other bonds. These ratings play a major role for both the issuers and the investors, creating the need for a good evaluation of bonds and the predicting of bond rating. Chapter 2 dealt with the problem of evaluation of bonds through a univariate ratio analysis, and chapters 3 and 4 with the prediction of bonds through multivariate models. Univariate ratio analysis as presented in chapter 2 may bring some answers and indications about the financial strength of a firm. However, the informational content of diagnostic ratio is better enhanced when used in a multivariate model. Such a multivariate model composed of diagnostic ratios would be more helpful and less cumbersome for bond ratings than univariate analysis. Various authors have attempted to explain and predict bond ratings based on multivariate analysis of the financial and/or statistical characteristics. As

shown in chapter 3, these models do an adequate job of capturing
the human judgments of bond raters. It was also shown that these
models suffer from (a) a diversity of approaches used in selecting
independent variables for the regression, discriminant, or multivariate profit models; (b) a lack of an economic rationale underlying
the choice of these variables; (c) a failure to account for the differences among the companies in their accounting for long-term
leases; and (d) the confusion of ex-ante predictive power with ex-
post discrimination. As a consequence, chapter 4 presented an
industrial bond rating prediction model aimed at correcting the
above limitations. This chapter is aimed at guiding the bond rater,
the bond issuer or any other analyst to an adequate implementation
of the model.

THE BOND RATING MODEL

MODEL'S PERFORMANCE

The methodology used was discriminant analysis to avoid some
of the pitfalls of the other techniques. Based on an economic rationale, the discriminant analysis model developed in this study correctly rated 72.93 percent of the ratings in an analysis sample
(1981), 67 percent of the ratings in a validation sample (1981),
67.19 percent of the ratings in a total estimating sample (1981), and
63.65 percent of the ratings in a control sample. Both validation
and predictive ability of the model were significant. Besides, two
results are noteworthy. First, most misclassified firms were classified in adjacent categories to the true ratings. Second, an examination of the *Credit Watch* list published by Standard and Poor for
five consecutive weeks following the availability of the information
on which the study is based, showed that seven of the firms put on
the list correspond to five of the misclassified firms. (See Exhibit
5.1.)

THE DISCRIMINANT FUNCTIONS

The discriminant model based on the estimating 1981 sample
yields a discriminant function for each of the five rating groups.

EXHIBIT 5.1 FIRMS MISCLASSIFIED AND ALSO ON THE CREDIT WATCH LIST

	Sample(s) in Which Misclassification Occurred	CREDIT WATCH RATING					
		March 29, 1982	April 5, 1982	April 12, 1982	April 19, 1982	April 26, 1982
Utilities, transportation						
Arizona Public Service Company	Analysis sample	/	/	/	/	Negative
Industrial, retailing						
Brunswick Corp.	Estimating sample Validation sample	Negative	Negative	Negative	Negative	Negative
Coca-Cola Co.	Estimating sample Validation sample	Negative	Negative	Negative		
Columbia Pictures Inds. Inc.	Estimating sample Validation sample	Positive	Positive	Positive	Positive	Positive
Lone Star Industries Inc.	Estimating sample Validation sample	Negative	Negative	Negative	Negative	Negative
Murphy (G.C.) Co.	Estimating sample Validation sample	Negative	Negative	/	/	/
Resorts International Inc.	Estimating sample Validation sample	Negative	Negative	Negative	/	/

These discriminant functions may be used to explain and/or predict bond ratings. They are as follows:

For an AAA rating:

$$Z = -31.6004 + 0.000737X_1 + 0.000119X_2 + 0.44234X_3 \\ + 0.62823X_4 + 7.26898X_5 + 0.68425X_6 + 0.06102X_7 \\ + 0.01802X_8 + 10.26302X_9$$

For an AA rating:

$$Z = -26.0425 + 0.000431X_1 - 0.000147X_2 + 0.48299X_3 \\ + 0.67906X_4 + 6.80279X_5 + 0.54641X_6 + 0.06600X_7 \\ + 0.01687X_8 + 9.76648X_9$$

For an A rating:

$$Z = -26.1304 + .000269X_1 - 0.000149X_2 + 0.58069X_3 \\ + 0.60516X_4 + 7.83642X_5 + 0.48850X_6 + 0.06777X_7 \\ + 0.00809X_8 + 8.18782X_9$$

For an BBB rating:

$$Z = -29.3824 + 0.000250X_1 - 0.000233X_2 + 0.71530X_3 \\ + 0.79864X_4 + 8.35763X_5 + 0.50766X_6 + 0.07116X_7 \\ + 0.00235X_8 + 4.27079X_9$$

For an BB rating:

$$Z = -31.3397 + 0.000265X_1 - 0.000295X_2 + 0.76589X_3 \\ + 0.80544X_4 + 9.15411X_5 + 0.48010X_6 + 0.05952X_7 \\ + 0.00705X_8 + 1.69732X_9$$

For an B rating:

$$Z = -34.8229 + 0.000242X_1 - 0.000357X_2 + 0.85499X_3 \\ + 0.84459X_4 + 9.24043X_5 + 0.49208X_6 + 0.06970X_7 \\ + 0.00099X_8 - 1.73660X_9$$

where:

X_1 = *Total assets.* Included as a representative of the total size of the firm (in millions).

X_2 = *Total debt.* Included as a measure of the total indebtness of the firm (in millions).

X_3 = *Long-term debt/total invested capital.* Included as a measure of the long-term capital intensiveness of the firm. By invested capital is meant the sum of the total debt, preferred stock and common equity (which includes common stock, capital surplus and retained earnings).

X_4 = *Short-term debt/total invested capital.* Included as a measure of the short-term capital intensiveness of the firm.

X_5 = *Current assets/current liabilities.* Included as a measure of the total liquidity of the firm.

X_6 = *Fixed charge coverage ratio.* Included as a measure of debt coverage.

X_7 = *Five-year cash flow as percentage of five-year growth needs.* Included as a measure of future liquidity.

X_8 = *Stock price/common equity per share.* Included as a measure of investors' expectations.

X_9 = *Subordination.* 1 for subordination, 0 for others. Included as a measure of the most relevant covenant in the indenture.

THE CLASSIFICATION PROCEDURE

The classification method consists simply of using the discriminant functions on new data as follows: For each firm which needs to be classified into a bond rating category, compute the classification score for each rating category from the discriminant function coefficients (multiply the data by the coefficients and add the constant term). The firm is then classified into the group for which the classification score is highest.[1]

To illustrate the classification procedure, let's use the following 1980 data for Frontier Airlines (the ratings given by Standard and Poor's was B).

X_1 = $312.8 (in millions)
X_2 = 116.1 (in millions)
X_3 = 48.7
X_4 = 4.1
X_5 = 0.9
X_6 = 3.5
X_7 = 52.8
X_8 = 104.7
X_9 = 1 (subordinated debt)

The classification scores for each rating category from the discriminant functions obtained by multiplying the coefficients by the data and adding the constant term are the following:

Z_{AAA} = 18.50916
Z_{AA} = 26.208
Z_A = 30.37737
Z_{BBB} = 38.72666
Z_{BB} = 41.09244
Z_B = 43.51933

Given that Z_B gives the highest classification score, the firm is classified by the model in the bond rating category B. Other examples are shown in Exhibit 5.2.

IMPLEMENTATIONS AND SUGGESTIONS

Given the sample classification procedure outlined in the previous paragraphs, the model may be useful to all those interested in explaining, predicting, and/or justifying bond ratings and evaluating the investment quality of bonds.

The issuing firm may use the classification procedure to explain the ratings assigned to its industrial bonds. Firms may be at a loss as to why their bonds have been assigned a given rating. The classification procedure provides a direct and easy way to check on their ratings. Conflicts between the ratings assigned by the rating agencies and this book's classification procedure may indicate that the rating agencies are concerned about qualitative factors not impounded in the model. Examples of factors include quality of management, growth plans, and so forth.

The issuing firm may use the classification procedure to predict the ratings that may be assigned to a new issue. Firms are generally at a loss when attempting to determine these ratings. The classification procedure outlined in this chapter provides a first idea of the ratings which may be assigned to them. Based on the results of the classification, firms may elect to go on with the new issue or attempt to first improve their financial conditions.

Investors may use the classification procedure to assess the investment quality of bonds. The model provides a direct and inexpensive way to classify bonds into five possible categories without

EXHIBIT 5.2   EXAMPLES OF FIRMS CORRECTLY
CLASSIFIED BY THE MODEL (INCLUDES Z
SCORES COMPUTED USING 1981
DISCRIMINANT FUNCTION)

NAME:	1 ASSETS	2 DEBT	3 CD/K	4 LTD/K	5 CR	6 FCC	7 5YRCFG	8 SPBV	SUBORDINATED
Bangor Punta	550.9	192.2	5.6	42.8	2.3	3.3	59.6	65.8	YES
Rohr Inds	292.7	92.7	0.8	53.7	2.6	1.6	39.7	91.4	YES
United Technlgs	6963.2	1381.3	12	23.5	1.5	2.5	35.9	127.4	NO
Frontier Airlines	312.8	116.1	4.1	48.7	0.9	3.5	52.8	104.7	YES
PSA	335.2	163.8	13.2	50.4	1.1	3.1	60.9	98.8	YES
PiedmontAviation	306.1	165.3	10.8	62	1.2	2.9	53	95	YES
Texas Air	325.9	170.6	3	63.5	2.3	4	58.8	85.6	YES
Zenith Radio	644.2	206	19.1	23.3	2.1	3.6	76.2	113.3	YES
Arvin Inds	304	88.4	2.1	32	3.9	2.8	178.6	71.6	NO
Bendix	2961.8	740.4	5.8	30.3	1.8	4	89.1	109.8	NO
Dana	1848	475.3	10.4	23.4	2.2	5.4	77.3	90.9	NO
Fruehauf	1516	467.1	8.1	39	1.7	2	113.7	67.7	NO
Anheuser-Busch	2254.5	807.2	13.7	32.7	1	5	58.2	148.7	NO
PpesiCo	3286.3	967.6	9.4	32.6	1.4	5.7	75.3	180.7	NO
GAF	909.9	314.3	16.1	29.8	2	1.9	60.6	49	NO
IdealBasicInds	753.4	254	0	41.2	1.9	8.1	66.7	112.9	NO
Jim Walter	2171.3	935.1	18.9	37.9	2	2.3	79	80.8	NO
Johns-Manville	2405.5	644.4	6.4	28.4	1.8	2.3	71.9	73.4	NO
Lone Star Inds	954.4	294.8	3.2	38.3	2.2	5.1	92.8	104.4	NO
Texas Inds.	313.3	137.4	4	48.3	1.8	7.8	80	198.7	YES
U.S. Gypsum	1069.6	154.7	3.3	15.9	2.4	12.8	101.3	88.6	NO
Amn.Cyanamid	2810.4	660.2	6.8	25.5	1.7	4.8	74.7	99.2	NO
Celanese	2380	579	3.2	31.8	1.9	4	98.3	79.9	NO
Diamond Shamrock	2622.1	820.8	3.4	37.4	2.2	5.6	68.4	169.7	NO
Int'l Minrl&Chems	1848.6	500	0.8	35.4	2	6.9	79.4	151.8	NO
Pfizer	3303.7	1046.2	17.1	24.1	2	4.8	100.3	236.4	NO
RichardsonMerrel	929.8	135.9	7.9	11.9	2.1	9.4	116.6	114.9	NO
Searle (G.D.)	1158.9	442.5	36.2	9.4	1.4	5.1	86.3	263.6	NO
SmithKline	1364	188.5	4.9	12.9	2.6	16.9	108.2	501.8	NO
Squibb	1885.8	605.8	12.5	26.4	2.1	4.2	83.8	140.6	NO
Syntex	675.3	162.2	8.9	19.4	2.6	4.9	117.3	240.4	NO
Upjohn	1505.8	312.8	8.6	21	2.4	8.2	108.6	245.3	NO
AMP	905.5	110.7	9.8	7.5	2.3	23.8	113.3	347.6	NO
ChampionSparkPlug	618.2	83.7	7.5	9.6	3	11	94.9	98.3	NO
E-Systems	228.3	40.4	1.3	25.9	2.6	6.6	213	244.1	YES
GK Technologies	745.1	224.7	10.3	31.9	1.9	5	60.1	232.2	NO
G.E.	17492.1	1961.3	9.9	10.2	1.3	9.4	104.1	159.8	NO
General Instrument	581.5	51.6	0.7	14.1	2.4	12.9	114.6	236.9	YES
Motorola	2050.6	426	3.8	24.6	2.4	6.6	81.6	195	NO
Raytheon	2754.1	128.6	5.5	7.1	1.3	27.1	93	324	NO
Square D	607.7	137.6	9.3	19.4	2.3	13.2	95.4	201.6	NO
Tandy	639.7	248.2	3.6	46.3	3.7	9.4	110.3	787.2	YES
Texas Instruments	2267.6	198.6	15.7	1.5	1.4	11.2	81.7	305.1	NO
Westinghouse Elec.	6867.5	472	4.2	12.2	1.3	10.7	81	95.8	NO
CFS Continental	213.4	59.4	6.1	36.9	2.3	3	74.5	58.6	NO
CPC International	2166.1	417.8	16	12.8	1.6	7.1	85.1	172.4	NO
Castle & Cooke	1211.8	427.2	11	36.1	2.1	1.6	54.6	91.6	NO
Esmark	2415.7	750.6	13.5	31.5	1.7	2.8	58.3	143.8	NO
Gen'l Mills	2012.4	468.5	6.1	25.4	1.7	7.5	84	138.4	NO

124

NAME:	ZSCORE(1) S&P AAA	ZSCORE(2) S&P AA	ZSCORE(3) S&P A	ZSCORE(4) S&P BBB	ZSCORE(5) S&P BB	ZSCORE(6) S&P B	S&P RATING
Bangor Punta	15.0791	21.15928	25.14527	30.69224	32.70627	33.56427	B
Rohr Inds	16.94737	23.28744	28.72407	34.90253	38.0684	39.38666	B
United Technlgs	18.99987	22.39174	20.23633	18.96305	17.51847	12.52578	AA
Frontier Airlines	6.808366	13.6823	17.386	21.68122	23.12083	24.03941	B
PSA	14.86752	22.2637	25.63874	32.1904	33.82687	35.36742	B
PiedmontAviation	18.50916	26.208	30.97737	38.72666	41.09244	43.51933	B
Texas Air	23.22075	29.95276	35.98292	43.71634	46.83948	49.31045	B
Zenith Radio	15.62565	21.65132	22.21691	27.31955	28.30304	27.81661	BB
Arvin Inds	36.82571	41.79819	44.39104	46.00535	44.79205	42.34535	BBB
Bendix	21.22035	25.75096	25.82669	25.03653	23.32347	19.50397	A
Dana	23.00946	27.44419	26.98161	26.72728	25.00568	20.87608	AA
Fruehauf	24.06122	30.01453	31.54423	32.59881	30.80847	28.36431	BBB
Anheuser-Busch	20.41598	25.6521	24.69446	24.58408	22.91357	19.04606	AA-
PpesiCo	23.45757	27.91916	26.95605	26.2899	24.85304	20.76921	AA
GAF	23.08706	28.90487	29.28396	30.92483	29.48447	26.22695	BBB
IdealBasicInds	22.93214	27.60193	29.36021	29.09225	28.09551	24.95903	A-
Jim Walter	31.4037	37.19167	37.62949	40.71325	39.65035	37.08647	BBB
Johns-Manville	17.46602	22.31376	22.65987	21.86704	20.12842	16.23276	A+
Lone Star Inds	25.38021	30.44444	32.07618	32.43599	31.29563	28.29968	BBB
Texas Inds.	19.41012	25.27288	28.33745	33.17214	35.31505	36.00077	B
U.S. Gypsum	22.55912	25.63067	24.84444	22.70277	20.20443	15.53595	AA
Amn.Cyanamid	18.35476	22.67925	22.21773	20.90318	18.96713	14.71056	AA-
Celanese	20.55126	25.24261	26.09992	25.34509	23.51206	20.03217	A-
Diamond Shamrock	26.43131	30.61812	31.16487	30.91788	30.34026	26.55082	A-
Int'l Minrl&Chems	23.08848	27.34332	28.05127	27.0211	25.90298	22.10348	A
Pfizer	30.83242	35.21984	32.74001	32.81329	31.47341	26.8635	AA
RichardsonMerrel	20.47478	24.31476	22.67886	20.40208	17.53077	12.60977	AA
Searle (G.D.)	30.15458	35.78519	30.33075	31.36184	29.17516	23.8045	AA
SmithKline	34.58712	36.43225	31.41479	27.11721	26.3924	19.13614	AA+
Squibb	25.44383	30.24984	29.51513	29.66396	28.22158	24.15608	AA
Syntex	27.09634	31.5994	30.06655	28.73527	27.35091	22.36801	AA
Upjohn	28.608	32.4885	30.6238	29.20911	27.7916	22.81163	AA
AMP	35.00149	36.41056	31.41945	28.0668	25.88072	19.39905	AA+
ChampionSparkPlug	24.98348	28.07688	26.74348	25.1224	22.97398	17.84682	AA
E-Systems	21.6593	26.9291	28.29843	30.64282	30.96846	30.58809	BB
GK Technologies	14.64306	20.22221	21.01146	24.63736	26.54658	26.60039	BB-
G.E.	27.64715	26.87742	20.79576	17.034	14.07736	8.004458	AAA
General Instrument	13.04732	16.45018	16.07275	16.31616	16.82436	14.56869	BB+
Motorola	23.95129	27.70181	26.92064	25.2086	24.07145	19.23133	AA
Raytheon	26.8139	27.42749	21.85675	16.62262	13.65328	6.832794	AA
Square D	28.75766	32.23633	30.36944	29.10003	27.32182	22.46702	AA
Tandy	45.89133	49.9055	48.41666	51.71138	57.64113	55.0072	BB-
Texas Instruments	19.21128	22.33679	16.67673	13.54026	9.910336	2.826304	AA
Westinghouse Elec.	15.26115	17.29061	14.41688	10.46531	7.328843	1.843242	AA-
CFS Continental	23.35567	28.97454	30.94343	31.97963	30.90995	28.04543	BBB
CPC International	20.8134	25.02335	21.96707	20.30591	17.85838	12.55965	AA
Castle & Cooke	23.82949	29.4493	30.43916	31.76416	30.97149	27.73978	BBB
Esmark	23.37236	28.50473	27.90919	28.34863	27.21201	23.29929	AA-
Gen'l Mills	20.38073	24.55881	23.8162	22.24234	20.28455	15.91571	AA

EXHIBIT 5.2—Continued

NAME:	1 ASSETS	2 DEBT	3 CD/K	4 LTD/K	5 CR	6 FCC	7 5YRCFG	8 SPBV	SUBORDINATED
Heinz (HJ)	1954.3	502.5	18.8	17.8	1.6	4.7	83	122.1	NO
Hershey Foods	691.8	228.9	12.5	28	1.6	7	66.1	107.5	NO
Hormel (Geo. A)	322.4	29.2	0.3	12.6	2	18.1	103.1	94.1	NO
Mayer (Oscar)	615.3	138.4	19.6	11.6	1.3	8.7	89.2	89.7	NO
McCormick	290.6	102.5	18.4	23.6	2.1	4.9	75.1	171.8	NO
Quaker Oats	1282.2	296.4	15.6	16.9	1.6	6	89.7	111.7	NO
Ralston Purina	2115.7	573.5	9.7	24.3	1.7	6.1	81	115.4	NO
Staley (AE) Mfg.	735.9	129.7	7.3	19.3	1.9	4.9	52.9	239.1	NO
Hilton Hotels	649.7	127.3	0.7	22.2	2.3	18.4	117.5	286.5	NO
Black & Decker	1115.6	140.4	7.6	13.9	1.9	8.6	93.2	168.4	NO
Combustion Eng.	2185	150.9	1.3	19.1	1.2	12.8	71.8	234.9	NO
Dover	429.3	65.2	9.3	9.9	2.5	22.4	117.4	337.3	NO
Scott & Fetzer	394.6	91.6	4.1	29.4	2.2	6.3	107.1	94.4	NO
Sunstrand	775.7	232.2	8.1	30.4	2.9	5.1	86	224.6	YES
Zurn Inds.	219.3	35.4	1.8	24.1	1.9	10.9	103.9	128.3	YES
General Signal	1055.9	127.2	6.3	11.1	2.3	14	76.4	181.8	NO
Bally Mfg.	654.9	244	0.9	45.5	2.4	4.8	39.4	238.8	YES
Columbia Pics.Inds.	487.7	179	19.7	25.9	2.1	5.8	161.2	166.9	YES
GulfResources&Chem	558.4	246.8	1.8	55.7	2.5	1.7	62.9	119.4	YES
Harsco	630.3	129.6	0.8	26.3	3	10.7	92.5	104	NO
RevereCopper&Brass	458.6	185.8	3.2	48.7	2.5	3.3	75.3	66.4	NO
Reynolds Metals	3077.8	921.5	1.9	39.5	2	4.8	89.4	65.4	YES
Borg-Warner	1946	362.2	14.1	10.5	1.6	5.3	142	77.5	NO
Condec	239.6	98.8	3.5	52.4	2.7	1.6	88.6	82.4	YES
CorningGlassWorks	1426.4	197.9	2.6	16	2.1	7	123.9	141.1	NO
Crane	1022.1	429.2	2.5	51	2.4	2.4	68.9	100.7	NO
Dayco	441	203.8	11.2	47.3	2.3	3	71.9	48	NO
Hoover Universal	327.4	77	0.7	33.5	1.8	6.5	72.3	113.4	NO
Monogram Inds.	220.2	94.4	5.5	48.7	2.9	4.8	181.6	93.1	YES
Norris INds.	344.3	24.9	0.1	8.8	3.6	26.2	126.2	106.8	NO
PPG Inds.	2690.9	589.5	3.8	25.7	2.6	8.8	85.8	87.9	NO
Robertson(H.H.)	299.2	77.3	25.5	19.6	1.5	3.6	82.9	91.6	YES
Snap-on Tools	305	61.1	13.7	12.4	2.4	17.6	96.8	305.3	NO
UMC Inds.	226.3	84.4	15.1	30.3	2.2	4.2	72.6	78.2	NO
Ashland Oil	3195.3	636	1.5	34.2	1.4	4.3	88.8	116.6	NO
Charter	1743.7	588.2	10.3	35.7	1.4	6.3	78.6	67.2	YES
Conoco	10364.9	1729.2	1.8	27.1	1.4	18.1	76.6	134.9	NO
Exxon	53055	6228	4.9	15.6	1.5	20.6	77.6	133.3	NO
Getty Oil	7397.6	589.1	8.2	5.1	1	79	83.8	181.5	NO
Gulf Oil	17624	1602	1	13.6	1.4	34.7	84.4	81	NO
Houston Natrl Gas	1793.3	445.1	1.9	33.3	1.6	5.3	87.7	231.3	NO
Inexco Oil	439.5	136.3	5.9	35.4	0.7	4.8	64.6	265.8	YES
Kerr-McGee	2621.5	395	1.3	23.4	1.3	5.6	64.1	162.6	NO
Marathon Oil	4549.5	892.1	0.2	32	1.1	14.3	62	175	NO
Mesa Petroleum	1172.7	518.8	5.7	47.3	0.7	9.7	62.6	419.8	YES
Pacific Resources	305.2	141	20.4	41.1	1.8	3.9	64	190.9	NO
Pennzoil	2362.2	771.7	0.5	43.6	1.8	5.7	84.4	261.7	NO
QuakerStt.OilRfnr	490.6	105.4	1.8	30	1.9	4.9	76.5	175.9	NO
Std Oil(Indiana)	18562.2	2777.3	1.3	22.6	1.2	18	89.6	212.4	NO

NAME:	ZSCORE(1) S&P AAA	ZSCORE(2) S&P AA	ZSCORE(3) S&P A	ZSCORE(4) S&P BBB	ZSCORE(5) S&P BB	ZSCORE(6) S&P B	S&P RATING
Heinz (HJ)	21.96102	26.92844	24.77329	24.5596	22.23544	17.73782	AA
Hershey Foods	21.83032	26.91674	26.44425	26.50261	24.69479	20.87642	AA
Hormel (Geo. A)	19.57638	22.05254	20.77792	17.27713	14.11935	9.088384	AA
Mayer (Oscar)	19.0403	23.90717	21.28164	20.40166	17.17223	12.51355	AA+
McCormick	27.1853	32.56105	31.1096	31.90091	30.55729	26.31878	AA
Quaker Oats	20.14298	25.01159	23.16865	22.35226	19.78624	15.26688	AA
Ralston Purina	20.68895	25.15412	24.29474	23.35363	21.33234	17.08623	AA+
Staley (AE) Mfg.	17.04627	21.46179	19.59769	16.97233	15.75836	10.06319	AA
Hilton Hotels	31.06027	33.50356	31.52934	28.65986	26.96439	21.77083	AA
Black & Decker	18.8439	22.72411	20.7107	18.02164	15.639	10.31187	AA+
Combustion Eng.	15.65483	18.70228	16.25593	11.89053	9.633141	3.882279	AA
Dover	35.95263	37.70498	33.35334	30.50393	28.52995	22.35796	AA-
Scott & Fetzer	23.0849	27.95421	28.80647	28.29912	26.45797	22.9584	A
Sunstrand	21.40176	26.45638	27.82792	32.04693	34.32248	33.52748	BB+
Zurn Inds.	10.27915	14.82519	16.23418	18.04958	18.33602	17.50875	BB
General Signal	22.56197	25.25138	22.79923	19.88911	17.78327	12.02518	AA
Bally Mfg.	17.04282	22.39909	25.38044	29.4509	32.6587	32.35422	BB
Columbia Pics.Inds.	24.69234	30.964	31.32146	36.91757	37.23661	37.49194	B
GulfResources&Chem	19.93669	26.41381	31.66037	38.09425	41.15274	42.69584	B
Harsco	27.92693	31.36593	32.1199	31.39972	30.11419	26.13107	A+
RevereCopper&Brass	28.79798	34.51048	37.80566	40.03517	39.72591	37.7471	BBB
Reynolds Metals	13.90321	18.87579	22.13084	26.21308	27.45054	27.98571	B
Borg-Warner	18.96311	23.6985	21.63949	20.01313	16.37372	11.88611	AA-
Condec	21.5787	28.2243	33.55625	40.40872	42.99477	44.81657	B
CorningGlassWorks	18.60805	22.53366	21.51149	18.57465	15.98728	18.0017	AA
Crane	28.70549	34.35996	37.51063	39.53823	39.53206	37.3974	BBB
Dayco	30.99551	37.19636	39.8468	43.30521	42.78132	41.04972	BBB
Hoover Universal	18.15942	23.00719	24.09911	22.82978	21.34197	17.60765	A
Monogram Inds.	30.69489	37.21722	42.02039	49.29497	50.74651	53.16576	B
Norris INds.	36.59681	37.14234	35.71251	33.56378	31.05485	26.05116	AA
PPG Inds.	26.21465	29.54313	29.65364	28.95272	27.42834	23.38004	A+
Robertson(H.H.)	13.39603	20.06114	19.7846	25.13905	25.31463	24.91869	BB
Snap-on Tools	33.88535	36.63905	32.7079	30.96224	29.28446	23.44737	AA
UMC Inds.	26.43437	32.08153	32.44627	34.12819	32.78773	29.55939	BBB
Ashland Oil	17.8058	22.37783	22.84142	21.27877	19.44518	15.73482	A
Charter	12.51379	18.22026	20.35158	24.92992	25.62408	26.08407	B
Conoco	29.30161	29.41346	26.73231	24.16019	21.93546	17.24262	AA
Exxon	60.66275	47.50268	34.77073	30.22046	28.11478	21.00453	AAA
Getty Oil	61.30801	53.72082	44.9076	41.25365	36.04386	30.35928	AAA
Gulf Oil	39.03006	34.46486	28.58608	24.56717	20.96234	15.49375	AAA
Houston Natrl Gas	20.74039	25.35246	25.00781	23.01893	21.80365	17.41124	AA+
Inexco Oil	5.211653	11.3854	12.06855	13.83964	15.0461	13.98679	BB-
Kerr-McGee	11.93528	15.96629	14.9366	11.48109	9.477372	4.353249	AA+
Marathon Oil	21.12479	23.67224	22.46474	19.74576	17.8868	13.36022	AA+
Mesa Petroleum	16.94341	22.43095	22.5034	24.99409	27.42809	26.44988	BB-
Pacific Resources	22.73718	29.60855	31.02564	37.98003	40.12692	40.67313	B
Pennzoil	26.94993	31.47091	31.91808	31.04599	30.68322	26.89554	A-
QuakerStt.OilRfnr	18.44107	23.27459	23.50811	21.70848	20.42265	16.06441	A
Std Oil(Indiana)	33.83761	31.35988	25.87604	21.73496	19.46953	13.66324	AAA

EXHIBIT 5.2—Continued

NAME:	1 ASSETS	2 DEBT	3 CD/K	4 LTD/K	5 CR	6 FCC	7 5YRCFG	8 SPBV	SUBORDINATED
Std Oil(Ohio)	11050.3	3892.3	1	54.7	1.5	9.6	51.1	401.5	NO
Std Oil Co. of Cal	20025.9	2111	0.8	16.4	1.5	27.8	110.9	125.8	NO
Sun	7970.2	975.3	1.8	18.8	1.3	10.1	91.8	116.9	NO
Superior Oil	2976.6	681.8	1.6	27.8	1.4	7	71.7	357.6	NO
UnionOilCo.ofCal.	6430.8	1241.2	0.8	26.9	1.7	12.5	86.8	184.4	NO
Witco Chemical	570.9	124	2.2	32.1	2.1	9	82.5	110.4	NO
Burroughs	3603.4	480.7	11.1	7.3	1.6	10.1	100.1	132.1	NO
Digital Equipment	2503.9	499.5	0.5	23.9	4.6	19.3	82.2	264.9	NO
IBM	25669.7	2217.9	3.9	8.7	1.6	25.8	82.6	254.5	NO
Savin	296.9	104.9	10.9	38.7	2.3	5	75.8	81.9	YES
Xerox	6977.5	1176.2	6.7	18.7	1.8	11.1	102.6	157.6	NO
Buttes Gas & Oil	316.6	215.1	8.4	72.3	1.3	1.6	47.8	228.8	YES
Global Marine	441	209.2	6.7	62.7	2.9	3	40.7	372.7	YES
Halliburton	4371.2	745.5	5	18.5	1.9	13.7	103.7	327.3	NO
Reading & Bates	630.1	171.7	1.2	33.2	1.5	4.2	58.8	260.1	NO
Rowan	388.4	130	4.3	34	1.7	3.5	72	529.6	YES
Boise Cascade	2486.2	724.7	1.7	35.3	1.7	3.8	61.1	83.6	NO
Champion Int'l	3152.4	907.5	1.7	34.9	1.9	5.5	69.8	91.2	NO
ChesapeakeCorp,VI	212.1	41.6	1.4	22.5	2.7	13.1	83.9	115.8	NO
Crown Zellerbach	2330.5	573.9	1.4	31.4	2.2	4.8	85	122.5	NO
Diamond Int'l	833	141.1	7.5	13.9	2	5.5	72.4	92.6	NO
Georgia-Pacific	4295	1503	7.2	35.8	1.8	3.7	69.7	152.7	NO
Gt.NorthernNekosa	1166.3	274.6	0.9	30	2.3	8.6	77.7	97	NO
Int'l Paper	4994	1036.9	2.4	23.2	2.2	4.5	80	75.7	NO
Kimberly-Clark	2248.8	367.5	3.3	19.1	1.7	17.2	86	97.7	NO
Mead	1759.9	512.9	7.3	31.1	1.4	5.9	111.1	88.5	NO
Potlatch	1013.5	359	1.3	40.7	1.8	3.4	66.1	109.2	NO
Saxon Inds.	474	266.6	12.8	55.7	2.7	1.4	46.2	43.2	YES
Scott Paper	1922	423.8	0.7	27.1	1.6	9.7	82.5	68.4	NO
Union Camp	1571.8	280.9	4.4	19.7	2	19.3	74.5	120.6	NO
Westvaco	1076.6	269.2	0.8	30.5	2.6	7.9	77.3	98.9	NO
Weyerhauser	5285	1508.6	2	32.6	2.1	6.2	88	160.6	NO
Chesebrough-Pond's	844.5	201.4	20.4	9.9	2	9	98.7	211.6	NO
Revlon	1981.1	482.4	17.5	12.9	1.9	7.7	88	200.7	NO
Filmways	248.2	136.4	8.9	60.9	1.4	1.6	44.6	109.5	YES
Times Mirror	1544.5	247.9	2.5	22.8	1.7	12.2	94.7	200.1	NO
Missouri Pacific	2521	1084.3	4.1	51.8	1.5	3.9	70.2	132	NO
Southern Pacific	5175.5	1667.4	3.5	41	1	2.1	71.3	53	NO
Union Pacific	5472.7	1184.1	1.4	29.3	1.2	7.6	69.7	198.4	NO
Kroger	1845.5	397.4	0.6	38	1.4	5.7	59.3	95.1	NO
Lucky Stores	1287.4	327.5	2.2	41	1.4	7.2	61.6	191.4	NO
American Stores	1209	452.8	6.9	50.2	1.3	9.4	18.1	125.4	NO
AssociatedDryGoods	981.6	190.2	4.1	23	1.8	4.2	79.4	72.5	NO
DWG	236.7	92.6	5.9	52.5	2.9	1.9	85.8	29.7	YES
Dayton-Hudson	1832.2	203	1.1	16.4	1.4	15.9	88.5	130.8	NO
Gordon Jewelry	364.4	89.7	10.1	23.5	2.5	7.8	72.1	79.8	YES
Mercantile Stores	597.5	132.8	0.4	29.1	2.7	7.5	84.5	69	NO
Nordstrom	244.3	79.8	2.3	39.2	2.6	6.8	59	177.3	YES
Scoa Inds.	304	99.7	4.4	45.1	2	6.8	115	196.9	NO

NAME:	ZSCORE(1) S&P AAA	ZSCORE(2) S&P AA	ZSCORE(3) S&P A	ZSCORE(4) S&P BBB	ZSCORE(5) S&P BB	ZSCORE(6) S&P B	S&P RATING
Std Oil(Ohio)	39.93289	41.05683	39.14233	38.26398	39.32221	34.78696	AA-
Std Oil Co. of Cal	40.40597	36.15415	30.17766	26.21703	22.96541	17.51079	AAA
Sun	18.17543	20.03547	17.629	13.94182	11.13389	6.00837	AA
Superior Oil	20.03006	23.65851	21.23091	17.43638	16.53488	10.67772	AA
UnionOilCo.ofCal.	25.48789	27.34574	25.56045	22.85419	21.05596	16.2143	AA
Witco Chemical	23.12741	27.48716	28.32151	27.57156	26.06449	22.42121	A+
Burroughs	18.6116	21.65694	18.34188	15.29909	12.11575	6.516425	AA+
Digital Equipment	47.8901	48.45055	47.4307	47.21005	47.74672	42.6193	AA
IBM	43.07506	37.07484	27.96167	22.68257	20.21899	13.007	AAA
Savin	18.83927	24.94154	27.97514	34.00287	35.68132	36.47414	B
Xerox	26.21272	28.16508	25.42317	23.03908	20.68226	15.64369	AA
Buttes Gas & Oil	23.50321	31.43555	36.32431	44.2893	47.96575	50.33468	B
Global Marine	33.0288	39.31318	42.7534	50.01364	55.19001	55.86116	B
Halliburton	28.71413	30.78714	27.08545	23.61978	21.9915	16.00736	AA
Reading & Bates	6.378608	11.851	13.07566	14.50713	16.26794	14.86467	BB-
Rowan	15.13503	20.63294	19.54585	20.39437	23.50536	20.80183	BB
Boise Cascade	17.45898	22.07941	23.18863	22.23165	20.8647	17.22945	A
Champion Int'l	21.08029	25.16539	26.04412	25.24122	23.91263	20.27394	A-
ChesapeakeCorp,VI	25.45335	28.65575	28.68109	27.20345	25.57316	21.15209	A
Crown Zellerbach	21.8908	26.12329	26.78072	25.67744	24.38317	20.45455	A
Diamond Int'l	14.54279	18.8566	17.76294	15.47422	13.13712	8.652425	AA
Georgia-Pacific	24.99184	29.15318	28.99929	28.81273	27.8496	23.99652	AA
Gt.NorthernNekosa	22.48468	26.44734	27.27793	26.24043	24.79171	20.92824	A+
Int'l Paper	19.5581	22.74469	22.40875	20.55107	18.73943	14.23805	AA-
Kimberly-Clark	22.02284	24.48618	23.08662	20.5533	17.7786	13.1336	AA
Mead	20.9537	26.03334	26.24814	25.69588	23.28622	19.97317	A
Potlatch	19.68592	24.99982	26.81755	26.54027	25.5713	22.3737	A+
Saxon Inds.	25.64325	32.64875	37.84987	47.00503	50.14055	52.43583	B
Scott Paper	17.09332	20.91828	21.19717	19.14302	16.78074	12.78661	A+
Union Camp	25.79819	28.03219	26.54365	24.52063	22.19532	17.4801	AA
Westvaco	24.28777	28.24346	29.31141	28.62496	27.47126	23.65309	A
Weyerhauser	26.19092	29.29064	28.9665	27.71467	26.56381	22.37725	AA
Chesebrough-Pond's	27.03816	31.33859	27.69668	26.83291	24.53904	19.16054	AA
Revlon	24.9496	29.03137	25.77286	24.59889	22.48608	17.1388	AA
Filmways	17.09584	24.70375	29.5443	36.86257	39.51974	41.61709	B
Times Mirror	21.57853	24.98641	23.55531	20.73447	18.64803	13.72952	AA
Missouri Pacific	26.37656	31.75388	33.78199	35.01648	34.46368	32.10336	BBB
Southern Pacific	17.02724	21.64934	22.69707	22.14018	20.34906	17.29835	A-
Union Pacific	18.43441	21.49768	19.99365	16.97327	15.28701	10.36655	AA
Kroger	16.66726	21.45543	22.68552	21.5567	20.09023	16.61884	A
Lucky Stores	21.48203	26.33506	26.9242	26.00891	25.08089	21.41432	A
American Stores	25.3958	30.45052	31.93616	33.3246	32.94913	30.2816	BBB+
AssociatedDryGoods	14.26914	19.05789	19.24532	17.41319	15.21655	10.94468	A+
DWG	23.66605	30.35206	36.05073	43.89823	46.44127	48.68128	B
Dayton-Hudson	18.25215	20.84917	19.1751	15.55915	12.70803	7.568318	AA
Gordon Jewelry	14.76709	19.70154	21.23866	25.33648	26.35675	25.80767	BB
Mercantile Stores	23.401	27.52245	28.92496	28.29064	26.92125	23.24423	A
Nordstrom	17.72272	22.84719	25.74438	29.93497	32.41285	32.23265	BB+
Scoa Inds.	31.37039	36.86135	38.23517	39.13023	38.30123	35.63914	BBB+

129

EXHIBIT 5.2—Continued

NAME:	ASSETS	DEBT	CD/K	LTD/K	CR	FCC	5YRCFG	SPBV	SUBORDINATED
	1	2	3	4	5	6	7	8	
Zayre	623.2	252	3.3	58	1.9	2	68.6	58.5	NO
Browning-FerrisInds	469.8	153.6	2.5	39.7	1.4	3.9	83.5	226.6	NO
Di Giorgio	330.6	138.9	19.2	37	1.9	2	69.8	62.4	YES
Dillingham	718.8	198	7	35.8	1.5	3.9	70.2	85.6	YES
EngelhardMinrls&Che	5693	1579.5	37.5	16	1.3	4.3	51	280.9	NO
Fischbach	369.6	73.7	22	17.6	1.8	3.4	110.9	102	YES
Humana	1292.6	745.5	3.3	70.2	1.4	2.1	25.3	527.3	NO
Nat'l Med. Enterps.	596.2	274.2	3.3	53.9	1.8	3	26.4	304.4	YES
TIGER INTERNATNAL	2144	1279.1	5.3	71.2	1.2	1.3	44	106.9	NO
NVF	1314.9	768.4	16.6	59.6	1.8	1.8	41.7	163	NO
LEVI STRAUSS	1346.8	167.6	7.5	10.6	2.3	23.9	138.7	216	NO
MCDONOUGH	226.3	26.3	8.2	7	2.8	11.9	138.5	105.6	NO
RIEGEL TEXTILE	232.8	45.6	1.2	25.3	3	12.6	108.8	69.6	NO
Goodyear Tire&Rub.	5492.9	1710.2	7.6	36	2.1	1.9	82.9	53.5	NO
Loews	8905.4	1258.2	14.3	39	2.2	3.9	247.8	97.6	NO
Reynolds Indus.	6643.8	1371.5	5.6	22	2.4	6.2	67	126.7	NO
Ariz. Publ. Service	2709.5	1297.2	4.7	46.7	0.6	1.8	31.7	80.8	NO
Carolina Pow.&Light	3935.1	1745	3	50	0.6	2.1	37.5	81.4	NO
Columbia Gas Sys.	3608.9	1181.5	1.8	47.9	0.9	3	74.5	103.7	NO
Continental Tlphn.	3058.3	1449.4	6.6	55.6	0.9	2.5	56.1	98.3	NO
Enserch	1965.9	597.8	1.6	41.4	1.3	3.3	63.8	205.9	NO
Ohio Edison	3707	1786.2	1.7	52.3	1	1.8	33	84	NO
Pacific Pow&Light	3288.9	1618.5	3.3	53.7	0.6	1.6	33.3	97.8	NO
Panhandle E. Pplin.	2799.5	982.7	4.5	46.3	1.1	3.3	64	151.7	NO
Penn. Pow.&Light	4056.5	1774.8	3	45.7	1.2	1.6	34.9	70.8	NO
Tex. Gas Trnsmssion	1290.7	304.7	3.2	33.1	1.1	4.8	90.1	132.9	NO
Transco	2808.1	1233.2	2.7	59.2	1	2.1	65.9	223.1	NO
United Telecommun.	4010.3	1875.8	9.8	51.7	0.7	3	61.1	109.1	NO
Western Union	1767.7	744.8	2.3	49.8	1	1	60.3	85.7	YES

NOTES: 1. TOTAL ASSETS
           2. TOTAL DEBT
           3. CURRENT DEBT TO CAPITAL
           4. LONG TERM DEBT TO CAPITAL
           5. CURRENT RATIO
           6. FIXED COST COVERAGE
           7. 5 YEAR CASH FLOW
           8. STOCK PRICE BOOK VALUE

NAME:	ZSCORE(1) S&P AAA	ZSCORE(2) S&P AA	ZSCORE(3) S&P A	ZSCORE(4) S&P BBB	ZSCORE(5) S&P BB	ZSCORE(6) S&P B	S&P RATING
Zayre	27.3018	33.77033	37.78666	40.6232	40.38688	39.13866	BBB-
Browning-FerrisInds	20.18433	25.7882	26.31366	25.12055	24.11663	20.33725	A-
Di Giorgio	17.65256	24.68193	27.07718	34.07719	35.46896	36.42418	B
Dillingham	8.585859	14.72696	17.32867	21.26331	22.25143	22.45765	B
EngelhardMinrls&Che	34.25521	38.66853	32.63257	34.27767	32.94647	27.50639	AA-
Fischbach	14.30393	20.708	20.58962	25.35445	25.37372	24.8807	BB
Humana	35.49366	41.61208	42.25329	43.29654	45.99949	42.46578	BB
Nat'l Med. Enterps.	17.02278	23.2375	26.09972	30.65541	34.33535	34.27279	BB-
TIGER INTERNATNAL	19.18317	26.35097	32.02541	39.69036	42.72587	45.38496	B
NVF	26.05265	33.25609	36.88433	45.56596	48.82943	50.69132	B
LEVI STRAUSS	24.2433	26.28973	24.45527	25.82228	25.45077	23.5906	AA
MCDONOUGH	15.66828	19.48702	19.37244	21.37142	21.0162	19.47723	BBB
RIEGEL TEXTILE	18.84419	22.74701	25.25321	28.6967	29.53621	29.30567	BB
Goodyear Tire&Rub.	26.20643	30.30995	31.04239	31.82612	30.56412	27.41595	BBB
Loews	47.15857	51.38886	51.06405	53.9726	51.2699	49.9087	BBB
Reynolds Indus.	25.03783	27.35807	25.85935	24.31282	22.99367	18.03851	AA
Ariz. Publ. Service	13.41083	19.07926	20.61063	20.39683	19.14279	16.17765	A-
Carolina Pow.&Light	15.33033	20.5873	22.30626	22.16842	21.01912	18.24406	A
Columbia Gas Sys.	18.79568	24.03948	25.66543	25.40749	24.02293	21.339	A
Continental Tlphn.	23.28092	29.13989	31.31811	32.97252	32.20625	30.22445	BBB
Enserch	18.81506	23.9794	24.57042	23.29767	22.46874	18.63946	A
Ohio Edison	17.84228	23.00579	25.26461	25.58529	24.93181	22.28238	BBB+
Pacific Pow&Light	16.36084	22.01851	24.08494	24.40827	23.57711	21.02787	BBB+
Panhandle E. Pplin.	21.04686	26.38936	27.45904	27.45272	26.49059	23.44984	A
Penn. Pow.&Light	17.1909	22.02111	23.69263	23.66681	22.77412	19.69924	A+
Tex. Gas Trnsmssion	15.47711	20.74561	21.05105	19.32754	17.22694	13.46724	A
Transco	15.25062	21.59291	25.03164	29.77382	32.30481	33.2836	B
United Telecommun.	23.70758	29.24007	30.39971	31.84086	30.7365	28.42672	BBB
Western Union	6.444119	13.073	17.09402	21.30361	22.78573	23.77668	B

resorting to the cumbersome and time consuming univariate ratio analysis.

The issuing firm may use the classification procedure to continuously check on their investment quality and to prevent being put on a credit watch list and/or any changes in their ratings.

CONCLUSIONS

Given the six discriminant functions and the single classification procedure outline in this chapter, bond raters, issuing firms, and/or bond analysts are provided a direct, inexpensive and empirically validated tool for explaining, predicting and/or justifying bond ratings and evaluating investment quality. The model is, however, only a first diagnostic tool to be supplemented by an analysis of qualitative factors on management, the firm, the industry, and the economy, which may also affect the investment quality of industrial bonds.

NOTES

1. You can also convert the classification scores to posterior probabilities: given that there are six rating categories and assuming that Z_{ij} is the classification score for the i variable firm for the j variable rating category, then the posterior probability that i belongs to group j is:

$$P_{ij} = \frac{\exp(Z_{ij})}{{}_k\Sigma_1^6 \exp(X_{ij})}$$

FINANCIAL STATEMENTS

STATEMENT OF CONSOLIDATED INCOME

The LTV Corporation and Subsidiaries
Year Ended December 31,
(In millions, except per share data)

	1981	1980	1979
Net Sales and Revenues	**$7,510.7**	$5,743.0	$5,658.0
Operating costs and expenses:			
Cost of products sold	**6,440.9**	5,104.5	4,998.0
Depreciation and amortization	**134.2**	120.9	124.9
Selling, general and administrative expenses	**378.6**	300.5	280.7
Interest expense and debt discount	**118.5**	144.0	151.6
Interest and other income	**(53.6)**	(57.5)	(40.9)
Gains from early extinguishment of debt	**(12.0)**	(29.9)	(10.0)
Total	**7,006.6**	5,582.5	5,504.3
Income from continuing operations before income taxes	**504.1**	160.5	153.7
Income taxes	**(99.1)**	(24.0)	(20.8)
Income from continuing operations	**405.0**	136.5	132.9
Income (loss) from discontinued operations	**(18.7)**	(8.6)	19.2
Extraordinary credit — tax benefit of operating loss carryforward	**—**	—	7.1
Cumulative effect on prior years of accounting change	**—**	—	14.3
Net Income	**$ 386.3**	$ 127.9	$ 173.5

Earnings (loss) per share:			
Fully diluted:			
Continuing operations	**$ 7.97**	$ 3.15	$ 3.28
Discontinued operations	**(0.38)**	(0.19)	0.47
Extraordinary credit	**—**	—	0.17
Accounting change	**—**	—	0.35
Net Income	**$ 7.59**	$ 2.96	$ 4.27
Primary:			
Continuing operations	**$ 8.38**	$ 4.24	$ 4.51
Discontinued operations	**(0.41)**	(0.29)	0.72
Extraordinary credit	**—**	—	0.26
Accounting change	**—**	—	0.54
Net Income	**$ 7.97**	$ 3.95	$ 6.03

See notes to consolidated financial statements.

STATEMENT OF CHANGES IN CONSOLIDATED FINANCIAL POSITION
The LTV Corporation and Subsidiaries
Year Ended December 31,
(in millions)

	1981	1980	1979
Source of Working Capital:			
Income from continuing operations	**$405.0**	$136.5	$132.9
Depreciation and amortization	**134.2**	120.9	124.9
Deferred income taxes (credit)	**64.5**	14.3	(5.4)
Gains from early extinguishment of debt	**(12.0)**	(29.9)	(10.0)
Amortization of debt discount and other	**20.3**	10.9	22.3
Total from Continuing Operations	**612.0**	252.7	264.7
Net income (loss) from discontinued operations	**(18.7)**	(8.6)	13.8
Total from Operations	**593.3**	244.1	278.5
Increase in long-term debt	**47.7**	212.9	109.3
Common and Series 1 stock issued for:			
Public offering of 4,000,000 shares	**92.8**	—	—
Conversion of convertible debentures and preferred stock	**78.5**	4.3	—
Employee option and benefit plans	**18.4**	7.0	3.7
Decrease (Increase) in net assets of discontinued meat and food operations	**14.9**	12.1	(14.2)
Disposition of investments and property	**24.4**	105.6	80.9
Proceeds from sale of benefits through a tax lease	**32.7**	—	—
Total Sources	**902.7**	586.0	458.2
Use of Working Capital:			
Property additions	**372.8**	227.9	317.5
Net assets of acquired businesses	**43.6**	26.0	—
Reduction in long-term debt:			
Conversion of convertible debentures to Common stock	**81.4**	—	—
Payments of long-term debt	**81.4**	284.2	112.8
Gain from early extinguishment of debt	**(12.0)**	(29.9)	(10.0)
Net reduction in long-term debt	**150.8**	254.3	102.8
Increase (decrease) in investments and other assets	**3.1**	28.6	(24.3)
(Increase) decrease in noncurrent employee compensation and benefits	**26.1**	11.0	(47.7)
Dividends	**1.1**	9.8	12.6
Other — net	**28.3**	9.3	5.0
Total Uses	**625.8**	566.9	365.9
Increase in Working Capital	**276.9**	19.1	92.3
Working Capital — beginning of year	**721.1**	702.0	609.7
Working Capital — end of year	**$998.0**	$721.1	$702.0
Changes in Components of Working Capital:			
Increase (decrease) in current assets:			
Cash and cash equivalents	**$ 74.2**	$(19.6)	$(10.9)
Receivables	**86.3**	58.6	82.5
Inventories	**181.6**	65.0	34.5
Prepaid expenses	**4.1**	(1.9)	7.2
(Increase) decrease in current liabilities:			
Notes payable to banks	**50.6**	24.9	65.2
Accounts payable and accrued liabilities	**(120.4)**	(107.3)	(102.2)
Current maturities of long-term debt	**0.5**	(0.6)	16.0
Increase in Working Capital	**$276.9**	$ 19.1	$ 92.3

See notes to consolidated financial statements.

CONSOLIDATED BALANCE SHEET
The LTV Corporation and Subsidiaries
December 31,
(In millions)

Assets	1981	1980
Current Assets		
Cash and cash equivalents	$ 143.7	$ 69.5
Receivables, less allowances for doubtful accounts of $18.8 in 1981 and $10.4 in 1980	871.2	784.9
Inventories:		
Products	899.1	715.7
Contracts in progress, less progress payments received of $117.8 in 1981 and $111.3 in 1980	184.2	181.6
Materials, purchased parts and supplies	540.7	484.0
Total	1,624.0	1,381.3
Less — Reduction of certain inventories to LIFO value	(469.9)	(408.8)
Total Inventories	1,154.1	972.5
Prepaid expenses	39.0	34.9
Total Current Assets	2,208.0	1,861.8
Investments and Other Assets		
Investments in and advances to steel group raw material affiliates	154.7	144.4
Notes receivable and other assets	84.4	89.9
Total Investments and Other Assets	239.1	234.3
Property, Plant and Equipment — at cost		
Land and land improvements	83.1	86.7
Buildings	223.9	217.0
Steel manufacturing equipment	2,365.2	2,246.3
Other manufacturing equipment	118.6	88.8
Furniture, fixtures and other	46.3	33.6
Ocean shipping vessels	162.4	92.5
Construction in progress	160.4	128.5
Total	3,159.9	2,893.4
Less — Allowances for depreciation	(1,274.3)	(1,268.3)
Total Property, Plant and Equipment	1,885.6	1,625.1
Net Assets Applicable to Wilson Foods Corporation	—	105.3
	$4,332.7	$3,826.5

See notes to consolidated financial statements.

Liabilities & Shareholders' Equity	1981	1980
Current Liabilities		
Notes payable to banks	$ —	$ 50.6
Accounts payable	472.6	469.1
Accrued employee compensation and benefits	430.9	390.5
Other accruals	215.4	179.0
Income taxes	72.4	32.3
Current maturities of long-term debt	18.7	19.2
Total Current Liabilities	1,210.0	1,140.7
Long-Term Debt	1,295.4	1,395.1
Deferrals and Non-Current Liabilities		
Employee compensation and benefits	336.7	357.8
Deferred income taxes	95.9	26.5
Other	88.5	79.6
Total Deferrals and Non-Current Liabilities	521.1	463.9
Commitments and Contingencies		
Preferred Stock with Mandatory Redemption	20.8	20.8
Shareholders' Equity		
Applicable to ongoing operations:		
Series 1 participating preference stock	0.4	1.0
Special stock, class AA	0.3	0.4
Common stock	24.1	17.9
Additional capital	618.1	438.6
Retained earnings	662.2	262.5
Excess of redemption value over par value of preferred stock with mandatory redemption	(19.7)	(19.7)
Total Applicable to Ongoing Operations	1,285.4	700.7
Applicable to Wilson Foods Corporation	—	105.3
Total Shareholders' Equity	1,285.4	806.0
	$4,332.7	$3,826.5

NOTES TO CONSOLIDATED FINANCIAL STATEMENTS
The LTV Corporation and Subsidiaries
December 31, 1981

SUMMARY OF SIGNIFICANT ACCOUNTING POLICIES

Principles of Consolidation

The consolidated financial statements include The LTV Corporation (LTV) and its majority owned subsidiaries (the Company). Investments in joint ventures and companies 20% or more owned are accounted for by the equity method. Equity in the net income of raw material ventures reduces "cost of products sold." All significant intercompany balances and transactions have been eliminated.

Reclassification for Discontinued Operations

The results of operations and net assets of the Company's meat and food products businesses, Wilson Foods Corporation (Wilson) and Briggs & Company (Briggs), have been reclassified and accounted for as discontinued operations in the consolidated financial statements and related notes.

Inventories

Steel and energy products and related raw materials are valued at cost determined for the most part by the "last-in, first-out" (LIFO) method (computed using the specific goods, multiple-pool method) which is lower than market value. Such inventories are stated at current value prior to reduction to LIFO value.

Fixed-price aerospace/defense contracts in progress are stated at accumulated costs, less amounts allocated to products delivered, based on the estimated total cost of the contracts determined under the learning curve concept which is based on a predictable decrease in unit cost as production techniques become more efficient through repetition. Related raw materials and purchased parts are stated at average cost, not in excess of market.

Property Costs and Depreciation and Amortization

Plant, equipment and ocean shipping vessels are depreciated principally by the straight-line method over the assets' estimated useful lives. For steel operations, the straight-line basis is modified to the extent that depreciation is increased at higher and decreased at lower operating levels.

When properties are retired or sold, their costs and the related allowance for depreciation are eliminated from the property and allowance for depreciation accounts. Generally for normal retirements, gains or losses are credited or charged against the allowance for depreciation; for abnormal retirements, gains or losses are included in income in the year of disposal.

Debt Discount and Expense

Unamortized debt discount is deducted from the face amount of the related debt. Debt discount and expense are amortized over the life of the related debt, using the "bonds outstanding" method.

Revenue Recognition

Sales of products, other than from fixed-price and cost reimbursement type aerospace contracts, are recognized when products are shipped to the customer.

Sales and profits from fixed-price aerospace/defense contracts are based on estimated final costs and are recorded at the time of delivery. Sales and fees from cost reimbursement aerospace/defense contracts are recognized using the percentage-of-completion method of accounting and are recorded as costs are incurred in the proportion that costs incurred bear to total estimated costs at completion. Incentive fees are recognized using the percentage-of-completion method when sufficient information is obtained to relate actual performance to target performance. Losses on contracts are recorded when identified.

Revenue from ocean shipping operations is recognized upon unloading inbound cargos (terminated voyage basis). For voyages in progress at the end of an accounting period, revenue and expenses, net of applicable operating differential subsidy, are deferred. Revenue from charter hire of vessels is recognized ratably over the term of the contract.

The ocean shipping operations also accrue revenue for an operating differential subsidy under an agreement with the United States government which expires in 1998. This subsidy compensates for the excess of certain vessel expenses over comparable vessel expenses of principal foreign competitors. The subsidy is accrued based on available information. The estimated accruals are revised and the income effect recognized when final subsidy rates or definitive information is received from the Maritime Administration (MARAD).

Retirement Plans

The Company has various retirement plans covering substantially all of its employees. Pension costs are accrued, including amortization (primarily over 40 years) of prior service costs. Contributions are made to Company sponsored pension plans in accordance with the minimum funding requirements of the Employee Retirement Income Security Act of 1974 (ERISA), and to multi-employer plans as required by collective bargaining agreements for the Company's seagoing, longshore and mining employees. Costs of life insurance and medical benefits which are provided to retired employees are expensed when paid.

Research and Development

Research and development costs are incurred under both Company-initiated programs and under contracts for specific programs with others, primarily the United States Government. Company-initiated programs include commercial and independent research and development. A large portion of the independent research and development is recoverable through overhead cost allowances on government contracts. Research and development costs incurred on Company-initiated programs totaled $40.7 million in 1981, $39.8 million in 1980 and $35.0 million in 1979. Those costs not recovered through contractual arrangements with others or through overhead cost allowances were charged to expense and totaled $11.7 million in 1981, $15.3 million in 1980 and $11.7 million in 1979.

Federal Income Taxes

In the computation of federal income taxes for financial reporting purposes, recognition is given to the income tax effect of timing differences between the reporting of transactions for financial reporting and for tax purposes. Investment and energy tax credits are recognized using the "flow through" method in the year they would be allowable for tax purposes in the absence of timing differences. The portion of proceeds, from the sale of tax benefits through tax leases, applicable to investment and energy tax credits is also recognized using the "flow through" method while the portion of proceeds applicable to depreciation is deferred and amortized over the life of the related assets.

Changes in Accounting Policies

Effective January 1, 1981, in accordance with Financial Accounting Standards Board Statement No. 43, the Company adopted the required policy of expensing the cost of extended vacations for certain steel group employees as earned. Previously, these costs were expensed when paid. The effects of this change on income from continuing operations in all years presented were immaterial. Expenses and accruals for other types of compensated absences were previously recognized in accordance with the requirements of Statement 43.

Results of operations for 1979 include a one-time credit of $14.3 million representing the cumulative effect of adopting the preferable accounting policy of capitalizing rehabilitation costs of blast furnaces.

CURRENT ASSETS

Receivables

Approximately $73.0 million of receivables at December 31, 1981 relate to long-term contracts, of which no significant amount is due or billable after one year. Unbilled receivables at December 31, 1981 and 1980 were not significant. There were no significant amounts included in receivables for claims subject to uncertainty as to realization.

Inventories

The percentage of inventories valued on the LIFO method was 76% and 73% for the years ended December 31, 1981 and 1980, respectively. The liquidation of LIFO inventory quantities carried as though acquired at lower costs which prevailed in earlier years decreased cost of products sold by approximately $15 million in 1981, $49 million in 1980 and $36 million in 1979.

At December 31, 1981, approximately $48 million was included in aerospace/defense contracts in progress for those deferred tooling, general and administrative costs which were recoverable under contract terms.

DEBT

At December 31, 1981 LTV and its subsidiaries individually could borrow up to approximately $346 million on a revolving basis under unused bank lines of credit. Subsequent to year-end, $100 million of the bank credit lines was terminated by the Company, and of the remainder $225 million is available through 1985. Security interests in receivables and inventories of certain subsidiaries ($366 million at December 31, 1981) were assigned as collateral. Interest is generally payable at ½ of 1 percent per annum above the lenders' prime commercial rates. Commitment fees of ½ of 1 percent per annum are generally payable based on the average daily unused portion of the bank credit commitments. Most of the banking arrangements provide for either the maintenance of average compensating balances approximating 10 percent of the credit line plus 10 percent of average outstanding borrowings or the payment of a fee for balance deficiencies. The funds on deposit under these arrangements are not subject to restriction on withdrawals.

The following is a summary of bank borrowings for 1981, 1980 and 1979 (in millions):

	1981	1980	1979
Borrowings during the year:			
Year-end balance	$ —	$ 50.6	$242.4
Month-end average	$ 33.3	$ 95.7	$313.3
Maximum at any month-end	$ 99.8	$ 206.4	$384.3
Interest rates:			
Year-end	16.15%	21.64%	16.18%
Average during the year	19.35%	17.25%	13.62%

Long-term debt consisted of the following at each year-end (in millions):

	Average Effective Interest Rate	1981	1980
LTV (Parent):			
5% Subordinated debentures due 1988	7.3%	$ 181.6	$ 181.6
6½% Subordinated debentures due 1988	10.2	27.5	29.4
6¼% Subordinated debentures due 1994	10.5	155.8	155.8
7½% Subordinated debentures due 1993 and 1994	12.0	206.1	206.1
11% Subordinated debentures due 2000 and 2007	11.6	92.0	92.0
12% Convertible Subordinated debentures due 2005, converted into common stock in 1981	12.0	—	75.0
9¼% Sinking Fund debentures due through 1997	11.6	63.5	70.1
Subsidiaries:			
6¼% Subordinated debentures due 1988 and 1994	9.3	33.5	36.1
5% Guaranteed Convertible Subordinated debentures due through 1988	5.0	54.3	61.1
3⅜% to 14% First Mortgage Bonds due from 1982 through 2011	9.6	426.6	461.1
10½% First Mortgage Bonds due through 2001 (90% Guaranteed by the Department of Commerce's Economic Development Admn.)	10.5	111.1	111.1
6½% to 9% Pollution Control Obligations due from 1985 through 2006	9.0	70.8	71.6
4.20% to 8.30% Government Insured Merchant Marine Bonds due from 1987 through 1997	9.5	32.1	38.0
7⅜% and 7½% First Preferred Vessel Mortgages due through 1990	12.2	27.5	—
Sundry mortgage and other notes		2.9	9.6
Capitalized lease obligations		43.0	44.8
Total Face Amount		1,528.3	1,643.4
Less: Unexpended pollution control funds		(76.9)	(78.9)
Unamortized discount		(137.3)	(150.2)
Current portion		(18.7)	(19.2)
Total Consolidated Long-Term Debt		$1,295.4	$1,395.1

Annual maturities through 1986 of long-term indebtedness (excluding capital leases) in excess of reacquired debentures available for sinking fund requirements were as follows at December 31, 1981 (in millions):

	Consolidated	LTV (Parent)
1982	$13.6	$ —
1983	22.8	0.1
1984	45.4	5.7
1985	59.6	11.0
1986	73.8	11.2

Future minimum lease payments for capital leases and noncancellable operating leases at December 31, 1981 were (in millions):

	Capital Leases	Operating Leases (exclusive of insurance and taxes)
1982	$ 9.3	$ 35.0
1983	8.9	32.0
1984	7.7	26.7
1985	6.0	21.3
1986	4.7	17.5
Later years	28.5	75.8
Total minimum lease payments	65.1	$208.3
Less amount representing interest	(22.1)	
Present value of net minimum lease payments	$43.0	

Charges to operations for rental expense on operating leases, less sublease rentals, were $66.0 million in 1981, $54.7 million in 1980 and $44.8 million in 1979.

Interest capitalized as part of the acquisition cost of certain construction projects amounted to $13.3 million in 1981, $12.2 million in 1980 and $18.0 million in 1979.

Substantially all land, buildings and equipment at the steel operations are pledged as collateral to the mortgage bonds. The Merchant Marine Bonds and First Preferred Vessel Mortgages are collateralized by first mortgages on vessels.

The unexpended pollution control bond funds are classified as reductions to long-term debt since these are funds from pollution control bond issues which are held by a trustee until utilized either for the repayment of principal and interest on the bonds when due or for the construction and installation of specified pollution control facilities.

Certain debt and lease instruments and MARAD regulations contain provisions which require, among other things, LTV and its subsidiaries to maintain minimum working capital and net worth amounts and financial ratios; which limit the amount of debt which can be incurred; and which limit the amount of retained earnings available for dividends by LTV and by its subsidiaries. At December 31, 1981, approximately $600 million of the retained earnings of LTV was available for the payment of cash dividends; while $440 million was transferrable to LTV from its subsidiaries (compared with LTV's total advances to and investments in net assets of its subsidiaries of approximately $2 billion). During 1981, LTV received $162 million of cash dividends from its subsidiaries.

EMPLOYEE COMPENSATION AND BENEFITS

The noncurrent liability for employee compensation and benefits includes approximately $204 million and $225 million at December 31, 1981 and 1980, respectively, for unfunded vested pension benefits assumed in the acquisition of The Lykes Corporation in 1978.

Costs under retirement plans were $203.1 million in 1981, $167.6 million in 1980 and $167.3 million in 1979. The accumulated plan benefits and plan net assets for the Company's defined benefit plans as of the most recent valuation dates (January 1, 1981 and 1980, respectively) were as follows (in millions):

	1981	1980
Actuarial present value of vested accumulated plan benefits	$1,572.5	$1,322.3
Net assets available for plan benefits	1,451.0	1,273.5
Excess	$ 121.5	$ 48.8
Actuarial present value of nonvested accumulated plan benefits	$ 193.8	$ 166.1

The increase during 1981 in pension expense and actuarial present value of accumulated plan benefits was primarily due to improvements in plan benefits.

The weighted average assumed rate of return used in determining the actuarial present value of accumulated plan benefits was 10 percent. The actuarial present values of accumulated plan benefits applicable to LTV, if it were to withdraw from its multi-employer plans, has not been determined by the sponsors of those plans.

PREFERRED STOCK WITH MANDATORY REDEMPTION

At December 31, 1981 and 1980, there were 921,288 shares of LTV's $5 par value, Series A preferred stock authorized and 205,964 shares oustanding (excluding 607,600 shares held in treasury). Outstanding shares decreased by 141,837 shares in 1979 as the result of exchanging two shares of $2.60 Series B preferred stock for each share of tendered Series A preferred stock. Holders of the Series A preferred stock are entitled to receive cumulative cash dividends of $5 per share annually, payable quarterly. In the event of liquidation, they would be entitled to receive $100 per share, plus accumulated dividends. The aggregate amount of such liquidation preference in excess of par value amounted to $19.7 million at December 31, 1981. Holders are also entitled to participate on a share-for-share basis in any assets remaining after the common stock and equivalent shares of Special stock, class AA have received $30 per share. The Series A preferred stock is subject to optional redemption of $100 per share plus accumulated unpaid dividends. LTV is required to redeem the remaining shares outstanding in 1991 (86,737) and 1992 (119,227). The holders of the $5 Series A preferred stock are entitled to one vote per share.

OTHER CAPITAL STOCK

Changes in the number of outstanding shares of other capital stock during the three years ended December 31, 1981 were as follows:

	Common Stock	Series 1 Participating Preference	Special Stock, Class AA	$2.60 Series B Preferred
Outstanding at January 1, 1979	23,757,459	1,383,107	902,296	4,154,786
Sold to Trustee of the LTV Employee Benefit Plans	370,128	—	—	—
Exercise of stock options	58,438	7,952	—	—
Series B preferred stock issued for Series A preferred stock	—	—	—	283,674
Stock dividends on Special stock, class AA	—	—	25,153	—
Conversion of convertible stocks	458,518	(365,380)	(63,890)	(194)
Outstanding at December 31, 1979	24,644,543	1,025,679	863,559	4,438,266
Sold to Trustee of the LTV Employee Benefit Plans	549,965	—	—	—
Exercise of stock options	48,113	—	—	—
Stock dividends on Special stock, class AA	—	—	20,903	—
Issued in purchase of businesses	—	—	—	31,167
Conversion and redemption from call of Series B preferred:				
Converted	9,943,390	1,296,964	—	(4,323,213)
Redeemed at $30 per share	—	—	—	(141,245)
Other conversions of convertible stocks and securities	606,792	(322,087)	(180,306)	(4,975)
Outstanding at December 31, 1980	35,792,803	2,000,556	704,156	—
Sold to Trustee of the LTV Employee Benefit Plans	779,430	—	—	
Exercise of stock options	178,171	300	—	
Common stock sold to the public	4,000,000	—	—	
Stock dividends on Special stock, class AA	—	—	19,676	
Conversion of 12% convertible subordinated debentures	6,168,907	—	—	
Other conversions of convertible stock and securities	1,269,283	(1,136,082)	(48,367)	
Outstanding at December 31, 1981	48,188,594	864,774	675,465	
Authorized at December 31, 1981	100,000,000	3,000,000	7,350,000	5,000,000
Held in treasury at December 31, 1981	642,828	—	—	—
Par value per share	$0.50	$0.50	$0.50	$1.00

The holders of Common stock are entitled to one vote per share.

At December 31, 1981 there were 5,519,753 total shares of Common stock reserved for issuance, of which 1,277,307 shares were reserved under stock option plans, 2,325,684 shares were reserved for conversion of 5% guaranteed convertible securities of a subsidiary at $23.36 per share, 12,848 shares were reserved for conversion of 4¾% debentures of a former subsidiary at $18.29 per share, 890,717 shares were reserved for conversion of Series 1 participating preference stock and 1,013,197 shares were reserved for conversion of Special stock, class AA.

Each share of Series 1 participating preference stock is convertible into 1.03 shares of Common stock. Holders are entitled to receive cash dividends equal to 110% of any cash dividend declared on the equivalent common shares into which the participating preference stock may be converted (effectively 113.3 percent of any cash dividends on Common stock at December

31, 1981). In the event of liquidation, after any preference in distribution in respect to the preferred stock, the holders of the Series 1 participating preference stock would be entitled to receive $10 per share plus accrued dividends. On or after January 31, 1984, this issue may be called for redemption at $6.00 per share plus accrued dividends. Holders of Series 1 participating preference stock are entitled to one vote per share.

Each share of Special stock, class AA is convertible into 1.5 shares of Common stock. The shares of Special stock are entitled to annual cumulative stock dividends of 3 percent payable in Special stock through 1992. No cash dividends are payable on the Special stock, class AA. The holders of the Special stock are entitled to a number of votes equal to the number of common shares into which their stock is convertible.

The Company also has authorized 7,650,000 shares of undesignated $0.50 par value Special stock, and 10,000,000 shares of undesignated $1 par value Preferred stock.

EMPLOYEE STOCK OPTIONS

LTV has employee stock option plans under which options are outstanding for terms of up to ten years from date of grant and are granted at prices not lower than the market price at date of grant. Common stock option data with respect to the two years ended December 31, 1981 were as follows:

	1981		1980	
	Shares	Price Range	Shares	Price Range
Outstanding, beginning of year	1,084,528	$ 6.50-$18.00	1,138,298	$ 6.50-$18.00
Granted	127,500	16.38- 22.63	110,500	10.38- 14.13
Terminated	(34,606)	8.50- 18.00	(116,157)	11.75- 15.06
Exercised	(178,171)	6.50- 17.31	(48,113)	7.75- 12.88
Outstanding, at end of year	999,251	6.75- 22.63	1,084,528	6.50- 18.00
Exercisable at December 31,1981	674,394	6.75- 16.13		

ADDITIONAL CAPITAL

Changes in additional capital during the three years ended December 31, 1981 were as follows (in millions):

	1981	1980	1979
Balance at beginning of year	$501.0	$498.3	$494.1
Distribution of net assets of Wilson Foods Corporation	(62.4)	—	—
Excess over par value of shares issued upon:			
Conversion or redemption of debentures and preferred stock, net	72.4	(5.4)	0.4
Stock dividends on Special stock, class AA	0.5	0.4	0.3
Sale of 4,000,000 shares of Common stock to the public	90.8	—	—
Sale of Common stock under Employee Option and Benefit Plans	17.8	6.7	3.5
Other	(2.0)	1.0	—
Balance at end of year	618.1	501.0	498.3
Less — Amount applicable to Wilson Foods Corporation	—	62.4	62.4
Balance applicable to ongoing operations	$618.1	$438.6	$435.9

RETAINED EARNINGS

Changes in retained earnings during the three years ended December 31, 1981 were as follows (in millions):

	1981	1980	1979
Balance at beginning of year:			
As previously reported			$ 40.1
Accounting change for compensated absences			(13.0)
As restated	$305.4	$187.7	27.1
Net income	386.3	127.9	173.5
Distribution of net assets of Wilson Foods Corporation	(27.9)	—	—
Dividends declared:			
Cash dividends on preferred stock	(1.1)	(9.8)	(12.6)
Stock dividends on Special stock, class AA	(0.5)	(0.4)	(0.3)
Balance at end of year	662.2	305.4	187.7
Less — Amount applicable to Wilson Foods Corporation	—	42.9	54.3
Balance applicable to ongoing operations	$662.2	$262.5	$133.4

TAXES ON INCOME

The provisions (credits) for taxes on income from continuing operations for each of the three years ended December 31, 1981 were as follows (in millions):

	1981	1980	1979
Current:			
Federal	$11.5	$ 1.7	$11.6
State	18.1	2.7	6.1
Foreign	5.0	5.3	1.4
Total	34.6	9.7	19.1
Deferred	64.5	14.3	(5.4)
Tax effect of net operating loss carryforward	—	—	7.1
Total	$99.1	$24.0	$20.8

The income tax effects of the factors accounting for the differences between the statutory federal income tax rate and the actual provisions on consolidated income from continuing operations for each of the three years ended December 31, 1981 were as follows (in millions):

	1981	1980	1979
Theoretical tax expense at 46%	$231.9	$73.8	$70.7
Increases (decreases) resulting from:			
Investment and energy tax credits	(109.5)*	(30.2)	(12.1)
Permanent differences between tax and book, primarily depreciation	(16.5)	(10.2)	(17.8)
Depletion	(8.5)	(8.3)	(11.7)
Domestic International Sales Corporation	1.4	(5.7)	(1.4)
Excess of equity in earnings of affiliated companies over dividends received, net of dividends received deduction	(8.2)	(2.2)	(7.7)
Permanent differences between tax and book bases of investments sold	—	(0.6)	(4.6)
Other items, net	8.5	7.4	5.4
Income tax provision	$ 99.1	$24.0	$20.8

*Includes $80 million of investment tax credits carried forward from prior years.

Deferred tax expense results from timing differences in the recognition of revenue and expense for tax and financial reporting purposes. The sources of these differences and the tax effect of each were as follows (in millions):

	1981	1980
Depreciation	**$33.1**	$ 4.0
Contributions to employee benefit plans	12.6	4.6
Plant closings	15.9	3.1
Other items, net	2.9	2.6
Deferred tax provision	**$64.5**	$14.3

The deferred tax credit in 1979 of $5.4 million represents the tax effect of items, principally pension costs and depreciation, which are reported in different periods for financial and for income tax purposes.

In 1979, an extraordinary credit of $7.1 million resulted from utilization of all available net operating loss carryforwards for financial reporting purposes.

For income tax reporting purposes, LTV had available net operating loss carryforwards of approximately $47 million at December 31, 1981, expiring $16 million in 1990 and $31 million in 1991. These carryforwards are restricted to offsetting future taxable income of the respective companies which generated the losses. Use of these loss carryforwards is dependent on future taxable income.

At December 31, 1981, LTV had available approximately $77 million of investment tax credit carryovers for tax reporting purposes. Of this amount $13 million, expiring in 1988 to 1992, is restricted to offsetting future taxes of the respective companies which generated the credits. The balance of the investment tax credit carryovers amounting to $64 million is not restricted as to use, and expires from 1992 to 1996. Use of these tax credits is dependent on future taxable income.

DISCONTINUED OPERATIONS

On July 31, 1981, LTV distributed the common stock of its wholly-owned subsidiary, Wilson Foods Corporation, to the holders of LTV's Common stock and Special stock, class AA. Accordingly, LTV's consolidated financial statements have been reclassified to treat meat and food operations as discontinued for all years presented. Sales of these discontinued operations during 1979, 1980 and the portion of 1981 prior to distribution were $2,338.8 million, $2,267.0 million and $1,312.0 million, respectively. Results of these discontinued operations in 1981 included losses of $6.1 million from operations and $12.6 million of costs associated with the shutdown of certain meat and food facilities. Results of discontinued operations in 1979 also included a $5.5 million credit from final disposition of other operations previously discontinued in 1977.

EARNINGS PER SHARE

Primary earnings per share amounts for 1981, 1980 and 1979 are after deducting preferred dividend requirements and are based upon share totals of 48,327,000, 29,929,000 and 26,673,000, respectively, representing the average number of shares of Common, Special stock, class AA and common equivalent shares outstanding during each year. Common equivalent shares primarily include Series 1 participating preference stock and shares issuable upon the exercise of employee stock options, when dilutive.

Fully diluted per share amounts for 1981, 1980 and 1979 are based on average share totals of 51,001,000, 45,281,000 and 41,063,000, respectively. Fully diluted shares are determined by increasing the average number of primary shares outstanding to reflect the cumulative effect of 3 percent annual stock dividends for the ensuing ten years on the Special stock, class AA and, where appropriate, the conversion of convertible securities together with related additions to income available for common and common stock equivalents for preferred dividends and interest expense, less applicable income taxes.

Had the December 1980 conversion of the Series B preferred stock into Common stock taken place on January 1, 1979 and the 1981 conversion of the 12% Convertible Subordinated debentures taken place at the date of issuance, May 1980, primary earnings per share from continuing operations for 1980 and 1979 would have been $3.31 and $3.46, respectively.

COMMITMENTS AND CONTINGENCIES

In conjunction with the distribution of Wilson Foods Corporation stock, LTV guaranteed the borrowings by Wilson Foods Corporation of up to $60 million through June 30, 1984 under the provisions of Wilson's bank credit agreement, which is secured by Wilson's accounts receivable. No borrowings were outstanding under the bank credit agreement at December 31, 1981. In addition, LTV continued as guarantor of future lease payments on some of Wilson's facilities for periods ranging from 7 to 16 years. Wilson's current payments under these leases approximate $3 million per annum.

A substantial number of aerospace/defense contracts and subcontracts are subject to price adjustments under their terms; none of which are expected to have a significant effect on the financial statements.

Certain government agencies have proposed adjustments affecting allowable costs charged to aerospace/defense contracts for which it is believed that adequate provision has been made.

LTV's steel operation has long-term raw material supply contracts with its joint ventures and with outside suppliers that commit LTV to annual future purchases of iron ore and coal at volumes which are less than its anticipated annual requirements. Such purchases in 1981 approximated $500 million. LTV is also committed to share in the costs to be incurred by its raw material joint ventures, to the extent funds so required are not generated by their operations.

The Company's steel operation is subject to a number of environmental laws and regulations. Uncertainties associated with the application of these laws and regulations promulgated and proposed thereunder create uncertainties as to their financial impact on LTV's steel operations, with respect to both operating costs and capital expenditures as well as the timing for the incurrence of such expenditures. However, LTV currently estimates that its capital cost of complying with the federal air and water requirements will be approximately $72 million in 1982 and average approximately $30 million per year (in future dollars to be paid) for the three year period 1983-1985, if the deferral referred to below is approved. Most of these environmental control expenditures are required to be made at the Company's major steelmaking and finishing plants by specified dates pursuant to the terms of a 1980 agreement with the United States Environmental Protection Agency ("EPA") and state environmental authorities (the "Environmental Agreement"). During 1981, the terms of the Environmental Agreement were incorporated into consent decrees entered against the Company's Steel Group in the U.S. District Courts for the Western District of Pennsylvania, the Northern District of Ohio and the Northern District of Indiana and thus formed the basis for the settlement of a number of environmental actions which previously had been pending against the Company's Steel Group.

Pursuant to the Steel Industry Compliance Extension Act of 1981 (the "Act"), the Company is seeking the approval of the EPA to defer the expenditure of approximately $45 to $65 million by the end of 1982 pursuant to the Environmental Agreement. Pending a decision on its application for deferral pursuant to the Act, the Company has continued to defer work on the projects which are the subject of its application and as of December 31, 1981 had not met a number of interim deadlines specified in the Environmental Agreement. Because of such deferral, the Company also will not be able to meet future progress deadlines for work on these projects. If the Company's failure to meet these deadlines are deemed by the EPA and the U.S. Justice

Department to constitute violations of the Environmental Agreement (and the related consent decree) which are not de minimis in nature, the EPA could deny the Company's application for deferral under the Act. Further, if agreement cannot be reached with respect to the deferral of these deadlines, pursuant to the Act or otherwise, and the Company's deferral of these projects is not sustained in court, the Company could be required to make some or all of such expenditures on an accelerated basis and could be subject to minimum penalties of $5,000 or $7,500, depending on the type of deadline, per day of delinquency per violation. Such penalties in the aggregate could be substantial in amount, although the Company is unable to predict whether or under what circumstance the EPA might attempt to impose any such penalties. In addition, the Company could be assessed penalties pursuant to Section 120 of the Clean Air Act equivalent to the economic benefit derived from failing to comply with the Clean Air Act requirements. However, Section 120 penalties do not begin to accrue until notification is issued by the EPA, and the Company has not been notified.

The Company is a party to civil class action litigation relating to a restatement of its earnings and those of its steel subsidiary for the years 1974 through 1977, after it had been determined that during such years its accounting for inventories and certain other items was incorrect in certain respects. In early 1982, the parties to the litigation reached an agreement to settle these and one other securities class action for approximately $7.8 million. The proposed settlement, which is subject to various court approvals, had been provided for as of December 31, 1981.

Further, in the ordinary course of business the Company is the subject of or party to various other pending or threatened litigation.

It is not possible to predict with certainty the outcome of the foregoing matters but after consultation with legal counsel, management of the company does not believe that they will materially affect the consolidated financial position of the company.

BUSINESS SEGMENTS

See page 50 for a table of business segment data for years 1979 through 1981.

The operations included in each segment and their primary products are listed below:

Steel — These operations include the production and sale of a diversified line of carbon steel products of hot and cold rolled sheet, tin mill and other flat rolled coated products, hot rolled and cold finished bars, tubular products, light plates and structural shapes, and the mining of coal and iron ore.

Energy Products and Services — These operations involve the manufacture and sale of oil and gas drilling and production equipment, the sale of tubular products and related oil field supplies.

Aerospace/Defense — These operations involve the design, development and production of missiles, space launch vehicles and commercial aircraft components; modification and production of military aircraft; and furnishing of related administrative and technical support services.

Ocean Shipping — These operations provide regularly scheduled liner services for the movement of cargo on established foreign trade routes to and from United States ports and Europe, Asia, South America, Africa and the Middle East.

Operating income was computed as total sales and revenue less cost of products sold and operating ex-

penses. Cost of products sold of the steel segment have been reduced by the equity in earnings of mining affiliates of approximately $55.2 million in 1981, $35.6 million in 1980 and $58.9 million in 1979. In computing operating income, none of the following items have been added or deducted: unallocated corporate expenses, interest expense, income taxes, credits for gains from early extinguishment of debt, non-operating interest and other income, discontinued operations, extraordinary items or accounting changes.

Sales between segments are made at prevailing market prices at the time of the sales.

Sales to federal, state and local government agencies or to unaffiliated customers outside the United States were less than 10% of consolidated sales and revenues.

Included in identifiable assets of the steel segment are investments in and advances to unconsolidated raw material joint ventures of $154.7 million in 1981, $144.4 million in 1980 and $133.6 million in 1979.

REPORT OF ERNST & WHINNEY, INDEPENDENT AUDITORS

To the Shareholders and Board of Directors
The LTV Corporation
Dallas, Texas

We have examined the consolidated balance sheet of The LTV Corporation and subsidiaries as of December 31, 1981 and 1980, and the related statements of consolidated income and changes in consolidated financial position for each of the three years in the period ended December 31, 1981. Our examinations were made in accordance with generally accepted auditing standards and, accordingly, included such tests of the accounting records and such other auditing procedures as we considered necessary in the circumstances.

In our opinion, the financial statements referred to above present fairly the consolidated financial position of The LTV Corporation and subsidiaries at December 31, 1981 and 1980 and the consolidated results of their operations and changes in their financial position for each of the three years in the period ended December 31, 1981, in conformity with generally accepted accounting principles consistently applied during the period subsequent to the change made as of January 1, 1979, with which we concur, in the method of accounting for blast furnace rehabilitation expenditures, as described in the summary of significant accounting policies in the notes to the financial statements.

Ernst + Whinney

Dallas, Texas
January 27, 1982

REPORT OF THE COMPANY

January 27, 1982

To the Shareholders:

LTV is responsible for the preparation of the accompanying financial statements of the Company and its subsidiaries. The financial statements have been prepared in conformity with generally accepted accounting principles appropriate in the circumstances and consistently applied, except as described in the Summary of Significant Accounting Policies note to the financial statements and, as such, include estimates and judgments. The financial statements have been examined by Ernst & Whinney, independent auditors, whose report appears on page 43.

The Company maintains an accounting system and related internal controls that we believe are sufficient to provide reasonable assurance that assets are safeguarded, transactions are executed and recorded in accordance with management's authorization and that the financial records are reliable for preparing financial statements. The concept of reasonable assurance is based on the recognition that the cost of a system of internal control must be related to the benefits derived and that the balancing of those factors requires estimates and judgment. The system is tested and evaluated regularly by the Company's internal auditors as well as by the independent auditors in connection with their annual audit.

The Board of Directors has an audit committee of Directors who are not members of management. The Committee meets with management, the internal auditors and the independent auditors in connection with its review of matters relating to the Company's annual financial statements; the Company's internal audit program; the Company's system of internal accounting controls; and the services of the independent auditors. The Committee periodically meets with internal auditors as well as the independent auditors, without management present, to discuss appropriate matters. In addition, the internal and independent auditors have full and free access to meet with the Committee — with or without management representatives present — to discuss the results of their examinations, the adequacy of internal accounting controls and the quality of financial reporting.

QUARTERLY FINANCIAL INFORMATION *(Unaudited)*

The following table presents unaudited sales and revenues and earnings by quarter for the years 1981 and 1980 (in millions, except per share data):

	First Quarter	Second Quarter	Third Quarter	Fourth Quarter	Total Year
Net sales and revenues					
1981	$1,752.1	$1,974.7	$1,950.1	$1,833.8	$7,510.7
1980	1,455.1	1,389.4	1,331.8	1,566.7	5,743.0
Operating income (1)					
1981	$ 101.9	$ 186.7	$ 185.2	$ 150.8	$ 624.6
1980	55.7	58.6	39.9	122.5	276.7
Income from continuing operations					
1981	$ 62.8	$ 129.3	$ 97.0(3)	$ 115.9(4)	$ 405.0
1980	29.2	27.7	11.0	68.6(5)	136.5
Net Income					
1981	$ 47.3	$ 126.1	$ 97.0(3)	$ 115.9(4)	$ 386.3
1980	26.4(2)	37.1	4.9	59.5(5)	127.9
Earnings per share					
Fully diluted					
Continuing income					
1981	$ 1.30	$ 2.59	$ 1.86	$ 2.22	$ 7.97
1980	0.72	0.66	0.28	1.47	3.15
Net income					
1981	$ 0.98	$ 2.53	$ 1.86	$ 2.22	$ 7.59
1980	0.65	0.87	0.06	1.28	2.96
Primary					
Continuing income					
1981	$ 1.37	$ 2.74	$ 1.93	$ 2.34	$ 8.38
1980	0.96	0.90	0.28	1.75(6)	4.24
Net income					
1981	$ 1.03	$ 2.67	$ 1.93	$ 2.34	$ 7.97
1980	0.86	1.25	0.06	1.52(6)	3.95

(1) See definition in BUSINESS SEGMENTS note to consolidated financial statements.
(2) Included pre-tax gains from early extinguishment of debt of $19.5 million in the first quarter of 1980.
(3) Results for the third quarter reflected an increase in the projected annual effective tax rate to 25 percent from the 15 percent provided in the first two quarters of the year. The increase in the projected full year tax rate resulted principally from projected increases in pre-tax income.
(4) Results for the fourth quarter reflected a reduction in the annual effective tax rate to 20 percent from the 25 percent rate provided for the first three quarters of the year. The reduction in the tax rate resulted principally from the realization of foreign and energy tax credits not previously anticipated.
(5) Included $13.1 million of pre-tax gains from the sale of a mine and certain plant facilities in the fourth quarter of 1980.
(6) Primary earnings per share for the fourth quarter of 1980 were lower by $0.62 as a result of the conversion of Series B preferred stock into common and Series 1 participating preference stock.

SUMMARY INFORMATION ON CHANGING PRICES (*Unaudited*)

Introduction

The high level of inflation experienced in the United States and abroad since 1970 distorts the comparability between companies and between years of reported historical-cost based results of operations and financial positions. As a result, generally accepted accounting principles in the United States require that major companies present supplemental information that attempts to measure the impact of inflation.

Two methods of computing the effects of inflation are required. They differ in how they value non-monetary assets; that is, those assets whose costs or values tend to increase or be maintained during inflation, such as inventories and fixed assets. The "constant dollar" method uses a rate of general inflation to revalue assets into consistent units of measure. The index used to approximate the general inflation rate is the Consumer Price Index for Urban Consumers (CPI-U), which is not necessarily indicative of changes in costs incurred by capital intensive industries. The "current cost" method recognizes that not all assets change in prices at the same rate. Instead, this method revalues a company's existing assets to their current in-place reconstructed cost.

Both methods of inflation-related accounting unrealistically attempt to reflect today's cost of replacement of existing productive facilities. In practice, businesses do not merely replace their existing facilities. Replacement may be made with other facilities having a different cost or having a greater production capacity. There are factors other than depreciation that also have to be considered in determining inflation adjusted cost of products sold. Labor, material and overhead costs can increase or decrease on a per unit basis when future technology or requirements are considered.

Subjective judgment and numerous assumptions are involved in developing the required disclosures; therefore, the following results, amounts and discussions should not be considered precise indicators of either the effects of inflation or the value of the assets of the Company.

Income Data Adjusted for Effects of Changing Prices

The statement of consolidated income for the year ended December 31, 1981 adjusted for changing prices is as follows (in millions):

Continuing Business Segments	Historical Cost	Constant Dollar	Current Cost
		(Average 1981 Dollars)	
Net sales and revenues	$7,510.7	$7,510.7	$7,510.7
Cost of products sold	6,440.9	6,474.4	6,455.7
Depreciation	134.2	222.4	324.1
Other costs and expenses	497.1	497.1	497.1
Interest and other income	(65.6)	(58.2)	(59.5)
Income taxes	99.1	99.1	99.1
	7,105.7	7,234.8	7,316.5
Income from continuing operations	405.0	275.9	194.2
Gain from change in purchasing power of net amounts owed	—	141.8	141.8
Income before discontinued operations and other items	$ 405.0	$ 417.7	$ 336.0

Management's Assessment of the Impact of Inflation on The LTV Corporation

Overall — The effects on The LTV Corporation and its shareholders of holding non-monetary assets has tended to be offset by holding large amounts of net monetary liabilities at relatively low coupon interest rates. Increases in cost of goods sold and depreciation expense caused income from operations to decrease to $275.9 million on a constant dollar basis and $194.2 million on a current cost basis compared with the $405.0 million reported in the primary financial statements. However, the offsetting gain from changes in purchasing power of net amounts owed caused net income (before discontinued operations) as calculated under the constant dollar and current cost methods to be $417.7 million and $336.0 million, respectively. The return on average continuing shareholders' equity in 1981 as computed under the constant dollar method was 20% compared with 41% reported using the primary financial statements.

Restated to value its major assets on a consistent current price level basis, LTV's inflation-adjusted balance sheet data presents a far different perspective on LTV's consolidated financial position than do the primary financial statements. On a constant dollar basis, LTV's debt-to-equity ratio at December 31, 1981 would be approximately 0.5-to-one compared with one-to-one on the historical cost basis in the primary financial statements.

Replacement of Non-Monetary Assets — Two of LTV's businesses are capital intensive (steel and ocean shipping). As outlined below under "Explanation of Methods and Adjustments", significant impacts on LTV's inflation-adjusted results of operations include an increase in depreciation expense and a reduction in gains on disposal of assets to reflect the relatively higher cost of new assets compared with the original cost of assets actually being used or sold. These reductions assume that facilities have to be or will be replaced. However, many of LTV's recent asset disposal decisions were made in accordance with management strategy to generate cash from less productive assets which can then be redeployed into products and services having more favorable long-term prospects. Also, as indicated in the operations review of this annual report, LTV has recently been able to make significant productivity improvements in key areas with relatively low investment in fixed assets. As a result, these required presentations tend to understate operating results.

Since most of LTV's inventories are valued using the LIFO method, inventory holding gains are already excluded from historical cost based results of operations.

Leveraging and Gain from Change in Purchasing Power of Net Amounts Owed — The minimum requirement of FASB Statement 33 is to display income from operations adjusted for the impact of holding nonmonetary inventory and fixed assets, and also to separately display the gain or loss from holding net monetary items. LTV has chosen to include its purchasing power gain when computing inflation-adjusted net income because, in the words of the Financial Accounting Standards Board, omitting this gain "... understates the increase in purchasing power earned for equity investors."

In LTV's tabulation of inflation-adjusted data, the current market value of the Company's debt has also been displayed. LTV has a relatively low level of interest cost when compared with the book value of its debt and with many other companies. This results because large amounts of LTV's long-term debt was borrowed at low rates during the 1960 s. At December 31, 1981, LTV had a weighted average long-term borrowing rate of approximately 10%. If the inflation-adjusted debt-to-equity ratio were also adjusted to reflect the current market value of LTV's long-term debt, a 0.29-to-one ratio would be the case at December 31, 1981.

This data underscores the shortcomings of traditional, historical-cost book value approaches to evaluation of a company's financial position. In the case of LTV, this data demonstrates that leveraging through low-cost debt can be a successful management strategy in combating inflation. However, management does not believe that additional debt would necessarily be beneficial or harmful. However, the data presented indicates that management should not bypass the opportunity to leverage if the proceeds can be used to generate a return higher than the cost of the debt.

Other — Sales and revenues as adjusted to constant dollars have increased substantially during recent years, 81% over 1977 and 18% over 1980. In the two years since 1979 (the first year after the merger with Lykes) sales growth has been two-fold in the energy products and services business segment while sales have declined slightly in the steel business segment due to the shutdown of unprofitable facilities.

The increase in general inflation over the increase in current costs of inventory and fixed assets indicates that specific prices since 1979 are increasing at a slower rate than the general inflation rate. This is a reversal of the trend that existed prior to 1976 when specific price increases traditionally exceeded the rate of general inflation.

Explanation of Methods and Adjustments

Inventories — Prior to reduction to LIFO value, the majority of the Company's detail inventory records are maintained on a current value basis which was used to estimate current cost. The remainder (primarily inventory of LTV's aerospace/defense operations) is assigned to contracts and is considered a monetary asset for both constant dollar and current cost purposes. No adjustment has been made to the historical cost balance sheet values of monetary inventory or to cost of sales for either method.

Property, Plant and Equipment — A considerable portion of the capital intensive steel and ocean shipping group's assets were acquired through mergers in 1968 and 1978. For constant dollar purposes, the date the assets were acquired by LTV and fair values assigned to those assets at that date were used to determine their constant dollar value.

Current cost amounts for property, plant and equipment were determined primarily by applying appropriate industrial construction indices to historical costs. To determine the current cost of property of acquired businesses, the indices were applied to the original cost of the property at the date originally purchased by the acquired company.

Depreciation — Depreciation expense under the constant dollar and current cost approaches was based on the restated asset values described above using the same depreciation methods and useful lives used in computing depreciation expense included in the primary financial statements.

The increase in current cost depreciation over constant dollar depreciation reflects the fact that a substantial portion of the Company's property was acquired through mergers and recorded at less than book value and is valued for constant dollar purposes at the cost to the Company at the acquisition date. As a result, the constant dollar value of property only reflects the effects of inflation on this property since the dates of the mergers.

Cost of Products Sold — For both the constant dollar and current cost methods, cost of products sold is estimated using historical LIFO based cost, which approximates current cost, adjusted primarily for reinstatement of the value of the liquidation of those LIFO quantities carried at lower costs.

Other Income — Under the constant dollar method, gains from property dispositions decreased as a result of increasing the net book value of the property sold to its constant dollar value at the date of sale. Under the current cost method, historical cost gains or losses were excluded from other income and were included in the calculation of holding gains.

Income Taxes — Income taxes are stated at historical cost for both constant dollar and current cost methods as required by the FASB.

Mining Reserves

Inflation accounting rules also require disclosure of information concerning mining reserves. The Company's steel operation owns various iron ore and coal mines in the United States and has equity interests in various ventures which own and operate iron ore, coal and limestone properties. A description of the quantities of reserves at December 31, 1981 and 1981 production is summarized as follows (in millions of tons):

	Proven Reserves	Steel Group's Share of Production
Consolidated Properties:		
Iron Ore (Gross Tons)*	3.5	0.5
Metallurgical Coal (Net Tons)	90.9	2.1
Equity Interest Properties:		
Iron Ore (Gross Tons)*	587.5	8.9
Metallurgical Coal (Net Tons)	39.3	1.0
Limestone (Gross Tons)	134.8	1.2

*Iron content equals approximately 64%.

Proven coal reserves sold in place during 1980 amounted to approximately 274 million gross tons. At December 31, 1981, the average market prices per ton of mined iron ore, metallurgical coal and limestone were $41.84, $50.35 and $3.13, respectively. These average market prices are not indicative of the value of the above reserves since significant costs will be incurred in extracting such reserves. Therefore, an aggregate value for the above reserves cannot be determined by multiplying the market price by the tons of mineral reserves.

Selected Financial Data Adjusted for the Effects of Changing Prices (average 1981 dollars in millions)

	1981	1980	1979	1978	1977
INCOME STATEMENT DATA (continuing business segments)					
Net sales and revenues:					
In historical dollars	**$7,510.7**	$5,743.0	$5,658.0	$3,066.3	$2,761.6
Adjusted for effects of general inflation	**7,510.7**	6,340.2	7,089.5	4,274.5	4,145.2
Income (loss) from operations:					
In historical dollars	**405.0**	136.5	132.9		
Adjusted for effects of general inflation	**275.9**	16.3	74.2		
Adjusted for specific price changes	**194.2**	(97.7)	(93.9)		
Gain from change in purchasing power of net amounts owed due to general inflation	**141.8**	233.9	281.9		
Net income (before discontinued operations, accounting changes and extraordinary items)					
Adjusted for effects of general inflation	**417.7**	250.3	356.1		
Adjusted for specific price changes	**336.0**	136.2	188.0		
Income (loss) from operations per fully diluted share:					
In historical dollars	**7.97**	3.15	3.28		
Adjusted for effects of general inflation	**5.43**	.51	1.87		
Adjusted for specific price changes	**3.83**	(2.01)	(2.23)		
Net income per fully diluted share (before discontinued operations, accounting changes and extraordinary items)				THIS INFORMATION IS NOT REQUIRED	
Adjusted for effects of general inflation	**8.21**	5.67	8.73		
Adjusted for specific price changes	**6.61**	3.16	4.64		
BALANCE SHEET DATA AT YEAR END					
Inventories:					
In historical dollars	**$1,154.1**	$ 972.5	$ 907.5		
Adjusted for specific price changes	**1,578.0**	1,446.1	1,508.4		
Properties, plant and equipment:					
In historical dollars	**1,885.6**	1,625.1	1,592.7		
Adjusted for specific price changes	**3,741.9**	3,711.2	4,086.0		
Long-term debt:					
In historical dollars	**1,295.4**	1,395.1	1,453.7		
Estimated market value	**842.4**	1,025.8	1,258.8		
Net assets (ongoing operations):					
In historical dollars	**1,285.4**	700.7	567.4		
Adjusted for effects of general inflation	**2,514.3**	1,877.9	1,703.8		
Adjusted for specific price changes	**3,614.9**	3,166.6	3,323.6		
Net assets per share (ongoing operations):					
In historical dollars	**25.95**	18.47	11.16		
Adjusted for effects of general inflation	**50.98**	50.34	52.31		
Adjusted for specific price changes	**73.30**	85.36	115.62		
OTHER DATA					
Holding gains on inventories and property, plant and equipment during the year:					
Increase in general inflation	**460.4**	611.1	694.5		
Increase in specific price changes	**407.9**	373.3	497.7		
Increase in general inflation over increase in specific prices	**52.5**	237.8	196.8		
Market price per common share at year-end:					
In historical dollars	**16⅜**	20¼	8	6⅝	6⅜
Adjusted for effects of general inflation	**15⅞**	21⅜	9½	8⅞	9⅜
Average consumer price index (1967 = 100)	**272.4**	246.8	217.4	195.4	181.5

MANAGEMENT'S REVIEW OF RESULTS

THREE-YEAR SUMMARY BY BUSINESS SEGMENT
(in millions)

| | Net Sales and Revenues | | | | | | Operating Income | | |
| | 1981 | | 1980 | | 1979 | | | | |
Segment	To Unaffiliated Customers	Between Segments	To Unaffiliated Customers	Between Segments	To Unaffiliated Customers	Between Segments	1981	1980	1979
Steel	$4,177.9	$607.7	$3,463.6	$336.6	$3,974.0	$200.7	$336.3	$ 69.4	$170.7
Energy Products and Services	2,078.5	2.5	1,214.6	3.4	795.1	6.1	220.2	114.2	68.8
Aerospace/Defense	797.3	—	652.0	—	554.8	—	38.8	57.5	51.5
Ocean Shipping	457.0	—	412.8	—	334.1	—	26.8	35.6	19.8
Intersegment eliminations	—	(610.2)	—	(340.0)	—	(206.8)	2.5	—	(7.3)
Total continuing operations	$7,510.7	$ —	$5,743.0	$ —	$5,658.0	$ —	624.6	276.7	303.5
Corporate income (expenses) net							(2.0)	27.8	1.8
Interest expense and debt discount							(118.5)	(144.0)	(151.6)
Income before taxes							$504.1	$160.5	$153.7

| | Identifiable Assets | | | Capital Expenditures | | | Depreciation and Amortization | | |
| | 1981 | 1980 | 1979 | 1981 | 1980 | 1979 | 1981 | 1980 | 1979 |
Segment									
Steel	$2,925.2	$2,695.7	$2,693.2	$239.7	$193.5	$279.6	$112.2	$104.3	$110.4
Energy Products and Services	755.1	466.4	349.2	26.7	10.5	4.5	6.7	4.0	2.6
Aerospace/Defense	368.4	332.9	230.9	34.6	13.6	12.4	7.1	7.0	6.6
Ocean Shipping	279.9	230.4	243.5	71.0	9.8	20.1	7.8	5.3	5.1
Corporate and other	73.4	50.5	29.5	0.8	0.5	0.9	0.4	0.3	0.2
Intersegment eliminations	(69.3)	(54.7)	(10.6)	—	—	—	—	—	—
Total continuing operations	4,332.7	3,721.2	3,535.7	$372.8	$227.9	$317.5	$134.2	$120.9	$124.9
Net assets of discontinued operations	—	105.3	116.7						
Total assets	$4,332.7	$3,826.5	$3,652.4						

The results of operations of LTV's four continuing business segments as outlined in the accompanying three-year summary of segment information provides the basis for the following discussion. The consolidated financial statements and the notes thereto, along with the Business Overview section of this annual report, should be read in connection with the following discussion. Each of LTV's business segments and definitions of terms are included in the Business Segments note to the consolidated financial statements. Operating income is based on income from continuing operations before interest and corporate expense, unusual credits and income taxes.

SALES AND OPERATING PERFORMANCE

1981 compared with 1980

Sales and revenues from continuing operations for 1981 of $7.5 billion increased 31% over such sales and revenues for 1980. Operating income from continuing operations increased by 126%, or by $347.9 million to $624.6 million. Sales and income increased primarily due to strong performances by the Steel and the Energy Products and Services groups, as outlined below.

Steel — Net sales and operating income for 1981 increased by $985 million and $267 million, respectively, from 1980. The increase in net sales resulted from increased shipments, increased sales of higher priced products and higher selling prices. Shipments of steel products in 1981 of 7.6 million tons increased 597,000 tons over 1980 shipments. Most of the increase in shipments occurred during the second and third quarters and included increases in flat rolled and tubular products reflecting some mid-year improvement in the automotive and appliance markets and the continuing high level of demand from the oil and gas industry in the United States throughout the year. Shipments of tubular products, which include casing, pipe and tubing utilized in the oilfield market, increased 21% in 1981. Markets for most other steel products, especially the consumer durable and industrial equipment markets, weakened significantly during the fourth quarter of 1981.

The increase in operating income resulted from the increase in volume, higher selling prices and improved product mix combined with relatively lower production costs due to higher production levels and productivity improvements. Raw steel production increased 1.16 million tons to 10.86 million tons in 1981. Although the Steel Group operated at 83% of capacity compared with 78% in 1980, it operated at only 59% of capacity during the fourth quarter of 1981 as a result of the deepening recession.

Steel Group product costs benefited from improved production at the Pittsburgh Works' electric furnaces, from the transfer of seamless round production to the Aliquippa Works, which has enabled it to substantially expand production of oil country tubular goods, and from various operating improvements at the Indiana Harbor Works which have resulted in increased efficiency and productivity. The 1981 period was penalized for costs related to a coal strike which occurred during most of the second quarter.

The liquidation of LIFO inventory quantities, carried as though acquired at lower costs which prevailed in earlier years, decreased cost of products sold by $17 million in 1981 compared with $48 million in 1980.

Energy Products and Services — Net sales of $2.1 billion for 1981 increased by 71% over 1980, while operating income of $220.2 million improved by $106.0 million over 1980, or by 93%. This improvement reflects the higher level of drilling activity in the U.S., increased selling prices, and increased production capacity and broadened product lines resulting from internal expansion and from acquisitions made in late 1980 and early 1981. Drilling activity in 1981 was strong as indicated by the average number of active drilling rigs in the U.S. which increased 36% over 1980. The Group's sales of drilling equipment more than doubled in 1981 while its sales of tubular products increased by approximately 83%. The volume of tubular products shipped was 41% greater in 1981 than in 1980.

Aerospace/Defense — Net sales of $797 million for 1981 increased by 22% over 1980, while operating income declined by 32% to $38.8 million. The increase in sales resulted from revenues from components for the new Boeing 757 and 767 airliners and a microwave communication project in Pakistan, delivery of modified A-7 military aircraft to Portugal, and new missile (MLRS) and space defense (ASAT) development programs. These were partially offset by fewer deliveries of McDonnell Douglas DC-10 and Boeing 747 aircraft components. The decline in operating income is due to replacing mature, more profitable subcontract business with new, and initially less profitable subcontract business. Also, during the fourth quarter, $9 million was provided for costs associated with developing advanced technology engine compartment nacelles for private aircraft and for cancellation of long-lead time material orders as a result of the A-7 aircraft being dropped from the 1982 defense budget.

Financial Statements

157

Ocean Shipping — Revenues of $457 million for 1981 increased by 11% over 1980, while operating income declined by 25% to $26.8 million. The increase in revenues was primarily due to higher rates and a significantly higher level of charter operations which now includes seven vessels under contract to the U.S. Department of Defense. Cargo volume improvements were greatest on the Far East (North) and the South and East Africa trade routes. Despite higher revenues, operating income declined due to extreme competition on the Group's Far East trade routes, the strengthened dollar which depressed export markets, and a slow start-up in government-impelled cargo which hurt trade routes servicing developing nations. All of these factors more than offset the favorable effect of the expanded charter operations. Two vessels encountered weather-related damages during the first quarter of 1981, which caused higher operating costs. In the fourth quarter, weakening worldwide economic conditions and a shortage of government-impelled cargo traffic depressed cargo traffic and caused an increase in vessel idle status.

1980 compared with 1979

Consolidated sales and revenues for 1980 of $5.7 billion increased $85.0 million over 1979 while operating income declined by $26.8 million to $276.7 million. Sales increases by the non-steel operations offset the decline in Steel Group sales. Although the energy products and services, aerospace and shipping operations increased their operating income (before eliminations) by $67.2 million (48%) over 1979, a decline in the operating results of the steel operations of 59% during 1980 caused consolidated operating income to decline by 9%.

Steel — Steel Group sales of $3.8 billion and operating income of $69.4 million, dropped from 1979 by $0.4 billion and $101.3 million, respectively. Shipments and production declined 18% and 15%, respectively, in 1980 compared with 1979, resulting in operating at 78% of capacity during 1980 compared with 86% in 1979. Demand for flat rolled products for the automotive and other consumer durable markets weakened during 1979 and declined further in 1980. The only major market with strengthened demand in 1980 compared with 1979 was the oil country market for

tubular goods, resulting in higher volume and selling prices. The Company was able to mitigate the cost impact of the lower production level in 1980 through cost-saving steps, including use of only electric arc and basic oxygen furnaces. Operating income in 1980 included $13 million of gains from sales of assets and $48 million from liquidation of LIFO inventory quantities, carried at lower costs which prevailed in earlier years, compared with $35 million of such liquidation benefits in 1979.

Energy Products and Services — The Energy Products and Services Group's improvement in sales to $1.2 billion and in operating income to $114.2 million resulted from record levels of activity in all segments of the oil and gas industry and reflected a substantial increase in drilling and production activity in the U.S. and Canada, and a strong demand for all products that are produced or sold by the Group. Both sales and income were favorably affected by increased volume and higher price realizations on virtually all products sold by the Group.

Aerospace/Defense — Sales of $652 million and operating income of $57.5 million for the Aerospace/Defense Group increased 18% and 12%, respectively, over 1979 and primarily reflect increased deliveries of A-7 aircraft and commercial aircraft subcontract work, offset in part by a lower level of aircraft overhaul and modernization work.

Ocean Shipping — The higher revenues of $413 million of the Ocean Shipping Group and the improved operating income of $35.6 million resulted from an 8% increase in the number of voyages completed, increased cargo tonnage, improved fleet utilization, primarily due to the chartering of five vessels to the Military Sealift Command, and the ability to reflect fuel price increases in shipping rates faster than was possible in 1979. Voyages originating on the Gulf Coast also contributed significantly to the improvement during 1980.

Interest and Corporate Office Expense

Interest expense decreased by $25.5 million during 1981 to $118.5 million. This decrease was primarily due to cash flow resulting from improved earnings and a four million share common stock offering which permitted all bank debt to be repaid in mid-1981, and due to the conversion in early 1981 of the 12% $75 million Convertible Subordinated debentures, which reduced interest expense.

Net corporate office expenses amounted to $2.0 million in 1981 versus income of $27.8 million in 1980. This change was primarily due to a reduction of $17.9 million between years in gains from early extinguishment of debt purchased for sinking fund purposes. Other increases in corporate-related costs were partially offset by an increase in interest income resulting from the cash flow on improved earnings and from the proceeds of the sale of four million shares of common stock.

Interest and corporate office expense for 1980 declined $33.6 million from 1979 primarily as a result of gains from the early extinguishment of debt purchased for sinking fund purposes of $29.9 million, compared with $10.0 million in 1979. Interest expense of $144.0 million for 1980 was 5% less than interest expense of $151.6 million in 1979, due to reductions in both bank debt and long-term borrowings.

See the notes to the consolidated financial statements for interest cost capitalized in years 1979 through 1981. Such amounts did not change significantly between years.

Income Taxes

LTV's effective book tax rate for 1981 was 20% compared with 15% for 1980 and 14% for 1979. The increase in 1981's effective tax rate was caused by higher levels of earnings, which increased in greater proportion than the investment tax credits and permanent book/tax differences available to reduce taxes. See the "TAXES ON INCOME" note to the consolidated financial statements for further information explaining LTV's tax rate and payment requirements for the years 1979 through 1981.

Discussion of Effects of Inflation

For information regarding the effects of inflation on LTV's consolidated operations, earnings and financial position, see pages 46 to 49 of this annual report.

Financial Position and Liquidity

The following completes the discussion of financial position and liquidity included in the "BUSINESS OVERVIEW" section of this annual report, which should be read in conjunction with the following.

Improved earnings and resulting cash flow coupled with the addition to capital of over $165 million from the conversion of debt into, and the sale of, common stock decreased the Company's reliance on debt financing during 1981.

Funds generated by operations ($612 million compared with $253 million in 1980) and proceeds from the issuance of common stock more than met 1981's needs for capital expenditures ($373 million compared with $228 million in 1980), repayment of debt and other requirements. There is no assurance that funds provided from operations in future years will remain at or exceed the 1981 or 1980 levels.

LTV (parent company) obtains cash from its operating subsidiaries to meet its liquidity needs. As indicated in the notes to the consolidated financial statements, the subsidiaries are restricted in the amount of cash that can be transferred to LTV. However, LTV's (parent company) near-term cash needs through 1988 for operating-type (general and administrative) costs and debt service (interest and principal) are minimal in relation to the amount of cash transferrable to LTV from its subsidiaries at December 31, 1981.

The Company's capital expenditures for 1982 are budgeted to be $354 million. Additional substantial capital expenditures are planned for years 1983 and after, including approximately $250 million to complete the two strand continuous caster at the Indiana Harbor Works and to complete the rebuild of two coke oven batteries at the Campbell Works in Youngstown, Ohio. At December 31, 1981, the Company had available $76.9 million of unexpended pollution control bond funds to finance certain environmental projects. The Company expects to be able to obtain similar long-term financing for a substantial portion of its pollution control expenditure requirements in future years.

The Company leases certain property and equipment under noncancellable lease arrangements. See the notes to the consolidated financial statements for further details.

Management believes it will have sufficient long-term liquidity to meet its operating requirements, its planned capital expenditure requirements (for expansion, replacement and environmental control spending) and its debt maturity requirements. Management cannot predict if it will be required to make unplanned additional expenditures to meet future foreign and domestic competition because such competition will depend upon a number of factors including inflation, labor relations and economic conditions in the United States and overseas, as well as United States Government protection against unfair foreign competition and the extent to which competitors make discretionary expenditures in the steel business.

FIVE-YEAR HIGHLIGHTS
(Dollars in millions, except per share data)

	1981	1980	1979	1978	1977
Summary of Operations for the Year:					
Sales and revenues					
Steel	$4,785.6	$3,800.2	$4,174.7	$2,410.6	$2,152.2
Energy Products and Services	2,081.0	1,218.0	801.2	261.4	231.5
Aerospace/Defense	797.3	652.0	554.8	491.3	462.6
Ocean Shipping	457.0	412.8	334.1	—	—
Sales between segments	(610.2)	(340.0)	(206.8)	(97.0)	(84.7)
Total	$7,510.7	$5,743.0	$5,658.0	$3,066.3	$2,761.6
Operating income					
Steel	$ 336.3	$ 69.4	$ 170.7	$ 43.1	$ 8.4
Energy Products and Services	220.2	114.2	68.8	18.6	12.9
Aerospace/Defense	38.8	57.5	51.5	47.5	38.8
Ocean Shipping	26.8	35.6	19.8	—	—
Eliminations between segments	2.5	—	(7.3)	—	—
Operating income	624.6	276.7	303.5	109.2	60.1
Interest and debt discount	(118.5)	(144.0)	(151.6)	(94.2)	(87.3)
Other income (expense) - net	(2.0)	27.8	1.8	2.1	(4.2)
Unusual credits	—	—	—	6.6	11.0
Income tax (charge) credit	(99.1)	(24.0)	(20.8)	(1.7)	1.0
Income (loss) from continuing operations	405.0	136.5	132.9	22.0	(19.4)
Income (loss) from discontinued operations, accounting changes and extraordinary items	(18.7)	(8.6)	40.6	13.7	(35.3)
Net income (loss)	$ 386.3	$ 127.9	$ 173.5	$ 35.7	$ (54.7)
Earnings (loss) per share (fully diluted):					
Continuing operations	$ 7.97	$ 3.15	$ 3.28	$ 1.19	$ (1.52)
Net income (loss)	7.59	2.96	4.27	1.89	(3.96)
Financial Position at Year-End:					
Working capital	$ 998.0	$ 721.1	$ 702.0	$ 609.7	$ 153.2
Total assets	4,332.7	3,826.5	3,652.4	3,476.8	1,857.0
Property, plant and equipment - net	1,885.6	1,625.1	1,592.7	1,516.7	976.4
Short-term debt (including current maturities)	18.7	69.8	94.0	175.3	67.7
Long-term debt	1,295.4	1,395.1	1,453.7	1,448.4	957.0
Preferred stock with mandatory redemption	20.8	20.8	20.8	35.1	50.9
Shareholders' equity applicable to ongoing operations	1,285.4	700.7	567.4	408.6	194.4
Total capital employed	2,738.2	2,202.5	2,082.1	1,922.7	1,223.0
Other Financial Information:					
Book value per share of common stock	$ 25.95	$ 18.47	$ 11.16	$ 5.78	$13.36
Ratio of current assets to current liabilities	1.82	1.63	1.66	1.59	1.29
Ratio of long-term debt to equity	1.01	1.99	2.56	3.54	4.92
Ratio of long-term debt to total capital employed	0.47	0.63	0.70	0.76	0.78
Expenditures for property	$372.8	$227.9	$317.5	$123.0	$79.0
Depreciation expense	134.2	120.9	124.9	75.6	63.8
Stock and Employee Data:					
Average number of fully diluted common and common equivalent shares outstanding (in thousands)	51,001	45,281	41,063	19,517	14,478
Common shares outstanding at year-end (in thousands)	48,189	35,793	24,645	23,757	13,311
Shareholders of record at year-end	53,700	59,400	60,900	65,200	32,500
Total employees at year-end	53,000	54,000	57,100	60,500	41,800

Note: Data for 1977 through 1980 have been revised to conform to 1981 presentation for discontinued operations. Stockholders' equity data for 1977 through 1980 and income data for 1978 and 1977 have also been restated for required retroactive application during 1981 of Statement of Financial Accounting Standards No. 43. Auditors' reports on LTV's financial statements for years 1977 through 1979 included consistency exceptions for changes in accounting policies, with which the auditors concurred, for interest costs (1979), blast furnace rehabilitation expenditures (1979), leases (1978), inventories (1978 and 1977), and steel mill roll costs (1978). The auditors' report in 1978 was originally qualified for a litigation-related contingency, which was subsequently removed.

STOCK INFORMATION

Transfer Agent and Registrar for Common Stock, Special Stock, Class AA, Accumulating Convertible, Series 1 Participating Convertible Preference Stock and $5 Series A Cumulative Preferred Stock:

Mercantile National Bank at Dallas
P. O. Box 225415
Dallas, Texas 75265

All such stocks are listed on the New York Stock Exchange.
The Common Stock is also listed on the Pacific Stock Exchange.

Market Prices and Dividends

The high and low sale prices of the Common Stock, Special Stock, Class AA, the Series 1 Participating Preference Stock and the $5 Series A Preferred Stock for the quarterly periods were as follows:

	Common Stock		Special Stock Class AA		Series 1 Participating Preference Stock		$5 Series A Preferred Stock	
	High	Low	High	Low	High	Low	High	Low
1980								
First Quarter	14⅞	7¾	21½	11⅝	14¼	7⅝	49½	41
Second Quarter	12	8⅞	18	14¼	11½	9¼	45	40¾
Third Quarter	14¼	9⅞	20½	15½	13⅞	10	49½	44¼
Fourth Quarter	20¾	12½	29½	19	20	12½	60	48
1981								
First Quarter	25	17¾	37	28	25	17¾	57	53
Second Quarter	26⅛	20⅛	38	32¼	25½	20½	55	50
Third Quarter	22¼	12⅝	33⅜	24	22	13⅛	50	42
Fourth Quarter	18⅝	14½	29	25	19	16	45⅞	41

In 1980 and 1981 LTV paid regular quarterly dividends of $1.25 per share on its $5 Series A Cumulative Preferred Stock and in December, 1980 and 1981, paid the regular 3% annual stock dividend on its Special Stock, Class AA.

As of February 19, 1982, the approximate number of stockholders of record of the Corporation was as follows:

Security	Holders
Common Stock	38,200
Series 1 Participating Preference Stock	10,000
Special Stock, Class AA	2,500
$5 Series A Preferred Stock	3,000

APPENDIX B

ESTIMATING SAMPLE 1981

APPENDIX B—ESTIMATING SAMPLE 1981

INDUSTRY Company	Bonds	S&P Ratings
AEROSPACE		
Bangor Punta	Subordinated debt	B+
Boeing	Subordinated debt	AA-
Fairchild Industries	Subordinated debt	A-
McDonnell Douglas	Subordinated debt	A-
Rohr Industries	Subordinated debt	B-
United Technologies	Senior Unsecured debt	AA
Grumman	Subordinated debt	BBB-
AIRLINES		
American Airlines	Equipment trust certificates	BBB-
Eastern Airlines	Equipment trust certificates	BB
Frontier Airlines	Subordinated debt	BB+
Ozark Airlines	Subordinated debt	B-
PSA	Subordinated debt	B
Pan American World Airways	Equipment trust certificates	B
Piedmont Aviation	Subordinated debt	B
Texas Air	Subordinated debt	B
Trans World	Subordinated debt	B+
APPLIANCES		
Singer	Senior unsecured debt	BB-
Whirlpool	Senior unsecured debt	AA-
White Consolidated Industries	Subordinated debt	BBB-
Zenith Radio	Subordinated debt	BBB-
AUTOMOTIVE		
Arvin Industries	Senior unsecured debt	BBB
Bendix	Senior unsecured debt	A
Eaton	Senior unsecured debt	A-
Ford Motor	Senior unsecured debt	A
Fruehauf	Senior unsecured debt	BBB
General Motors	Senior unsecured debt	AA+
International Harvester	Senior unsecured debt	B
PACCAR	Senior unsecured debt	AA-
Questor	Senior preferred stock	BB

INDUSTRY Company	Bonds	S&P Ratings
BEVERAGES		
Coca-cola	Senior unsecured debt	AAA
Heublein	Senior unsecured debt	A
PepsiCo	Senior unsecured debt	AA
Schlitz (Jos.) Brewing	Senior unsecured debt	BB
Wometco Enterprises	Subordinated debt	BBB-
BUILDING MATERIALS		
Certain Teed	Industrial revenue bonds	BB+
GAF	Senior unsecured debt	BB+
Ideal Basic Industries	Senior unsecured debt	BBB-
Interpace	Industrial revenue bonds	A
Jim Walter	Senior unsecured debt	BBB-
Lone Star Industries	Senior unsecured debt	BBB
Manville	Senior unsecured debt	A
National Gypsum	Industrial revenue bonds	A+
Owens-Corning Fiberglas	Senior unsecured debt	A+
Sherwin-William	Senior unsecured debt	BB
Texas Industries	Subordinated debt	B+
U.S. Gypsum	Senior unsecured debt	AA
CHEMICALS		
Air Products & Chemicals	Senior unsecured debt	A+
Akzona	Senior unsecured debt	BB+
Allied	Senior unsecured debt	A
American Cyanamid	Senior unsecured debt	A+
Celanese	Senior unsecured debt	A-
Dexter	Industrial revenue bonds	
Diamond Shamrock	Senior unsecured debt	A-
Du Pont	Senior unsecured debt	AA
Hercules	Senior unsecured debt	A
International Minerals & Chemical	Senior unsecured debt	A
Koppers	Industrial revenue bonds	A
Lubrizol	Industrial revenue bonds	AA
Monsanto	Senior unsecured debt	A
Morton-Norwich Products	Senior unsecured debt	A
National Distillers & Chemical	Senior unsecured debt	A

INDUSTRY		
Company	Bonds	S&P Ratings
Olin	Industrial revenue bonds	A
Rohm and Haas	Senior unsecured debt	A
SCM	Senior unsecured debt	BBB
Stauffer Chemical	Senior unsecured debt	A
Sun Chemical	Industrial revenue bonds	BBB-
Texasgulf	Senior unsecured debt	A+
Witco Chemical	Senior unsecured debt	A+
CONGLOMERATES		
Avco	Senior unsecured debt	BB+
City Investing	Senior unsecured debt	BB
Colt Industries	Industrial revenue bonds	A
Fuqua Industries	Subordinated debt	B-
Gulf & Western Industries	Industrial revenue bonds	BBB
Kidde	Senior unsecured debt	BBB
LTV	Senior unsecured debt	B
Lear Siegler	Subordinated debt	BBB
Martin Marietta	Senior unsecured debt	AA-
Northwest Industries	Senior unsecured debt	A
Rockwell International	Senior unsecured debt	AA
Teledyne	Senior unsecured debt	A
Textron	Senior unsecured debt	AA-
Whittaker	Subordinated debt	B+
Zapata	Subordinated debt	B
CONTAINERS		
American Can	Senior unsecured debt	A-
Brockway Glass	Senior unsecured debt	A
Continental Group	Senior unsecured debt	A
Crown Cork & Seal	Senior unsecured debt	AA
Kerr Glass Mfg.	Industrial revenue debt	BBB
Maryland Corp.	Senior unsecured debt	A
Owens-Illinois	Senior unsecured debt	A
DRUGS		
Abbott Laboratories	Senior unsecured debt	AA
American Hospital Supply	Senior unsecured debt	AA
Bristol-Myers	Senior unsecured debt	AAA

INDUSTRY Company	Bonds	S&P Ratings
Cooper Laboratories	Subordinated debt	B
Mallinckrodt	Subordinated debt	A-
Merck	Senior unsecured debt	AAA
Pfizer	Senior unsecured debt	AA
Schering-Plough	Industrial revenue bonds	AAA
Searle (G.D.)	Senior unsecured debt	AA-
Smithkline	Senior unsecured debt	AA
Squibb	Senior unsecured debt	A+
Syntex	Industrial revenue bonds	AA-
ELECTRICAL, ELECTRONICS		
AMP	Senior unsecured debt	AA+
Champion Spark Plug	Senior unsecured debt	AA-
E-Systems	Subordinated debt	BBB-
Emerson Electric	Industrial revenue bonds	AAA
General Electric	Senior unsecured debt	AAA
General Instrument	Subordinated debt	A
Gould	Senior unsecured debt	A
Grainger (W.W.)	Industrial revenue bonds	AA
Harris	Senior unsecured debt	A
Intel	Subordinated debt	A-
Loral	Subordinated debt	BBB
M/A-COM	Subordinated debt	BB+
Mitel	Industrial revenue bonds	AAA
Oak Industries	Senior unsecured debt	BB+
RCA	Senior unsecured debt	BBB+
Raytheon	Senior unsecured debt	AA
Sanders Associates	Subordinated debt	BB+
Tandy	Subordinated debt	A-
Texas Instruments	Senior unsecured debt	AA
Varian Associates	Subordinated debt	B+
Westinghouse Electric	Senior unsecured debt	AA-
FOOD PROCESSING		
Archer-Daniels-Midland	Senior unsecured debt	A
Borden	Senior unsecured debt	A+
CPC International	Senior unsecured debt	AA
Campbell Soup	Senior unsecured debt	AAA
Campbell Taggart	Senior unsecured debt	A+
Castle & Cooke	Senior unsecured debt	BBB-

INDUSTRY Company	Bonds	S&P Ratings
Central Soya	Senior unsecured debt	BBB
Dart & Kraft	Senior unsecured debt	AA
Dekalb AgResearch	Industrial revenue bonds	A
Esmark	Senior unsecured debt	BBB
Foremost-McKesson	Industrial revenue bonds	A-
General Foods	Senior unsecured debt	AA
General Host	Subordinated debt	B-
General Mills	Senior unsecured debt	A+
Hershey Foods	Senior unsecured debt	A+
Hormel (Geo. A.)	Senior unsecured debt	A
International Multifoods	Senior unsecured debt	BBB+
Kellogg	Senior unsecured debt	AAA
Norton Simon	Senior unsecured debt	BBB+
Peavey	Industrial revenue bonds	BBB+
United Brands	Subordinated debt	B
FOOD AND LODGING		
Caesars World	Senior unsecured debt	BB-
McDonald's	Senior unsecured debt	AA
Ramada Inns	Subordinated debt	B-
Resort International	Subordinated debt	BBB-
GENERAL MACHINERY		
Black & Decker Mfg.	Senior unsecured debt	A+
Clark Equipment	Senior unsecured debt	A
Cooper Industries	Industrial revenue bonds	A
Eagle-Picher-Industries	Industrial revenue bonds	A
Figgie International	Senior unsecured debt	BB
Midland Ross	Senior unsecured debt	A
Rexnord	Senior unsecured debt	A
Scott & Fetzer	Senior unsecured debt	A
Zurn Industries	Subordinated debt	BBB+
INSTRUMENTS		
General Signal	Senior unsecured debt	AA
Itek	Subordinated debt	B+
Johnson Controls	Senior unsecured debt	A
Tektronix	Senior unsecured debt	A
Western Pacific Industries	Subordinated debt	BB-

INDUSTRY Company	Bonds	S&P Ratings
LEISURE TIME INDUSTRIES		
AMF	Senior unsecured debt	A-
Bally Mfg.	Subordinated debt	BBB-
Brunswick	Subordinated debt	BBB-
Columbia Pictures Industries	Subordinated debt	BBB-
MGM Grand Hotels	Collateral trust debentures	BB
Polaroid	Senior unsecured debt	A+
Twentieth Century-Fox Film	Senior unsecured debt	BBB
Warner Communications	Senior unsecured debt	AA
METALS & MINING		
Aluminum Co. of America	Senior unsecured debt	A
AMAX	Senior unsecured debt	A+
ASARCO	Senior unsecured debt	A-
Gulf Resources & Chemical	Subordinated debt	B
Harsco	Senior unsecured debt	A+
Kennametal	Industrial revenue bonds	A+
Revere Copper & BRASS	Industrial revenue bonds	BBB
Reynolds Metals	Subordinated debt	BB
UNC Resources	Subordinated debt	BB-
MISC. MANUFACTURING		
ACF Industries	Equipment trust certificates	AA-
American Standard	Senior unsecured debt	A+
Avery International	Senior unsecured debt	A
Borg-Warner	Senior unsecured debt	AA-
Condec	Subordinated debt	B-
Corning Glass Works	Senior unsecured debt	AA
Crane	Senior unsecured debt	BBB
Dayco	Industrial revenue bonds	BB+
Dennison Mfg.	Senior unsecured debt	A
Guardian Industries	Industrial revenue bonds	BBB
Hoover Universal	Senior unsecured debt	A
Minnesota Mining & Mfg.	Senior unsecured debt	AAA
Monogram Industries	Subordinated debt	B
Norton	Senior unsecured debt	A
PPG Industries	Senior unsecured debt	A+
Parker-Hannifin	Senior unsecured debt	A
Robertson (H. H.)	Subordiated debt	BBB-

INDUSTRY Company	Bonds	S&P Ratings
Snap-on Tools	Industrial revenue bonds	AA
Standex-International	Subordinated debt	BB
Todd Shipyards	Subordinated debt	B
Trane	Senior unsecured debt	A
Tyco Laboratories	Subordinated debt	B+
Tyler	Subordinated debt	BBB
UMC Industries	Senior unsecured debt	BBB
Vulcan Materials	Senior unsecured debt	A
Wheelabrator-Frye	Senior unsecured debt	A
NATURAL RESOURCES (FUEL)		
Alaska Interstate	Subordinated debt	B+
Amerada Hess	Subordinated debt	BBB+
Apache	Subordinated debt	B+
Ashland Oil	Senior unsecured debt	BBB+
Atlantic Richfield	Senior unsecured debt	AA+
Belco Petroleum	Subordinated debt	BBB-
Charter	Subordinated debt	B-
Cities Services	Senior unsecured debt	A+
Crystal Oil	Subordinated debt	B
Dorchester Gas	Subordinated debt	BBB-
Exxon	Senior unsecured debt	AAA
Getty Oil	Senior unsecured debt	AAA
Gulf Oil	Senior unsecured debt	AAA
Houston Natural Gas	Senior unsecured debt	A+
Inexco	Subordinated debt	BB-
Kaneb Services	Subordinated debt	BBB
Kerr-McGee	Senior unsecured debt	A+
Lear Petroleum	Subordinated debt	B
Louisiana Land & Exploration	Industrial revenue bonds	A
MAPCO	Subordinated debt	BBB-
Marathon Oil	Senior unsecured debt	A
Mesa Petroleum	Subordinated debt	BB+
Mobil	Senior unsecured debt	AA
Natomas	Senior unsecured debt	BBB
Occidental Petroleum	Senior unsecured debt	BBB+
Pennzoil	Senior unsecured debt	A-
Petro-Lewis	Subordinated debt	B+
Petrolane	Senior unsecured debt	A+
Phillips Petroleum	Senior unsecured debt	AA+
Pittston	Senior unsecured debt	A

| INDUSTRY | | |
Company	Bonds	S&P Ratings
Pogo Producing	Subordinated debt	BB+
Quaker State Oil Refining	Senior unsecured debt	A-
Shell Oil	Senior unsecured debt	AA+
Standard Oil Co. (Indiana)	Senior unsecured debt	AAA
Standard Oil Co. (Ohio)	Senior unsecured debt	AA
Standard Oil Co. of California	Senior unsecured debt	AAA
Sun	Senior unsecured debt	AA
Superior Oil	Senior unsecured debt	AA
Tesoro Petroleum	Subordinated debt	B
Texaco	Senior unsecured debt	AA+
Texas Oil & Gas	First mortgage bonds	AA-
Union Oil Co. of California	Senior unsecured debt	AA
OFFICE EQUIPMENT, COMPUTERS		
Control Data	Senior unsecured debt	BBB
Data General	Senior unsecured debt	A
Digital Equipment	Senior unsecured debt	AAA
Honeywell	Senior unsecured debt	A+
International Business Machines	Senior unsecured debt	AAA
Lanier Business Products	Subordinated debt	BB+
Mohawk Data Sciences	Subordinated debt	B+
Nashua	Senior unsecured debt	BBB
Pitney-Bowes	Senior unsecured debt	A
Prime Computer	Subordinated debt	B
Savin	Subordinated debt	B
Storage Technology	Subordinated debt	BB-
Wang Laboratories	Subordinated debt	BB+
Xerox	Senior unsecured debt	AA
OIL SERVICE & SUPPLY		
Big Three Industries	Senior unsecured debt	A+
Buttes Gas & Oil	Subordinated debt	B
Dresser Industries	Senior unsecured debt	AA
Geosource	Senior unsecured debt	A+
Global Marine	Senior subordinated debt	B+
Halliburton	Senior unsecured debt	AA
Hughes Tools	Senior unsecured debt	AA-
NL Industries	Senior unsecured debt	A
Smith International	Senior unsecured debt	A
Texas International	Subordinated debt	B

INDUSTRY		S&P
Company	Bonds	Ratings
Tidewater	Subordinated debt	BBB-
Western Co. of North America	Subordinated debt	BB-
PAPER		
Boise Cascade	Senior unsecured debt	A
Champion International	Senior unsecured debt	A-
Chesapeake Corp. of Virginia	Industrial revenue bonds	A
Crown Zellerbach	Senior unsecured debt	A-
Diamond International	Senior unsecured debt	AA
Federal Paper Board	Senior unsecured debt	BBB-
Georgia-Pacific	Senior unsecured debt	A+
Great Northern Nekoosa	Senior unsecured debt	A+
Hammermill Paper	Subordinated debt	BBB
International Paper	Senior unsecured debt	AA-
Kimberly-Clark	Senior unsecured debt	AA
Potlatch	Industrial revenue bonds	A
St. Regis Paper	Senior unsecured debt	A
Saxon Industries	Subordinated debt	B-
Scott Paper	Senior unsecured debt	A-
Westvaco	Senior unsecured debt	A
PERSONAL CARE PRODUCTS		
Chesebrough-Pond's	Senior unsecured debt	AA
Economics Laboratory	Subordinated debt	BBB
Procter & Gamble	Senior unsecured debt	AAA
Purex Industries	Subordinated debt	A-
PUBLISHING, RADIO & TV BROADCASTING		
American Broadcasting	Senior unsecured debt	A
CBS	Senior unsecured debt	AA
Harte-Hanks Communications	Subordinated debt	BB+
Metromedia	Subordinated debt	BBB
Storer Broadcasting	Subordinated debt	BB-
RAILROADS		
Burlington Northern	Equipment trust certificates	AA
Missouri Pacific	Senior unsecured debt	BBB
Norfolk & Western Railway	Equipment trust certificates	AAA

INDUSTRY Company	Bonds	S&P Ratings
Santa Fe Industries	Subordinated debt	A-
Soo Line Railroad	Equipment trust certificates	AAA
Southern Pacific	Senior unsecured debt	A-
Southern Railway	Equipment trust certificates	AAA
Union Pacific	Senior unsecured debt	AA

REAL ESTATE & HOUSING

Kaufman & Broad	Subordinated debt	BB-

RETAILING (Food)

Albertson's	Industrial revenue bonds	A
American Stores	Senior unsecured debt	BBB+
Fisher Foods	Subordinated debt	B+
Jewel	Industrial revenue bonds	A
Kroger	Senior unsecured debt	A
Lucky Stores	Senior unsecured debt	A
Pneumo	Industrial revenue bonds	BBB-
Safeway Stores	Senior unsecured debt	A
Southland	Senior unsecured debt	A
Supermarkets General	Industrial revenue bonds	BBB

RETAILING (Nonfood)

Allied Stores	Senior unsecured debt	A+
Associated Dry Goods	Senior unsecured debt	A+
Carter Hawley Hale Stores	Senior unsecured debt	BBB+
DWG	Subordinated debt	B-
Dayton Hudson	Senior unsecured debt	AA
Federated Department Stores	Senior unsecured debt	AAA
Gordon Jewelry	Subordinated debt	BBB-
Lionel	Subordinated debt	B
May Department Stores	Senior unsecured debt	AA
Melville	Subordinated debt	A-
Murphy (G. C.)	Senior unsecured debt	BBB+
Nordstrom	Industrial revenue bonds	BBB+
Penny (J. C.)	Senior unsecured debt	A+
SOCA Industries	Industrial revenue bonds	A-
Sears, Roebuck	Senior unsecured debt	AA
Toys "R" Us	Subordinated debt	A-
Walgreen	Subordinated debt	A-

INDUSTRY Company	Bonds	S&P Ratings
Wickes	Senior unsecured debt	BB
Woolworth (F. W.)	Senior unsecured debt	BBB+
Zayre	Senior unsecured debt	BBB-
SERVICE INDUSTRIES		
ARA Services	Subordinated debt	A-
Alco Standard	Industrial revenue bonds	A-
American Medical International	Subordinated debt	BBB
Amfac	Subordinated debt	BBB-
Comdisco	Subordinated debt	BB+
Computer Sciences	Subordinated debt	B+
Di Giorgio	Subordinated debt	B+
Dillingham	Subordinated debt	BB-
Edwards (A. G.) & Sons	Subordinated debt	BBB
Fischbach	Subordinated debt	BBB-
Flexi-Van	Collateral trust debentures	BBB
Fluor	Industrial revenue bonds	AA
Gelco	Subordinated debt	BB-
Humana	First mortgage bonds	BB
Kay	Subordinated debt	B-
Lifemark	Subordinated debt	BB+
National Medical Enterprises	Subordinated debt	BBB
Ogden	Subordinated debt	BB+
PHH Group	Senior unsecured debt	AA-
Phibro	Senior unsecured debt	AA-
Purolator	Industrial revenue bonds	A
Ryder System	Collateral trust debentures	BBB+
SeaCo	Subordinated debt	BBB-
Sysco	Industrial revenue bonds	A
Tiger International	Subordinated debt	B
Waste Management	Industrial revenue bonds	A
SPECIAL MACHINERY		
American Hoist & Derrick	Subordinated debt	BB+
Bucyrus-Erie	Senior unsecured debt	A
Caterpillar Tractor	Senior unsecured debt	AA
Deere	Senior unsecured debt	AA-
Dover	Senior unsecured debt	AA-
FMC	Senior unsecured debt	A
Joy Mfg.	Senior unsecured debt	A+

INDUSTRY		
Company	Bonds	S&P Ratings

STEEL

Armco	Senior unsecured debt	A
Bethlehem Steel	Senior unsecured debt	A
Copper Weld	Senior unsecured debt	A
Inland Steel	First mortgage bonds	A
NVF	Subordinated debt	B
National Steel	First mortgage bonds	A-
Nucor	Industrial revenue bonds	AA-

TEXTILES, APPAREL

Brown Group	Senior unsecured debt	A
Burlington Industries	Senior unsecured debt	A
Collins & Aikman	Industrial revenue bonds	A
Dan River	Senior unsecured debt	BB+
Genesco	Senior unsecured debt	B
Interco	Senior unsecured debt	A+
Levi Strauss	Industrial revenue bonds	AA
Phillips-Van-Heusen	Subordinated debt	B+
Riegel Textile	Subordinated debt	BBB-
Springs Mills	Industrial revenue bonds	BBB
Stevens (J. P.)	Subordinated debt	BB+
U.S. Shoe	Senior unsecured debt	A
West Point Pepperell	Subordinated debt	A-

TIRE & RUBBER

Armstrong Rubber	Senior unsecured debt	BBB-
Firestone Tire & Rubber	Senior unsecured debt	BBB
Goodrich (B. F.)	Senior unsecured debt	BBB-
Goodyear Tire & Rubber	Senior unsecured debt	BBB

TOBACCO

American Brands	Senior unsecured debt	A+
Loews	Senior unsecured debt	BBB
Philip Morris	Senior unsecured debt	A
Reynolds (R. J.) Industries	Senior unsecured debt	AA
U.S. Tobacco	Industrial revenue bonds	A

INDUSTRY Company	Bonds	S&P Ratings
TRUCKING		
Consolidated Freightways	Senior unsecured debt	AA
Leaseway Transportation	Industrial revenue bonds	A
Tele Com	Subordinated debt	B
UTILITIES		
American Telephone & Telegraph	Senior unsecured debt	AAA
Arizona Public Service	First mortgage bonds	A-
Arkla	First mortgage bonds	AA-
Carolina Power & Light	First mortgage bonds	A
Central Telephone & Utilities	First mortgage bonds	A
Century Telephone Enterprises	Subordinated debt	B
Columbia Gas System	Senior unsecured debt	A
Commonwealth Edison	First mortgage bonds	A
Consolidated Edison Co. of New York	First mortgage bonds	A
Consolidated Natural Gas	Senior unsecured debt	AA
Consumers Power	First mortgage bonds	BBB-
Continental Telephone	Senior unsecured debt	BBB
Duquesne Light	First mortgage bonds	BBB+
ENSERCH	Senior unsecured debt	A
Flordia Power & Light	First mortgage bonds	A+
Gulf States Utilities	First mortgage bonds	BBB
Illinois Power	First mortgage bonds	AA
InterNorth	Senior unsecured debt	A+
Long Island Lighting	First mortgage bonds	BBB
MCI Communication	Subordinated debt	B+
Mid-Continental Telephone	Subordinated debt	BBB-
Northern Indiana Public Service	First mortgage bonds	A
Ohio Edison	First mortgage bonds	BBB-
Pacific Power & Light	First mortgage bonds	BBB

APPENDIX **C**

CONTROL SAMPLE 1980

APPENDIX C—CONTROL SAMPLE 1980

INDUSTRY Company	Bonds	S&P Ratings
AEROSPACE		
Bangor Punta	Subordinated debt	B
Fairchild Industries	Subordinated debt	BBB-
Grumman	Subordinated debt	BB
McDonnell Douglas	Subordinated debt	BBB
Rohr Industries	Subordinated debt	B
United Technologies	Senior unsecured debt	AA
AIRLINES		
American Airlines	Equipment trust certificates	BBB-
Continental Air Lines	Subordinated debt	B
Delta Air Lines	Industrial revenue bonds	A
Eastern Airlines	Equipment trust certificates	BB
Frontier Airlines	Subordinated debt	B
PSA	Subordinated debt	B
Pan American World Airways	Equipment trust certificates	BB
Piedmont Aviation	Subordinated debt	B
Texas Air	Subordinated debt	B
USAir	Subordinated debt	BB-
Western Air Lines	Subordinated debt	B
World Airways	Equipment trust certificates	B
APPLIANCES		
Singer	Senior unsecured debt	BB-
Sunbeam	Senior unsecured debt	A
Whirlpool	Senior unsecured debt	A
White Consolidated Inds.	Subordinated debt	BB
Zenith Radio	Subordinated debt	BB
AUTOMOTIVE		
American Motors	Subordinated debt	B
Arvin Industries	Senior unsecured debt	BBB
Bendix	Senior unsecured debt	A
Chrysler	Senior unsecured debt	B
Dana	Senior unsecured debt	AA
Eaton	Senior unsecured debt	A-
Federal Mogul	Senior unsecured debt	A
Ford Motor	Senior unsecured debt	AA

179

INDUSTRY Company	Bonds	S&P Ratings
Fruehauf	Senior unsecured debt	BBB
General Motors	Senior unsecured debt	AAA
International Harvester	Senior unsecured debt	BBB
PACCAR	Senior unsecured debt	A+
Questor	Senior preferred stock	BB
Sheller-Globe	Subordinated debt	B
Smith (A. O.)	Senior unsecured debt	A-
BEVERAGES		
Anheuser-Busch	Senior unsecured debt	AA-
Coca-Cola	Senior unsecured debt	AAA
General Cinema	Subordinated debt	BB
Helleman (G.) Brewing	Senior unsecured debt	A
Heublein	Senior unsecured debt	A
PepsiCo.	Senior unsecured debt	AA
Schlitz (Jos.) Brewing	Senior unsecured debt	BB
Wometco Enterprises	Subordinated debt	BB
BUILDING MATERIALS		
California Portland Cement	Industrial revenue bonds	A
Certain Teed	Industrial revenue bonds	A
GAF	Senior unsecured debt	BBB
General Portland	Senior unsecured debt	BBB
Ideal Basic Industries	Senior unsecured debt	A-
Insilco	Subordinated debt	BB
Interpace	Industrial revenue bonds	A
Jim Walter	Senior unsecured debt	BBB
John-Manville	Senior unsecured debt	A+
Lone Star Industries	Senior unsecured debt	BBB
Masco	Senior unsecured debt	A
National Gypsum	Industrial revenues bonds	A+
Owens-Corning Fiberglas	Senior unsecured debt	A+
Sherwin Williams	Senior unsecured debt	BB
Texas Industries	Subordinated debt	B
U. S. Gypsum	Senior unsecured debt	AA
CHEMICALS		
Air Products & Chemicals	Senior unsecured debt	A+
Akzona	Senior unsecured debt	BB+

INDUSTRY Company	Bonds	S&P Ratings
Allied Chemicals	Senior unsecured debt	A
American Cyanamid	Senior unsecured debt	AA-
Avery International	Senior unsecured debt	A
Celanese	Senior unsecured debt	A-
Diamond Shamrock	Senior unsecured debt	A-
Dow Chemical	Senior unsecured debt	A+
Du Pont	Senior unsecured debt	AAA
Ferro	Senior unsecured debt	A
Grace (W. R.)	Senior unsecured debt	BBB+
Hercules	Senior unsecured debt	A
International Minerals and Chemical	Senior unsecured debt	A
DRUGS		
Mallinckrodt	Subordinated debt	BBB
Merck	Senior unsecured debt	AAA
Pfizer	Senior unsecured debt	AA
Richardson Merrell	Senior unsecured debt	AA
Searle (G. D.)	Senior unsecured debt	A+
Smith Kline	Senior unsecured debt	AA
Squibb	Senior unsecured debt	A+
Sterling Drug	Senior unsecured debt	AAA
Syntex	Industrial revenue bonds	A
Upjohn	Senior unsecured debt	AA
Warner Lambert	Senior unsecured debt	AAA
ELECTRICAL, ELECTRONICS		
AMP	Senior unsecured debt	AA+
Ampex	Subordinated debt	B
Champion Spark Plug	Senior unsecured debt	AA
E-Systems	Subordinated debt	BB
Emerson Electric	Industrial revenue bonds	AAA
General Electric	Senior unsecured debt	AAA
General Instrument	Subordinated debt	BB+
Gould	Senior unsecured debt	A
Harris	Senior unsecured debt	A
Intel	Subordinated debt	BBB
McGraw-Edison	Senior unsecured debt	A-
Motorola	Senior unsecured debt	AA
North American Philips	Senior unsecured debt	A

INDUSTRY Company	Bonds	S&P Ratings
Oak Industries	Subordinated debt	B
Raytheon	Senior unsecured debt	AA
Sanders Associates	Subordinated debt	B
Square D	Industrial revenue bonds	AA
Tandy	Subordinated debt	BB-
Texas Instruments	Senior unsecured debt	AA
Varian Associates	Subordinated debt	B
Westinghouse Electric	Senior unsecured debt	AA-
FOOD PROCESSING		
Amstar	Senior preferred stock	BBB
Beatrice Foods	Senior unsecured stock	AAA
Borden	Senior unsecured debt	A+
CFS Continental	Industrial revenue bonds	BBB
CPC International	Senior unsecured debt	AA
Campbell Soup	Senior unsecured debt	AAA
Campbell Taggart	Industrial revenue bonds	A+
Carnation	Senior unsecured debt	AAA
Castle & Cooke	Senior unsecured debt	BBB
Central Soya	Senior unsecured debt	A
Consolidated Foods	Senior unsecured debt	AA
DPF	Subordinated debt	B
Dekalb AgResearch	Industrial revenue bonds	A
Esmark	Senior unsecured debt	BBB
Foremost-McKesson	Subordinated debt	BB+
General Foods	Senior unsecured debt	AAA
General Mills	Senior unsecured debt	A+
Greyhound	Senior unsecured debt	A
Heinz (H. J.)	Senior unsecured debt	A
Hershey Foods	Senior unsecured debt	A+
Hormel (Geo. A.)	Senior unsecured debt	A
International Multifoods	Senior unsecured debt	BBB+
Kellogg	Senior unsecured debt	AAA
Kraft	Senior unsecured debt	AAA
Mayer (Oscar)	Senior unsecured debt	AA-
McCormick	Industrial revenue bonds	A
Nabisco	Senior unsecured debt	AA
Norton Simon	Senior unsecured debt	A
Peavey	Industrial revenue bonds	BBB+
Pillsbury	Senior unsecured debt	A
Quaker Oats	Senior unsecured debt	A+

INDUSTRY Company	Bonds	S&P Ratings
Ralston Purina	Senior unsecured debt	AA
Staley (A. E.) Mfg.	Senior unsecured debt	A
Standard Brands	Senior unsecured debt	A
Stokely-Van Camp	Senior unsecured debt	BBB
United Brands	Subordinated debt	B

FOOD & LODGING

Company	Bonds	S&P Ratings
ARA Services	Subordinated debt	BBB
Caesars World	Senior unsecured debt	B
Hilton Hotels	Collateral trust debentures	A+
Holiday Inns	First mortgage bonds	BBB
McDonald's	Senior unsecured debt	A+
Ramada Inns	Subordinated debt	B
Resorts International	Subordinated debt	BB
Sambo's Restaurants	Industrial revenue bonds	B

GENERAL MACHINERY

Company	Bonds	S&P Ratings
A-T-O	Senior unsecured debt	BB
Black and Decker Mfg.	Senior unsecured debt	AA
Combustion Engineering	Senior unsecured debt	A
Cooper Industries	Industrial revenue bonds	A
Cummins Engine	Senior unsecured debt	BBB+
Dover	Senior unsecured debt	AA-
Eagle-Picher Industries	Industrial revenue bonds	A
Hobart	Industrial revenue bonds	A
Ingersoll-Rand	Senior unsecured debt	A
Joy Mfg.	Senior unsecured debt	A+
Midland Ross	Senior unsecured debt	A
Parker-Hannifin	Senior unsecured debt	A
Research-Cottrell	Industrial revenue bonds	BBB
Rexnord	Senior unsecured debt	A
Scott and Fetzer	Senior unsecured debt	A
Sunstrand	Subordinated debt	BB+
Zurn Industries	Subordinated debt	BB

INSTRUMENTS

Company	Bonds	S&P Ratings
Bausch and Lomb	Industrial revenue bonds	A
General Signals	Senior unsecured debt	AA
Itek	Subordinated debt	B

INDUSTRY Company	Bonds	S&P Ratings
Johnson Centrols	Senior unsecured debt	A
Sybron	Senior unsecured debt	A
Talley Industries	Senior unsecured debt	BB-
Tektronix	Senior unsecured debt	A
LEISURE TIME INDUSTRIES		
AMF	Senior unsecured debt	BBB
American Greetings	Senior unsecured debt	A
Bally Mfg.	Subordinated debt	BB
Brunswick	Subordinated debt	BB
Columbia Pictures Inds.	Subordinated debt	B
MGM Grand Hotels	Collateral trust debentures	BB+
Outboard Marine	Senior unsecured debt	BB
Polaroid	Senior unsecured debt	A+
Twentieth Century-Fox Film	Senior unsecured debt	BBB
Warner Communications	Senior unsecured debt	A+
METALS & MINING		
Aluminum Co. of America	Senior unsecured debt	A
AMAX	Senior unsecured debt	A+
ASARCO	Senior unsecured debt	A-
Gulf Resources and Chemical	Subordinated debt	B
Hanna Mining	Senior unsecured debt	A
Harsco	Senior unsecured debt	A+
Kennametal	Industrial revenue bonds	A+
Kennecott	Senior unsecured debt	BBB
Phelps Dodge	Senior unsecured debt	BBB+
Revere Copper and Brass	Industrial revenue bonds	B
Reynolds Metals	Subordinated debt	B
St. Joe Minerals	Industrial revenue bonds	AA
UNC Resources	Subordinated debt	BB
MISC. MANUFACTURING		
ACF Industries	Equipment trust certificates	AA-
American Standard	Senior unsecured debt	A+
Apache	Subordinated debt	B
Armstrong World Industries	Senior unsecured debt	AA
Borg-Warner	Senior unsecured debt	AA-
Condec	Subordinated debt	B

INDUSTRY Company	Bonds	S&P Ratings
Corning Glass Works	Senior unsecured debt	AA
Crane	Senior unsecured debt	BBB
Dart Industries	Senior unsecured debt	A
Dayco	Industrial revenue bonds	BBB
Dennison Mfg.	Senior unsecured debt	A
Emhart	Senior unsecured debt	A
Guardian Industries	Industrial revenue bonds	BBB
Hoover Universal	Senior unsecured debt	A
Monogram Industries	Subordinated debt	B
Norris Industries	Industrial revenue bonds	AA
Norton	Senior unsecured debt	A
PPG Industries	Senior unsecured debt	A+
Pullman	Senior unsecured debt	BBB
Robertson (H. H.)	Subordinated debt	BB
Snap-on Tools	Industrial revenue bonds	AA
Stanley Works	Senior unsecured debt	A+
Trane	Senior unsecured debt	A
Tyco Laboratories	Subordinated debt	B
Tyler	Subordinated debt	BB+
UMC Industries	Senior unsecured debt	BBB
Vulcan Materials	Senior unsecured debt	A
Wheelabrator-Frye	Senior unsecured debt	A
NATURAL RESOURCES (FUEL)		
Amerada Hess	Subordinated debt	BBB
Ashland Oil	Senior unsecured debt	A
Atlantic Richfield	Senior unsecured debt	AA
Belco Petroleum	Subordinated debt	BB
Charter	Subordinated debt	B
Cities Service	Senior unsecured debt	A
Conoco	Senior unsecured debt	AA
Exxon	Senior unsecured debt	AAA
Getty Oil	Senior unsecured debt	AAA
Gulf Oil	Senior unsecured debt	AAA
Houston Natural Gas	Senior unsecured debt	A+
Inexco Oil	Subordinated debt	BB-
Kerr-McGee	Senior unsecured debt	AA
MAPCO	Subordinated debt	BB
Marathon Oil	Senior unsecured debt	AA
Mesa Petroleum	Subordinated debt	BB-
Mobil	Senior unsecured debt	AA

INDUSTRY Company	Bonds	S&P Ratings
Natomas	Senior unsecured debt	BBB
Occidental Petroleum	Senior unsecured debt	BBB
Pennzoil	Senior unsecured debt	A-
Petro-Lewis	Subordinated debt	B
Pittston	Subordinated debt	A-
Quaker State Oil Refining	Senior unsecured debt	A
Shell Oil	Senior unsecured debt	AA+
Standard Oil (Indiana)	Senior unsecured debt	AAA
Standard Oil (Ohio)	Senior unsecured debt	AA-
Standard Oil Co. of California	Senior unsecured debt	AAA
Sun	Senior unsecured debt	AA
Superior Oil	Senior unsecured debt	AA
Tesoro Petroleum	Subordinated debt	B
Texaco	Senior unsecured debt	AA+
Texas Oil and Gas	First mortgage bonds	A+
Union Oil Co. of California	Senior unsecured debt	AA
Witco Chemical	Senior unsecured debt	A+

OFFICE EQUIPMENT, COMPUTERS

Company	Bonds	S&P Ratings
AM International	Senior unsecured debt	BB
Burroughs	Senior unsecured debt	AA+
Control Data	Senior unsecured debt	BBB
Data General	Senior unsecured debt	A-
Diebold	Industrial revenue bonds	A
Digital Equipment	Senior unsecured debt	AA
Honeywell	Senior unsecured debt	A+
International Business Machines	Senior unsecured debt	AAA
Memorex	Subordinated debt	B
NCR	Senior unsecured debt	A+
Nashua	Senior unsecured debt	BBB
Pitney-Bowes	Senior unsecured debt	A
Savin	Subordinated debt	B
Sperry	Senior unsecured debt	A
Storage Technology	Subordinated debt	B
Wang Laboratories	Subordinated debt	B
Xerox	Senior unsecured debt	AA

OIL SERVICE & SUPPLY

Company	Bonds	S&P Ratings
Baker International	Senior unsecured debt	A
Big Three Industries	Senior unsecured debt	A+

INDUSTRY Company	Bonds	S&P Ratings
Buttes Gas and Oil	Subordinated debt	B
Dresser Industries	Senior unsecured debt	A+
Global Marine	Senior Subordenated debt	B
Halliburton	Senior unsecured debt	AA
Huges Tool	Senior unsecured debt	A+
McDermott	Senior unsecured debt	A
NL Industries	Senior unsecured debt	A
Rowan	Subordinated debt	BB
Santa Fe International	Subordinated debt	BB-
Smith International	Senior unsecured debt	A
Texas International	Subordinated debt	B
Western Co. of N. America	Subordinated debt	B
PAPER & FOREST PRODUCTS		
Bemis	Senior unsecured debt	BBB
Boise Cascade	Senior unsecured debt	A
Brown	Industrial revenue bonds	BB
Champion International	Senior unsecured debt	A-
Chesepeake Corp. of Virginia	Industrial revenue bonds	A
Crown Zellerbach	Senior unsecured debt	A
Diamond International	Senior unsecured debt	AA
Federal Paper Board	Senior unsecured debt	BBB
Georgia-Pacific	Senior unsecured debt	AA
Great Northern Nekoosa	Senior unsecured debt	A+
Hammermill Paper	Subordinated debt	BB
International Paper	Senior unsecured debt	AA-
Kimberly-Clark	Senior unsecured debt	AA
Mead	Senior unsecured debt	A
Potlatch	Industrial revenue bonds	A+
St. Regis Paper	Industrial revenue bonds	A
Saxon Industries	Subordinated debt	B
Scott Paper	Senior unsecured debt	A+
Union Camp	Senior unsecured debt	AA
Westvaco	Senior unsecured debt	A
Weyerhauser	Senior unsecured debt	AA
PERSONAL CARE PRODUCTS		
Chesebrough-Pond's	Senior unsecured debt	AA
Economics Laboratory	Subordinated debt	BB+
Proctor and Gamble	Senior unsecured debt	AAA

INDUSTRY		
Company	Bonds	S&P Ratings
Purex Industries	Subordinated debt	BBB
Revlon	Senior unsecured debt	AA

PUBLISHING, RADIO & TV BROADCASTING

American Broadcasting	Senior unsecured debt	A
CBS	Senior unsecured debt	AA
Filmways	Subordinated debt	B
Harte-Hanks Communications	Subordinated debt	BB-
Macmillan	Senior unsecured debt	A-
Metromedia	Subordinated debt	BB+
Storer Broadcasting	Subordinated debt	AA
Time	Senior unsecured debt	AA
Times Mirror	Senior unsecured debt	AA
Viacom International	Subordinated debt	B

RAILROADS

Burlington Northern	Equipment trust certificates	AA
Chicago and North Western Trans	Equipment trust certificates	A
Florida East Coast Railway	First Mortgage bonds	BB
Missouri Pacific	Senior unsecured debt	BBB
Norfolk and Western Railway	Equipment trust certificates	AAA
St. Louis-San Francisco Railway	First mortgage bonds	BBB
Santa Fe Industries	Subordinated debt	BBB
Soo Line Railroad	Equipment trust certificates	AA+
Southern Pacific	Senior unsecured debt	A-
Southern Railway	Equipment trust certificates	AAA
Union Pacific	Senior unsecured debt	AA

REAL ESTATE & HOUSING

Kaufman and Broad	Subordinated debt	B
U. S. Home	Senior unsecured debt	BB+

RETAILING (FOOD)

Fisher Foods	Subordinated debt	B
Kroger	Senior unsecured debt	A
Lucky Stores	Senior unsecured debt	A
Pneumo	Industrial revenue bonds	BBB-
Safeway Stores	Senior unsecured debt	A
Southland	Senior unsecured debt	A

INDUSTRY Company	Bonds	S&P Ratings
RETAILING (NONFOOD)		
Allied Stores	Senior unsecured debt	A+
American Stores	Senior unsecured debt	BBB+
Associated Dry Goods	Senior unsecured debt	A+
Carter Hawley Hale Stores	Senior unsecured debt	A
DWG	Subordinated debt	B
Dayton-Hudson	Senior unsecured debt	AA
Edison Brothers Stores	Industrial revenue bonds	A+
Federated Department Stores	Senior unsecured debt	AAA
Gordon Jewelry	Subordinated Debt	BB
K Mart	Senior unsecured debt	AA
May Department Stores	Senior unsecured debt	AA
Melville	Subordinated debt	BBB
Mercantile Stores	Senior unsecured debt	A
Meyer (Fred)	Subordinated debt	BB
Murphy (C. G.)	Senior unsecured debt	A
Nordstrom	Subordinated debt	BB+
Penney (J. C.)	Senior unsecured debt	A+
Scoa Industries	Industrial revenue bonds	BBB+
Sears, Roebuck	Senior unsecured debt	AA
Walgreen	Subordinated debt	BBB
Wickes	Senior unsecured debt	BBB
Woolworth (F. W.)	Senior unsecured debt	A
Zayre	Senior unsecured debt	BBB-
SERVICE INDUSTRIES		
American District Telegraph	Industrial revenue bonds	A
American Medical International	Subordinated debt	BB+
Amfac	Subordinated debt	BB
Browning-Ferris Industries	Senior unsecured debt	A-
Comdisco	Subordinated debt	BB-
Computer Sciences	Subordinated debt	B
Di Giorgio	Subordinated debt	B
Dillingham	Subordinated debt	B
Engelhard Minerals and Chemicals	Senior unsecured debt	AA-
Fischbach	Subordinated debt	BB
Flexi-Van	Collateral trust debentures	BBB
Gelco	Subordinated debt	B
Hospital Corp. of America	First mortgage bonds	A
Humana	First mortgage bonds	BB
Kay	Subordinated debt	B

INDUSTRY		
Company	Bonds	S&P Ratings
National Medical Enterprises	Subordinated debt	BB-
Ogden	Subordinated debt	BB
Purolator	Industrial revenue bonds	A
Ryder System	Collateral trust debentures	BBB+
Sea Containers	Subordinated debt	BBB-
Seaboard World Airlines	Subordinated debt	B
Super Valu Stores	Industrial revenue bonds	A
TIRE & RUBBER		
Goodyear Tire and Rubber	Senior unsecured debt	BBB
Uniroyal	Subordinated debt	A
TOBACCO		
American Brands	Senior unsecured debt	A+
Loews	Senior unsecured debt	BBB
Philip Morris	Senior unsecured debt	A
Reynolds (R. J.) Industries	Senior unsecured debt	AA
U.S. Tobacco	Industrial revenue bonds	A
TRUCKING		
Consolidated Freightways	Senior unsecured debt	AA
Leaseway Transportation	Industrial revnue bonds	A
UTILITIES		
Arizona Public Service	First mortgage bonds	A-
Arkansas Louisiana Gas	First mortgage bonds	AA-
Baltimore Gas and Electric	First mortgage bonds	AA-
Carolina Power and Light	First mortgage bonds	A
Central Telephone and Utilities	First mortgage bonds	A
Cincinnati Bell	Senior unsecured debt	AAA
Cleveland Electric Illuminating	First mortgage bonds	AA-
Columbia Gas System	Senior unsecured debt	A
Commonwealth Edison	First mortgage bonds	A
Consolidated Edison of N. Y.	First mortgage bonds	A
Consolidated Natural Gas	Senior unsecured debt	AA
Consumers Power	First mortgage bonds	BBB
Continental Telephone	Senior unsecured debt	BBB
Enserch	Senior unsecured debt	A
Florida Power and Light	First mortgage bonds	A+

INDUSTRY Company	Bonds	S&P Ratings
General Telephone and Electronics	Senior unsecured debt	BBB
Gulf States Utilities	First mortgage bonds	A
InterNorth	Senior unsecured debt	A+
Long Island Lighting	First mortgage bonds	BBB
Mid-continent Telephone	Subordinated debt	BB
Northern States Power	First mortgage bonds	AA
Ohio Edison	First mortgage bonds	BBB+
Pacific Power and Light	First mortgage bonds	BBB+
Panhandle Eastern Pipe Line	Senior unsecured debt	A
Pennsylvania Power and Light	First mortgage bonds	A+
Public Service Co. of Indiana	First mortgage bonds	AA
Rochester Telephone	First mortgage bonds	AA
Southern New England Telephone	Senior unsecured debt	AA
Texas Gas Transmission	Senior unsecured debt	A
Texas Utilities	Industrial revenue bonds	AA
Union Electric	First mortgage bonds	A-
United Telecommunications	Senior Unsecured debt	BBB
Western Union	Subordinated debt	B

INDEX

About the Author

AHMED BELKAOUI is Professor of Accounting at the University of Illinois' Chicago campus. He is the author of *Accounting Theory, Conceptual Foundations of Management Accounting, Theorie Comptable, Cost Accounting, Socio-Economic Accounting* and numerous articles.

DATE DUE

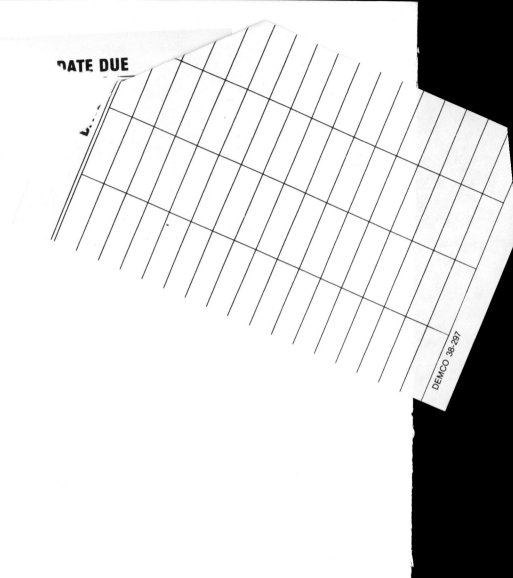

DEMCO 38-297